Key Stage 3

Religious Education Directory

Source *to* Summit

Year 9

SERIES EDITOR
Andy Lewis

Rebecca Jinks
Laura Skinner-Howe
Mateusz Boniecki
Ann-Marie Bridle

Great Clarendon Street, Oxford, OX2 6DP, United Kingdom

Oxford University Press is a department of the University of Oxford. It furthers the University's objective of excellence in research, scholarship, and education by publishing worldwide. Oxford is a registered trade mark of Oxford University Press in the UK and in certain other countries.

© Oxford University Press 2025

The moral rights of the authors have been asserted

First published in 2025

All rights reserved. No part of this publication may be reproduced, stored in a retrieval system, transmitted, used for text and data mining, or used for training artificial intelligence, in any form or by any means, without the prior permission in writing of Oxford University Press, or as expressly permitted by law, by licence or under terms agreed with the appropriate reprographics rights organization. Enquiries concerning reproduction outside the scope of the above should be sent to the Rights Department, Oxford University Press, at the address above.

You must not circulate this work in any other form and you must impose this same condition on any acquirer

British Library Cataloguing in Publication Data
Data available

978-1-382-03638-2

978-1-382-03636-8 (ebook)

10 9 8 7 6 5 4 3 2 1

The manufacturing process conforms to the environmental regulations of the country of origin.

Printed in the UK by Bell & Bain Ltd, Glasgow

The manufacturer's authorised representative in the EU for product safety is Oxford University Press España S.A. of el Parque Empresarial San Fernando de Henares, Avenida de Castilla, 2 – 28830 Madrid (www.oup.es/en).

Nihil obstat: Fr Martin Hardy STL, Censor Deputatus

Imprimatur + Alan Williams SM, Bishop of Brentwood

18th December 2024

The Nihil obstat and Imprimatur are a declaration from the Catholic Church that the parts of this publication concerned with doctrine and morals are free from error. It is not implied that those who have granted the Nihil obstat and Imprimatur agree with the contents, opinions or statements expressed.

This resource has been officially endorsed to confirm that it meets the requirements of the *Religious Education Directory: To know You more clearly*. The Catholic Education Service has reviewed this resource and confirms that, as appropriate: it meets the expected outcomes for the relevant age-phase covered by this resource; it provides an age-related sequence of learning that enables all pupils to make progress in religious education; it ensures pupils are developing each of the three ways of knowing (understand, discern, respond) at all points in their learning; it gives appropriate weight to each of the knowledge lenses, allowing pupils to make meaningful connections between scriptural texts (hear), Catholic beliefs (believe), prayer and liturgy (celebrate) and the relationship of faith to life (live); as part of the live lens it provides students with the study of a rich mix of philosophical and ethical issues, artistic expression, and lived religion elements in each year of their study; it is reflective of the global nature of Catholicism and is inclusive of the diverse cultural expressions of Catholic faith and life; it presents learning in an age appropriate sequential way designed to maximise progress.

This endorsement has been approved by the Department of Education and Formation of the Catholic Bishops Conference of England and Wales.

CONTENTS

In Chapters 1 to 5, students can choose to study **any two** of the Ethical, Lived Religion and Artistic Expression Options.

Introduction		5

Chapter 1: Creation and Covenant — 8

1.1	What do the Genesis creation stories teach about human life?	10
1.2	Why is creation *imago Dei* important?	12
1.3	What's the value of morality and freedom?	14
1.4	What is the sanctity of life?	16
1.5	What does St Paul teach about the dignity of the human body?	18
1.6	What is the Sacrament of Matrimony?	20
1.7	What happens in a Catholic wedding ceremony?	22
1.8	Ethical Option: What are the ethical implications of IVF?	24
1.9	Artistic Expression Option: How can art reflect human dignity?	26
1.10	Lived Religion Option: How does the hospice movement support human dignity?	28
	Assessment	30

Chapter 2: Prophecy and Promise — 32

2.1	How can we read the Bible allegorically?	34
2.2	Who was Hannah?	36
2.3	Why is Hannah important?	38
2.4	What is the Magnificat?	40
2.5	How did holy women keep alive the hope of salvation?	42
2.6	How is God's choice of Mary important?	44
2.7	How do Marian dogmas show the importance of Mary?	46
2.8	What does it mean to say Mary is Ever Virgin?	48
2.9	How do Marian titles fulfil Mary's prophecy?	50
2.10	Ethical Option: How does the Magnificat inspire those who are oppressed?	52
2.11	Artistic Expression Option: How do devotional images show Catholic beliefs about Mary?	54
2.12	Lived Religion Option: How is Josephine Bakhita a woman of the Magnificat?	56
	Assessment	58

Chapter 3: Galilee to Jerusalem — 62

3.1	What does the Gospel of Mark teach about discipleship?	64
3.2	What does the story of the Rich Young Man teach?	66
3.3	What are the costs and rewards of discipleship?	68
3.4	How did the disciples sometimes fail?	70
3.5	How were women important in Jesus' ministry?	72
3.6	How did Jesus' female followers demonstrate discipleship?	74
3.7	What is a vocation?	76
3.8	What is meant by religious life?	78
3.9	What is the Sacrament of Holy Orders?	80
3.10	Ethical Option: Why are only men ordained as Catholic priests?	82
3.11	Artistic Expression Option: How is the calling of the twelve depicted in art?	84
3.12	Lived Religion Option: What is the role of lay people in the Catholic Church?	86
	Assessment	88

	Chapter 4: Desert to Garden	**92**
4.1	What was the Temple in Jerusalem?	94
4.2	What was Herod's Temple?	96
4.3	Why is the Day of Atonement relevant for Christians?	98
4.4	Why was Jesus' sacrifice necessary?	100
4.5	What is redemption?	102
4.6	What is the New Covenant?	104
4.7	How is Jesus both High Priest and Temple?	106
4.8	Ethical Option: Can all sins be forgiven?	108
4.9	Artistic Expression Option: How does art depict reconciliation?	110
4.10	Lived Religion Option: What is Pax Christi?	112
	Assessment	**114**

	Chapter 5: To the Ends of the Earth	**118**
5.1	What does the Bible teach about the early Church?	120
5.2	How is the Church the communion of saints?	122
5.3	What do Catholics believe about the Church on earth?	124
5.4	Is the Church on earth holy?	126
5.5	Who leads the Church on earth?	128
5.6	What do Catholics believe about the Church in heaven?	130
5.7	What do Catholics believe about the Church being purified?	132
5.8	How do Catholics show devotion to saints and angels in the liturgy?	134
5.9	How do Catholics show devotion to saints and angels in prayer?	136
5.10	Ethical Option: Should Catholics use shrines and relics in worship?	138
5.11	Artistic Expression Option: How are saints represented in art?	140
5.12	Lived Religion Option: How do Catholics around the world show devotion to Mary?	142
	Assessment	**144**

	Chapter 6: Dialogue and Encounter	**146**
6.1	What does *Meeting God in Friend and Stranger* teach?	148
6.2	What does a commitment to the common good mean?	150
6.3	How does CSAN support respect for the person?	152
6.4	How does SVP support social wellbeing and development of society?	154
6.5	How does CAFOD work for peace and security?	156
	Assessment	**158**

	Glossary	**159**
	Index	**162**
	Acknowledgements	**167**

INTRODUCTION

Welcome to the third, and final, book in the *Source to Summit* series. The team who have worked on this book are excited to complete this three-year, three-book journey with you as you learn all about the story of the Bible, the story of Christianity and the story of the Church today. This book has been written to make every student feel comfortable and welcomed into this story – whether you are Catholic yourself, or studying this story as a member of a Catholic school.

Source to Summit

We have used a play on words for our title. It is based on a quote from the Catechism of the Catholic Church which describes the Eucharist as 'the source and summit of the Christian life' (CCC 1324). We wanted to highlight the journey that is at the heart of this book, which is the story of the Church from the source – the very moment of creation – to the complete and full revelation found in Jesus Christ, and then on to how the early Church was established, eventually becoming the vibrant faith that is practised today by around 1.3 billion Catholics all over the world.

We will look at how the ancient stories told in the Bible continue to influence how modern Catholics live their lives today, guiding how they choose to live and interact with the world and with others. We will look at how they have inspired artists to try to express and communicate their feelings about God to others. As well as learning about these stories you will be encouraged to reflect on their meaning and how they might fit with your own beliefs and values.

The Bible and other key books

In this book we have used the English Standard Version – Catholic Edition of the Bible. It is this translation that will be used in the new Lectionary, a Catholic book that contains the readings to be used at Mass for each day of the year.

We have included quotes from the Bible, with their references. For a fuller understanding, we would encourage you to look up the reference in your class Bible, and to read around the quotes to understand them in context.

We also quote and refer to other sources and publications, such as the Catechism of the Catholic Church (CCC) – a book that summarises the beliefs of the Church – and the Youth Catechism of the Catholic Church or YOUCAT (YC) – a version of the Catechism written to help young people better understand the beliefs of the Church.

Dialogue and Encounter

Chapter 6 will look at how the Catholic Church enters into dialogue (discussion and debate) with people from different denominations, religions and worldviews. In the school year, there will be time for you to study other religions and worldviews. Your teacher should be able to find resources that cover these outside of this book.

How to use this book

We have tried to make the books in this series as easy to use as possible.

Each chapter is introduced with an **overview** of the big ideas and questions that you will cover in your lessons for that half-term.

We have written each **title** as a question to help you work out the main enquiry or focus for the lesson.

Each double-page lesson has a clear **objective** so you can know exactly what you are trying to achieve.

Throughout the book, and during Key Stage 3, you will return to ideas and topics again and again. These **links** will help you to make connections so you can build on what you have learned.

Sometimes we have encouraged you to go beyond the textbook and **read more** of a religious text to explore its possible meanings more fully.

We have given definitions for **useful vocabulary** to help you understand the text. Test yourself on these key words to make sure you know what they mean.

We will often quote from the Bible or Catechism. Sometimes we will use callout boxes to help you understand the **quotations**.

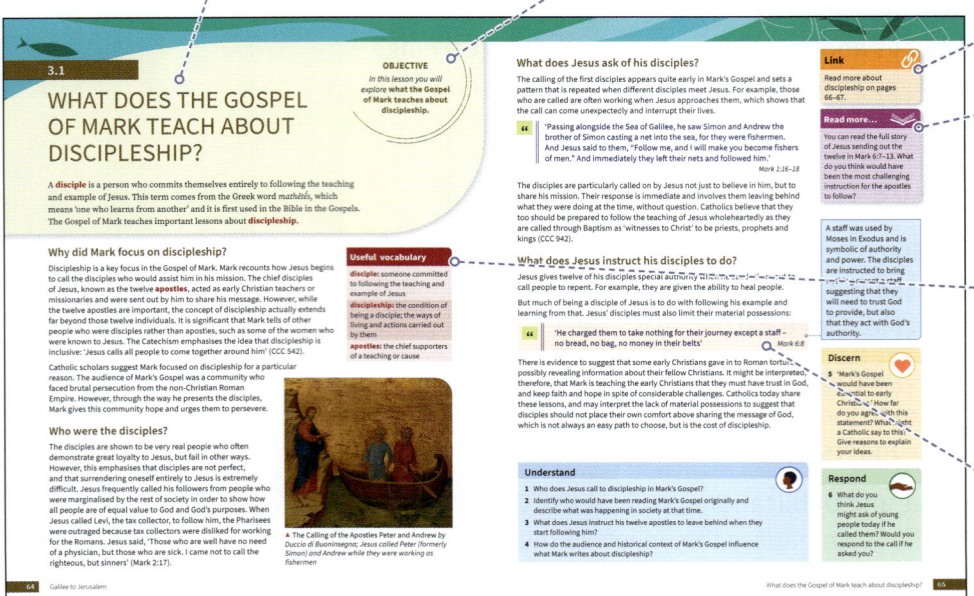

Introduction

There are three types of activity in each lesson.

Understand

These questions check that you have understood what you have learned.

Discern

These questions encourage you to judge wisely. For example, they might ask you to look at different points of view, decide which you agree with more, and explain your reasons for making that judgement.

Respond

These questions allow you to reflect on what you have learned and to consider how this learning fits with your own personal viewpoint. You might consider whether what you have learned will have an impact on how you live and act.

At the end of each chapter you can use these **Assessment** pages to test yourself on what you have learned.

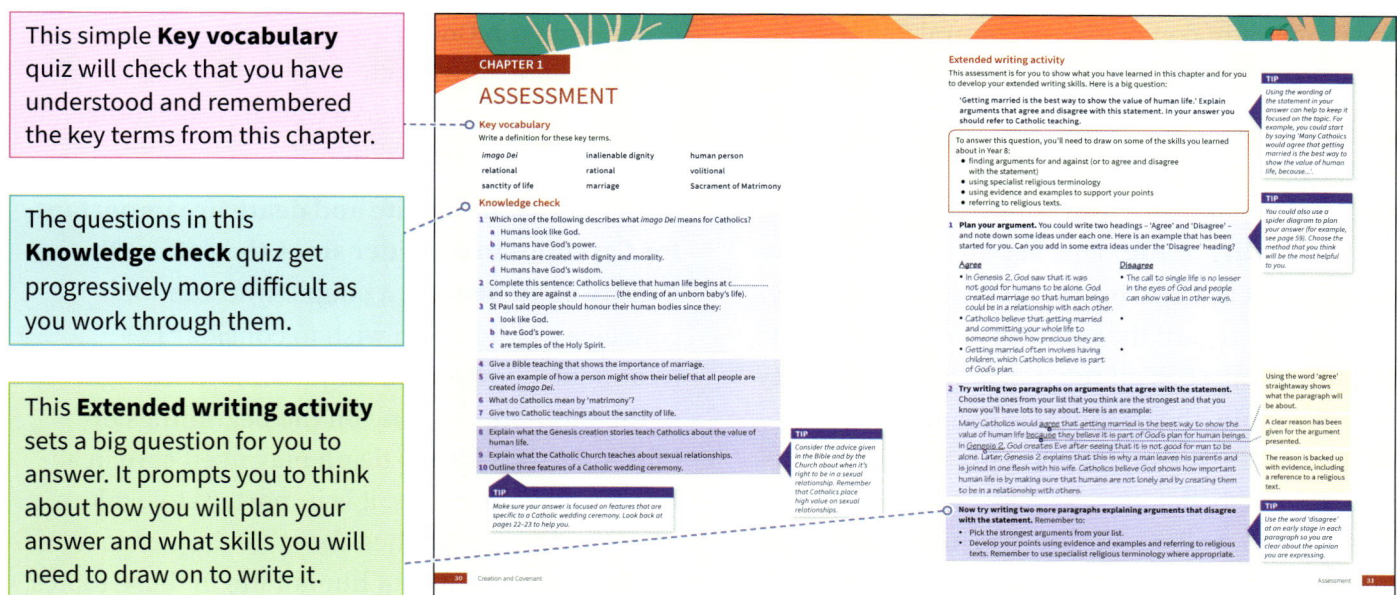

This simple **Key vocabulary** quiz will check that you have understood and remembered the key terms from this chapter.

The questions in this **Knowledge check** quiz get progressively more difficult as you work through them.

This **Extended writing activity** sets a big question for you to answer. It prompts you to think about how you will plan your answer and what skills you will need to draw on to write it.

The activities and Assessment pages in the book will help you to check that you are learning, understanding and remembering the story from *Source to Summit*, which is the central story of the Catholic Church. We hope you enjoy using this book in your RE lessons this year.

Andy Lewis
RE Teacher and Series Editor

Introduction 7

CHAPTER 1:
CREATION AND COVENANT

Introduction

The more we read the Genesis creation stories, the more we learn about **the nature of God and the nature of human life**. In creating humans *imago Dei* – which is Latin for 'in the image of God' – God shows the unique bond between humans and their creator, as well as the dignity and worth of human life.

This dignity is not something that Catholics would take lightly. **Catholics believe that they have a special vocation to protect the dignity of all** – from the youngest to the oldest person, from the moment of conception to natural death. The dignity of all people is a belief that cannot just be held in a person's mind – it must be lived.

Catholics believe that all human life is a gift from God and is therefore holy: this belief is known as the **sanctity of life**. This has an impact on how people treat a foetus or a person close to death; how people regard the equality of all people and how they approach all relationships. **This dignity is inalienable**: this means it is not earned and it cannot be taken away; **it is simply part of being human**. The belief in creation *imago Dei* is the reminder that all people are **'not just something, but someone'** (CCC 357). Catholics believe that if everyone respected this idea, the world could be transformed.

For Catholics, creation *imago Dei* is a reminder that God has given every life a purpose and blessing. Every person is free, but also able to think rationally in order to make moral decisions. Catholics recognise that this ability is not something to hold on to but rather to be used for the good of society.

The Genesis creation stories also teach the **importance of lifelong, committed relationships** in the form of marriage; Catholics believe **God creates humans to be in relationship with each other and with God**. This is seen through the Sacrament of Matrimony – the lifelong union of a man and woman to serve God and each other through their lives together.

Issues surrounding life and death are important for Catholics to consider since they affect the dignity of all people. A couple who cannot conceive a child could wish to consider IVF treatment – how would they do this in the light of the Church's teaching on the beginnings of life? A person close to death may need care in a hospice. For Catholics, it is important to explore what the Church teaches about the importance of dignity and the value of human life in these topics, compassionately understanding their importance for all those who are affected by them.

1.1

WHAT DO THE GENESIS CREATION STORIES TEACH ABOUT HUMAN LIFE?

OBJECTIVE
*In this lesson you will explore **what the Genesis creation stories teach us about how special human life is.***

In Genesis 1 and 2, there are two accounts of creation. The creation stories help Catholics to understand the value, meaning and purpose of human life.

Why are there two accounts of creation?

While Genesis 1 and 2 have the same theme – creation – there are differences between the stories. Many people suggest the stories of the Old Testament were first repeated and retold between communities and passed on to future generations. The stories were eventually written down by numerous different people, so there are differences in the two accounts.

Genesis 1:26–28

Genesis 1 is described as a Priestly account. It is more formal and structured, likely written by priests. God creates the universe over days, building up creation until the making of human life. Catholics may see this as God firstly creating the home that humans will need, before placing them in this home at the end, which shows their importance. In Genesis 1, humans are created by God's spoken word.

Useful vocabulary

imago Dei: a Latin phrase meaning 'in the image of God', the idea that humans reflect God's nature

> 'Then God said, "Let us make man in our image, after our likeness. And let them have dominion over the fish of the sea and over the birds of the heavens and over the livestock and over all the earth and over every creeping thing that creeps on the earth."
>
> So God created man in his own image, in the image of God he created him; male and female he created them.
>
> And God blessed them. And God said to them, "Be fruitful and multiply and fill the earth and subdue it."'
>
> *Genesis 1:26–28*

Genesis 1 reveals that God creates humans *imago Dei* – in God's image and likeness. For Catholics, this does not mean humans look like God, but that they have a special dignity and worth; they are capable of knowing and having a relationship with God, they have the ability to think or reason, and they understand right from wrong.

Humans have a responsibility to other humans and to the whole of creation; they are given 'dominion' – the power to rule over the whole of creation.

Men and women are created at the same time in Genesis 1.

God gives humans the responsibility to reproduce to continue God's creation.

Creation and Covenant

Genesis 2:7

Genesis 2 is described as a Yahwist account. It is a descriptive story, where God is presented differently: God is physically involved in creating man and breathing life into him.

> The man is firstly formed, from the earth.

> " 'then the LORD God formed the man of dust from the ground and breathed into his nostrils the breath of life, and the man became a living creature.'
> *Genesis 2:7*

> God gives life to the man with breath. Catholics believe this is God giving man his soul, something that God does not give to any other animal, showing how important human life is.

▲ Adam and Eve in the Garden – *a mural from St Mathias Mulumba Kalemba Metropolitan Cathedral in Tanzania*

Genesis 2:20–23

Genesis 2:20–23 teaches that woman was made second, but shows the connection between humans.

> God willed humans to have company. The woman is formed from the man, showing their interconnectedness.

> " 'But for Adam there was not found a helper fit for him. So the LORD God caused a deep sleep to fall on the man, and while he slept took one of his ribs and closed up its place with flesh. And the rib that the LORD God had taken from the man he made into a woman and brought her to the man. Then the man said,
>   "This at last is bone of my bones
>   and flesh of my flesh;
>   she shall be called Woman,
>   because she was taken out of Man." '
> *Genesis 2:20–23*

> Man and woman are both made by God; both are connected through their creation. Humans are made to be in relationship with each other.

Are men and women equal?

The Church teaches that men and women are equal since they both share equally in God's purposes for the world:

> " ' "In creating men 'male and female', God gives man and woman an equal personal dignity." "Man is a person, man and woman equally so, since both were created in the image and likeness of the personal God".'
> *Catechism of the Catholic Church 2334*

Understand

1. Describe what happens in:
   a) Genesis 1:26–28, b) Genesis 2:7, c) Genesis 2:20–23.
2. Explain two differences in the detail of how humans are made in the accounts of Genesis 1 and 2.
3. Explain how the author's voice differs in the accounts of Genesis 1 and 2.
4. Why does the Church teach that men and women have equal dignity? Use a quotation from each of Genesis 1 and 2 to explain your answer.

Discern

5. 'Humans are God's most important creation.' How far do you agree the accounts in Genesis 1 and 2 support this statement? Give reasons to agree and disagree, using quotations from the Genesis accounts to support your ideas.

Respond

6. How does the idea that human life is a particularly special thing make you feel? Does it make a difference to how you see friends and family? What about people in your wider community?

What do the Genesis creation stories teach about human life?   11

1.2

WHY IS CREATION *IMAGO DEI* IMPORTANT?

OBJECTIVE
In this lesson you will learn **why Catholics believe it is important that humans are created in God's image and likeness.**

The Genesis creation accounts make it clear that humans are created differently to all other parts of creation because nothing else is created in God's image. For Catholics, this gives human life great value and meaning and influences the way that they value their own life, and their behaviour towards and their treatment of others.

What does belief in creation *imago Dei* tell humans about their own lives?

Catholics believe that being created *imago Dei* means that humans have a special dignity and value which has been given to them by God. As God chose to create through pure love, Catholics believe that every person is an expression of God's love. This gives all humans meaning and purpose.

> 'Being in the image of God the human individual possesses the dignity of a person, who is not just something, but someone.'
> *Catechism of the Catholic Church 357*

This means that every person has dignity – no one is an object or a thing. Every person has been created by God for a purpose. Being created *imago Dei* also means that a person is a unique individual, called to live among others and to be in a relationship with God. This means that it is never right to set anyone aside or place yourself above others – every person has equal dignity.

> 'God did not create man a solitary being.'
> *Catechism of the Catholic Church 383*

As Catholics believe humans are created through love by a loving God, then humans are called to reflect that love through expressing love to others. Humans are made to love and be loved. In Genesis 2, woman is created as a companion for man, showing that God knows the importance for humans of being in a relationship. This aspect of human creation shows that humans are **relational**.

> 'The dignity of the human person is … fulfilled in his vocation to divine beatitude.'
> *Catechism of the Catholic Church 1700*

Catholics believe all humans have come from God, who is complete love and holiness. Humans have the same destiny too – to be with God. A 'vocation to divine beatitude' means the call to holiness that every person has: a blessed life with God and infinite joy.

Useful vocabulary

relational: concerning the way in which two or more people are connected; in Catholicism this is the relationship between humans, and between humans and God

volitional: based on free choice or free will

rational: based on reason or logic

Creation and Covenant

> '… man is endowed with freedom'
>
> *Catechism of the Catholic Church 1705*

All humans have a free choice – they can accept or reject God; they can choose to do good or to do wrong – human actions are **volitional**. Catholics believe God will guide that person, but that person has freedom to accept or reject God's help. The Catechism teaches that humans have a right to exercise their freedom but that this doesn't mean that a person can do everything. Humans also have a responsibility to make moral choices. If a person is immoral in their freedom, they cause disorder and suffering.

> 'God created man a **rational** being'
>
> *Catechism of the Catholic Church 1730*

Being rational means being able to think in a reasoned and logical way. Humans are given this gift as part of their creation *imago Dei*. Humans can use reason to help them to know how to make moral choices.

Link

You could read more about making moral choices on pages 14–15.

What does belief in creation *imago Dei* tell Catholics about their relationship with the world and others?

Creation *imago Dei* is not just an idea. For Catholics it is a driving force behind how they view their own lives, the lives of others and their role within the whole of God's creation. Creation *imago Dei* has moral implications: it helps Catholics to find value but also to understand the responsibilities given to them by God. This can be seen in the following ways:

- All life is sacred: the belief that all life is sacred is the belief that every single person, no matter who they are, is created in God's image and is precious to God. For Catholics, every life is holy and so deserves to be respected.
- Humans are the stewards, not owners, of life: God gives life and gives humans the responsibility to care for life. The belief that life is a precious gift from God affects not only how Catholics care for themselves, but also how they care for others.

▼ *Catholics believe that all people are created* imago Dei

Understand

1. What makes humans different to the rest of God's creation?
2. Give one way that being created *imago Dei* makes a person:
   a. someone, not something
   b. relational
   c. volitional
   d. rational.
3. Explain why being created *imago Dei* means Catholics understand every human life to be sacred.
4. Explain why being created *imago Dei* means Catholics understand that humans are stewards, not owners, of life.

Discern

5. 'The world would be a better place if everyone remembered that humans are created *imago Dei*.' How far do you agree with this statement? What would the Catholic view be? Give reasons to explain your ideas.

Respond

6. Do you think you recognise your own and other people's dignity, irrespective of how they appear, act or feel? Give some examples from your own life to add to your answer.

1.3

WHAT'S THE VALUE OF MORALITY AND FREEDOM?

OBJECTIVES
*In this lesson you will explore **how Catholics discern what morality is and why they believe moral choices matter.***

Catholics believe that, as a result of being created *imago Dei,* humans have a sense of morality: the ability to know when actions are right or wrong. The Catholic Church teaches that although people are able to choose freely between right and wrong, they should consider how their choices impact the whole community in which they live.

How do moral choices impact a community?

All humans make moral choices every day. These might be as simple as not pushing in at the lunch queue, or handing in money found on the floor. Catholics believe making positive **moral** choices reflects a good personal **ethic**, but that it also has a 'communal dimension'. This means that an individual's moral choices will have an effect on others and the community in a bigger picture. If no one pushes in at the lunch queue, then all of the school community benefits: everyone takes their turn and people feel the system is fair.

- The Church teaches that 'Every **human person**, created in the image of God, has the natural right to be recognized as a free and responsible being' (CCC 1738). While this means that all humans can make choices about how they behave, it doesn't mean doing or saying whatever they want. When humans make moral choices, they should consider the dignity and value of others.
- The Church also teaches that humans should work towards creating a fair society in which freedom can flourish by protecting 'the economic, social, political, and cultural conditions that are needed for a just exercise of freedom' (CCC 1740).

Catholics believe a single human sin does not exist in isolation: sin breeds more sin, and this can corrupt a community, creating 'social sin' (CCC 1869). If one person sins, then others may be tempted to as well, as that becomes acceptable in society. This means society itself and institutions within society begin to act in a sinful way, damaging the lives of individual humans and their relationship with each other, and with God.

How can Catholics know what is moral?

The Catechism guides Catholics towards acting in a moral way by setting out certain points that need to be explored in making a moral choice in CCC 1750–1754:

- **The chosen object** – this is the act carried out and the end result of the moral choice that has been made.

> **Useful vocabulary**
>
> **moral:** concerned with right and wrong behaviour
>
> **ethic:** principles or beliefs about what is right and wrong
>
> **human person:** for Catholics, a living being possessing both a physical body and spiritual soul

▲ *Can the intention and circumstances of a wrong action make a difference to the morality of that action?*

Creation and Covenant

- **The end in view or the intention** – this is what motivates the moral choice; it is the reason that a person decides to behave in a certain way. A person might do a good deed, which is intended to bring goodness: this is therefore morally good. A person may also do a good deed to get praise from other people or to receive a reward: their intention is selfish and therefore morally wrong, even though their action may produce goodness.
- **The circumstances of the action** – this is the situation in which the decision is made, and the actual consequences of the choice or action. The circumstances increase or reduce the 'moral goodness or evil' (CCC 1754) in the action. It might help us to consider how responsible a person is for their actions. The circumstance can't change whether the action is morally right or wrong, but if a person was afraid for their personal safety, or stole a loaf of bread rather than £100,000, this would reduce the 'evil'.

Example 1:
A parent steals food from a supermarket to feed their children, as they are unable to afford food.

Chosen object: feeding their children.

End view or intention: to ensure that their children are fed. However, the action of stealing is morally wrong.

Circumstances: they are hungry and need to eat. It might be that the parent felt they had no choice but to steal because they were desperate. We might feel very sorry for this person. A society that leaves a person in this situation isn't a fair or just society. While the action of stealing is always wrong, these circumstances seem to reduce the severity of the theft.

Example 2:
A person challenges discrimination in their workplace because they have heard colleagues using discriminatory language.

Chosen object: calling out discrimination.

End view or intention: to ensure that all people are treated with respect, irrespective of gender, sexuality, ethnicity, disability or social class.

Circumstances: this person is standing up to people in their workplace, who could treat them unfairly as a result. However, they challenge discrimination because it is wrong and an offence against the dignity of the person. This action is morally right.

Understand
1. What does 'morality' mean?
2. What does it mean to say that moral choices have a communal dimension?
3. What does it mean to say that humans are both 'free and responsible' (CCC 1738)?
4. Identify two potential impacts of individual sin on society.
5. Summarise the three points that the Catholic Church asks humans to consider in judging morality.
6. Choose an example of a good or evil act and explain how each point could be used to judge the morality of the act.

Discern
7. 'If we're free, we should be able to do whatever we want.' Explain how a Catholic might respond to this statement and give a reason why someone might disagree with them. Which argument do you think is more persuasive?

Respond
8. Think of a time when you faced a moral decision. Using the three points on morality outlined on these pages, assess how good or bad your decision was. Do you think these points could be useful to your future decisions?

What's the value of morality and freedom?

1.4

WHAT IS THE SANCTITY OF LIFE?

OBJECTIVES
*In this lesson you will explore **Catholic beliefs about the sanctity of life and life beginning at conception.***

The Bible gives clear teaching that, from the moment of human creation, human life is a gift from God and is holy. This belief is known as the **sanctity of life**. Respecting the sanctity of life has a significant impact on how Catholics respond to moral issues and the care of those who are ill or disabled.

Why do Catholics believe in the sanctity of life?

The Bible contains many teachings that help Catholics to understand that human life is blessed and holy, such as the commandment not to kill in Exodus 20:13 and the description in 1 Corinthians 6:19 that every person's body is a 'temple of the Holy Spirit'.

The Catechism teaches that:

> 'Human life is sacred because from its beginning it involves the creative action of God and it remains for ever in a special relationship with the Creator, who is its sole end. God alone is the Lord of life from its beginning until its end'
>
> *Catechism of the Catholic Church 2258*

Therefore, Catholics believe that only God gives life and only God can take it away. If a human takes the decision to end a human life, they have made a decision that is rightfully God's and so undermines the belief in the sanctity of life. The Catechism says that humans must protect and nurture what God has created:

> 'We are stewards, not owners, of the life God has entrusted to us. It is not ours to dispose of.'
>
> *Catechism of the Catholic Church 2280*

Useful vocabulary

sanctity of life: the idea that human life is a holy gift from God

When does the human right to life begin?

The Catholic Church teaches that life begins at conception: the moment the sperm fertilises the egg. From this early moment, the Catholic Church would say that life has begun, and the human right to life is in place. This comes from a teaching in Jeremiah that says 'Before I formed you in the womb I knew you, and before you were born I consecrated you' (Jeremiah 1:5). Catholics (and some non-Catholics) argue that the fertilised egg contains all the genetic information and unique qualities of an individual, therefore they believe that life begins at conception.

Link

You could read more about what the calling of Jeremiah shows about the sanctity of life in *Source to Summit: Year 8* pages 38–39.

Creation and Covenant

There are other non-Catholic views about when life begins below.
- Some people might say this is when the heart begins to beat (around 3 weeks after conception).
- Others might argue that this is when brain activity begins (about 6 weeks after conception).
- Others might say that life begins at birth.

The Catholic Church believes that life should be protected from the moment it begins, stating that a person has a 'right to life and physical integrity from the moment of conception until death' (CCC 2273). This means that a foetus (even in the earliest stages of development) has the right to have their life protected – as much right as you do now, and as much right as a person who might die in the next few moments.

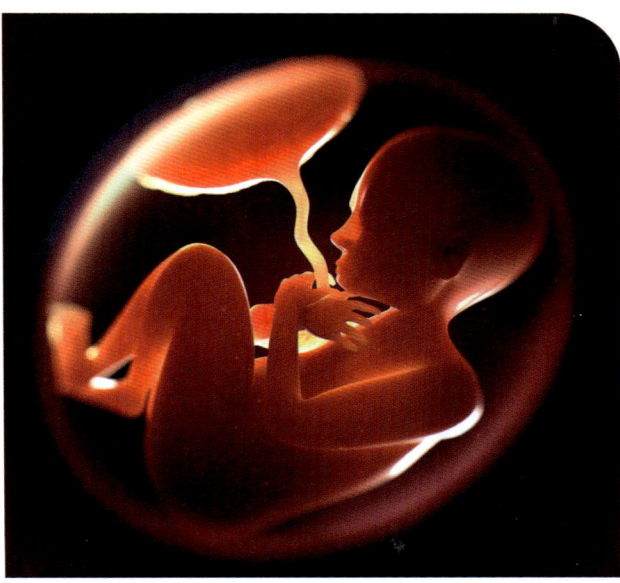

▲ Catholics believe that life begins at conception and the rights of a foetus should be protected

Other people might suggest that while life does begin at conception, the rights of a foetus are different to the rights of people who are already alive. They might argue that, for example, the mother has more rights than the foetus, since she is already alive. This might be used to justify a woman's choice to have an abortion, which is when a pregnancy is terminated (ended) and the foetus dies. The woman is considered to have autonomy over her body, meaning that she can make her own choices and, as the foetus is dependent on her body for survival, the woman can make decisions that will affect the foetus.

The Catholic Church teaches that in all circumstances, abortion goes against the sanctity of life and denies the fundamental right to life of all people. However, the Church teaches that if a doctor acts to save the life of a pregnant woman (primary intention) and as the secondary effect, the foetus dies, this is not an abortion since it was not the intention of the doctor to end the pregnancy. This is known as St Thomas Aquinas' principle of Double Effect.

Understand

1. What does 'sanctity of life' mean?
2. Choose two Bible teachings that support belief in the sanctity of life. Explain how they show the value of life.
3. Why does the Catholic Church believe life begins at conception?
4. When does the Catholic Church say that a person has the right to life?
5. What does the Catholic Church teach about abortion?

Discern

6. 'Human life begins at conception, therefore abortion is always wrong.' Give at least one argument to agree and one argument to disagree with this statement. Include a Catholic response where you discuss the belief in *imago Dei*. Evaluate the strengths and weaknesses of each argument and reach a final judgement.

Respond

7. When do you think life begins? Back up your idea with reasons.

What is the sanctity of life? 17

1.5

WHAT DOES ST PAUL TEACH ABOUT THE DIGNITY OF THE HUMAN BODY?

OBJECTIVE
*In this lesson you will explore **why the dignity of the human body is particularly important when considering sexual relationships.***

We know now that Catholics believe that all human life is sacred and holy. This teaching has a wide-ranging impact on all aspects of human life and human relationships, including discussions about sexual behaviour. The Catholic Church teaches that the dignity of the human body means physical relationships should only be entered into as part of **marriage**.

Every person has inalienable dignity

To say that every human has **inalienable dignity** means that there is no situation where that person's dignity can be taken away. Human life has inalienable dignity in all aspects of human experience, from sexual relationships to the care of a person who is terminally unwell.

Catholics believe that being valued in this way is a fundamental part of being human because dignity was given by God at creation. In Genesis 1 and 2, God showed how precious human life was by creating it *imago Dei*, by breathing life and a soul into Adam and by giving human life special purpose and responsibility. Catholics believe human creation is the work of God and it cannot be undone – all human life has dignity and worth, no matter the condition of the life.

Human dignity is part of sexual relationships

Because human life has this dignity and worth, Catholics believe that their physical bodies are precious. In particular, having a sexual relationship is something that Catholics feel should be respected and valued.

Corinthians records the letters that St Paul wrote to the early Church in Corinth, guiding those Christians on particular issues. 1 Corinthians 6 teaches that physical bodies should be used to do God's work on earth. St Paul acknowledges that people might feel that they can do whatever they like, but reminds them that not everything humans choose is good and so they should allow God to guide them in making moral choices. St Paul emphasises sexual relationships in this extract.

> **Useful vocabulary**
>
> **marriage:** in Catholicism, a binding lifelong relationship in which a man and a woman live by promises made to each other and to God
>
> **inalienable dignity:** a state of value attached to human life that cannot be challenged or removed

▲ *Catholics believe human relationships are an important expression of God's love*

Creation and Covenant

> 'Flee from sexual immorality ... the sexually immoral person sins against his own body. Or do you not know that your body is a temple of the Holy Spirit within you, whom you have from God? ... So glorify God in your body.'
>
> 1 Corinthians 6:18–20

St Paul reminds his readers that their bodies are gifts from God and should be used to honour God.

This means sexual behaviour that is not as God intended it. In Genesis 1 and 2, God's command is to reproduce and to be joined in a relationship. Catholics believe God created sex as an expression of love, to unite a married couple and create new life. St Paul teaches that sex outside marriage is wrong.

Sexual relationships are a gift from God to a married couple

In Genesis 2, following the creation of Eve, the unity of man and woman is explored:

> 'Therefore a man shall leave his father and his mother and hold fast to his wife, and they shall become one flesh.'
>
> Genesis 2:24

This is often associated with marriage, as the woman is clearly described as 'his wife'. The reference to 'one flesh' could be a reminder that in God's eyes a couple become one when they marry, but it can also be read as a reference to their sexual union.

For Catholics, sex is created by God and given to married couples as the highest and most intimate expression of human love, but also an expression of God's love for humans.

Gaudium et Spes 24 says 'man can only find himself by making a sincere gift of himself'. Catholics believe that the purpose of human life can be found by giving of themselves (showing love) to others. In the Catholic Church, a sexual relationship within marriage is the very definition of making a sincere gift of oneself. The Church teachings therefore are informed by St Paul's message to the Church of Corinth that sex should be treated with high regard and dignity.

Read more...

You can read the full extract about human dignity as part of sexual relationships in 1 Corinthians 6:12-20. Do you think what the passage says about sexual relationships is relevant for Catholics today?

Understand

1. What does it mean to describe human dignity as 'inalienable'?
2. What do the accounts of the creation of humans in Genesis 1 and 2 teach about the dignity of human life?
3. What does St Paul teach about the sacred nature of human life in 1 Corinthians 6? In your answer, you could refer to the idea of *imago Dei*.
4. Explain what the Church teaches about sexual relationships with reference to Genesis 2.

Discern

5. 'Sexual relationships are a gift from God.' Give two arguments to agree and two to disagree with this statement, showing Catholic teaching in your answer.

Respond

6. Do you think it is important to believe that humans have inalienable dignity? Why?

1.6

WHAT IS THE SACRAMENT OF MATRIMONY?

OBJECTIVE
In this lesson you will explore what Catholics believe about marriage.

Marriage, or matrimony, is a lifelong commitment that Catholics believe is a vocation: a calling from God and a life of service. It unites a man and woman both in law and in the eyes of God. Catholics believe that marriage is a part of God's plan for humans and as a sacrament, an important sign of God's love on earth, as well as an expression of human love.

Why is marriage important to Catholics?

We read earlier in the Genesis 2 creation story how God sees that man needs a companion. Woman is created as a companion to man and later we are told that together they create a special bond and are encouraged to reproduce.

For Catholics, these teachings of unity, companionship and procreation from the Genesis creation stories show that marriage has always been God's plan for humans. For those people who are called by God to marriage, this is an important way to fulfil the purpose that God has given to them.

Jesus emphasised the importance of marriage in his teaching in Mark 10:1–12, where he was questioned about divorce. He explained that divorce was not part of God's plan for humans; God intended unity and companionship for humans:

> 'And he left there and went to the region of Judea and beyond the Jordan, and crowds gathered to him again. And again, as was his custom, he taught them.
>
> And Pharisees came up and in order to test him asked, "Is it lawful for a man to divorce his wife?" He answered them, "What did Moses command you?" They said, "Moses allowed a man to write a certificate of divorce and send her away." And Jesus said to them, "Because of your hardness of heart he wrote you this commandment. But from the beginning of creation, 'God made them male and female.' 'Therefore, a man shall leave his father and mother and hold fast to his wife, and the two shall become one flesh.' So they are no longer two but one flesh. What therefore God has joined together, let not man separate."'
>
> Mark 10:1–9

Read more…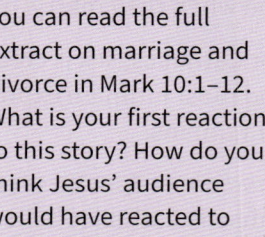

You can read the full extract on marriage and divorce in Mark 10:1–12. What is your first reaction to this story? How do you think Jesus' audience would have reacted to this teaching?

▲ Catholics believe that matrimony is God's will

Creation and Covenant

What do Catholics believe about marriage?

Catholics believe that marriage is a gift from God to unite a man and woman. It must be freely entered into and ordered to the good of the spouses: in other words, both people must give to the marriage, so that both may receive from the marriage. Catholics view marriage as:

- **Exclusive:** marriage is between one man and one woman and they promise to give themselves to each other and be faithful for the rest of their lives.
- **Life-giving:** one of the purposes of marriage is so the couple can have children and educate them so that they learn to love God and others. In having children, the Catechism recognises that the couple are showing the same special ability to create life that God did. Life-giving also involves giving their life to their spouse in service and love so that they both receive goodness from the marriage.
- **Permanent:** marriage is a lifelong commitment: Catholics promise to keep their **vows** until death. Following Mark 10:6–9, the Church only in particular circumstances recognises divorce.
- **A sacrament:** sacraments are outward signs of God's sacred love so the couple's marriage is not just a way of showing their love – it expresses God's love to humanity too: 'Since God created him man and woman, their mutual love becomes an image of the absolute and unfailing love with which God loves man' (CCC 1604).

The **Sacrament of Matrimony** is one of the seven sacraments of the Church. Together with the Sacrament of Holy Orders, it is a Sacrament at the Service of Communion, often called a sacrament of vocation.

Catholics see matrimony as a Service of Communion because they believe that Jesus becomes part of the relationship between husband and wife, helping them to live closely to him by loving and serving each other in their relationship and within their family. The Church therefore believes that marriage takes on a great symbolism of the love Jesus has for his Church: 'Christian marriage in its turn becomes an efficacious sign, the sacrament of the covenant of Christ and the Church' (CCC 1617).

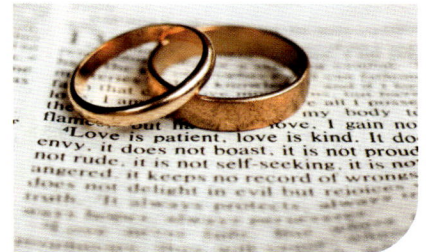

▲ Catholics read about the importance and purpose of marriage in the Bible and the Catechism

Useful vocabulary

vows: solemn promises that cannot be broken

Sacrament of Matrimony: the Sacrament at the Service of Communion in which a man and woman make the lasting commitment of marriage

Link

You could read more about the Sacrament of Holy Orders on page 80.

Discern

6 'No one can promise to be married for life.' Present arguments for and against this statement, including what a Catholic view is. Evaluate the strengths and weaknesses of the arguments and reach a final judgement.

Respond

7 What do you think about the four qualities of marriage? Do they have equal importance to you?

Understand

1 Why is matrimony considered a sacrament?
2 What evidence is there in Genesis 1 and 2 to suggest that marriage is part of God's plan for humans? You can look back at pages 10–11 to help you.
3 What did Jesus teach that showed that God's plan for marriage is lifelong?
4 What are the four qualities or purposes of marriage, according to the Catholic Church?
5 Why do Catholics see matrimony as a Service of Communion?

What is the Sacrament of Matrimony? **21**

1.7

WHAT HAPPENS IN A CATHOLIC WEDDING CEREMONY?

OBJECTIVE
*In this lesson you will learn about **what happens in the Sacrament of Matrimony.***

The Sacrament of Matrimony is one of two Sacraments at the Service of Communion, or vocational sacraments. Sacraments are sacred rites which make God's invisible saving power visible and present to those who receive them. They express God's love for humanity, and in the Sacrament of Matrimony the love of the couple particularly echoes the love that God has for all people.

Origins of the Sacrament of Matrimony

As we have seen, Catholics believe the union of a man and a woman in marriage is deeply significant, and its origins come from the Book of Genesis in the Bible. Although there has always been a legal element to marriage, it was described as a sacrament by St Augustine in the fourth century AD, and this understanding gradually became common in the following centuries.

How do a couple prepare to get married in the Catholic Church?

When at least one of the two people getting married is a baptised Catholic, the couple can marry in the Catholic Church. They will meet with the parish priest to discuss their hope to be married in the Church. In most cases, the couple will be asked to undertake a programme of preparation, not just for their wedding day but for their married life together. This will include learning about Catholic teaching on matrimony and they will discuss matters such as the upbringing of children in the Catholic faith. They will also choose the readings for the wedding ceremony, choose the hymns and music and write a prayer to say at the wedding.

What happens in the Sacrament of Matrimony?

For Catholics, the rites of matrimony can happen within a Mass (known as a Nuptial Mass) or as a separate wedding ceremony, according to the choice of the bride and groom.

▲ *The couple receive Holy Communion during a Nuptial Mass*

22   Creation and Covenant

A Nuptial Mass will begin with the Welcome and the Liturgy of the Word, which is when God's word is heard through the couple's chosen readings. These will include a Psalm and an extract from a Gospel, as well as other Old Testament or New Testament readings. These are usually based on the theme of love and the importance of marriage. The priest's sermon will express Catholic beliefs about matrimony.

Following this, the celebration of marriage happens. This has a legal aspect as well as a religious nature. The priest will follow the *Order of Celebrating Matrimony* from the Roman Missal.

The questions before the consent

The priest will ask questions to ensure that the couple are prepared to enter this commitment fully, asking the couple to confirm that:
- They are freely choosing to get married. The marriage can't be a proper marriage if someone is forcing them to get married.
- They will love and honour each other for the rest of their lives.
- The couple will accept children from God and bring them up following the law of Christ and his Church.

The civil declaration of freedom

The priest then asks the bride and groom to confirm they are free lawfully to marry. This is a legal requirement of all wedding ceremonies in England and Wales.

The consent

Following this, the bride and groom make a promise using words such as:

> 'I call upon these persons here present to witness that I, (name), do take thee, (name), to be my lawful wedded wife/husband, to have and to hold from this day forward for better, for worse, for richer, for poorer, in sickness and in health, to love and to cherish till death do us part.'

In this promise, they are showing that they will continue to love and care for each other, no matter the obstacles that life will throw at them, such as illness and poverty. This shows the exclusive and permanent nature of their marriage.

The blessing and giving of rings

The priest blesses the wedding rings and the bride and groom give them to each other. As the couple place the wedding rings on each other's fingers, they say words such as:

> '(Name), receive this ring as a sign of my love and fidelity [faithfulness]. In the name of the Father, and of the Son, and of the Holy Spirit.'

The wedding rings are a sign of the never-ending love between the couple.

Following this, there are bidding prayers which will usually ask God's blessing on the bride and groom, as well as praying for the wider needs of the Church.

If this is a Nuptial Mass, the Mass will continue in the ordinary way for a Mass. A marriage register is signed, which is a legal document to record that the marriage has been legally performed.

Understand

1. What are the origins of the Sacrament of Matrimony?
2. Give three ways in which a bride and groom prepare for their wedding ceremony.
3. Create a table listing the four beliefs about marriage: exclusive; life-giving; permanent; a sacrament. For each one, explain:
   a. its meaning
   b. where it is seen in the wedding ceremony.

   Complete the table using information from pages 20–23.

Discern

4. 'The commitment to have children is the most important part of getting married.' How far do you agree with this statement? What might a Catholic say to this? Explain your ideas with reference to the different parts of the wedding ceremony.

Respond

5. Do you think that preparing for marriage is important? Give reasons for your opinion.

1.8 ETHICAL OPTION

WHAT ARE THE ETHICAL IMPLICATIONS OF IVF?

OBJECTIVE
In this lesson you will explore **the ethical implications of IVF in relation to the belief in the sanctity of life.**

In this chapter, you have learned about how Catholics value human life from conception to natural death, and considered the belief that all humans are created *imago Dei*. You will now explore the impact that these values and beliefs may have on a Catholic's moral response to in vitro fertilisation (IVF).

In vitro fertilisation (IVF)

Some couples who wish to have children struggle to conceive a baby naturally and so need additional support to conceive their child. In vitro fertilisation (IVF) is one technique that can be used to help people experiencing fertility problems to have a baby. For IVF to occur, a woman will have eggs taken from her ovaries. These will be fertilised with sperm in a laboratory. Embryos (fertilised eggs) are then transferred into the woman's womb. If the transfer is successful, the woman will test positive for pregnancy and the pregnancy will continue as a natural conception would.

Ethical implications of IVF for Catholics

The Catholic Church understands the sorrow that many couples face when they struggle to conceive a child. The Church recognises the joy that children can bring to a marriage and the importance of procreation as a reason for sacramental marriage. The Church would therefore always want to support and comfort a couple who are experiencing issues with fertility. However, the use of IVF raises serious ethical implications for Catholics.

The 1987 document *Donum Vitae* (The Gift of Life) was published by the Catholic Church to clarify that using technology to assist with conception is only permitted if it helps or assists the act of sexual intercourse in marriage, not if it replaces it. For example, it is permitted to use a drug to stimulate ovulation (releasing an egg) so that a woman is more likely to conceive when she has sex. However, as IVF replaces the act of a couple making love, the Church teaches that it should not be used. The Church emphasises the right of a child to be born as an act of love between parents.

The Catholic Church is also concerned about other aspects of IVF. During IVF treatment, many eggs are usually fertilised and sometimes multiple embryos are placed into the woman's womb. This may result in multiple pregnancies (for example carrying twins or triplets). In some instances where there are multiple pregnancies, this might cause serious health risks for the woman or the unborn babies. In these cases, selective termination (abortion of one or more foetuses) would not be acceptable to the Catholic Church as it denies the sanctity of life from conception.

Likewise, after a couple is successful with IVF, they may still have fertilised eggs in storage. If they do not want to use these embryos, they are often disposed of or used for research. All of these scenarios are problematic for Catholics because they violate the inalienable dignity of life that they believe every person has from the moment of conception.

Further developments of IVF

How IVF is used has developed over time. A fairly new but still rare use is known as the idea of 'saviour siblings'. This is when a couple use IVF to screen and conceive a child that is genetically suited to helping an existing child who needs a transplant or stem cell donation to save their life. The embryo would be screened to ensure that it is the best match for their sibling.

Case study: Molly and Adam Nash

Molly Nash was born with a rare disorder called Fanconi anaemia which caused her to experience bone marrow failure. Her parents decided to use IVF to conceive another child, using a new technique called embryo selection. This meant that embryos went through genetic testing to check for the genetic abnormality that causes Fanconi anaemia, and an embryo without this abnormality was used. Molly's brother, Adam, was born in August 2000. After his birth, stem cells from his umbilical cord were given to Molly, which reversed her bone marrow failure. Adam has been described as the first 'saviour sibling'.

▲ Adam and Molly Nash

Since the birth of Adam Nash, other 'saviour siblings' have been born through IVF, and saved the lives of their siblings. However, there are concerns about this advance in technology:
- The embryos that carry genetic abnormalities would be disposed of.
- The wellbeing of children conceived to save the life of a sibling could be affected; for example, they might feel resentful of this.
- The Catholic Church does not want any child to suffer or die, but is concerned that the creation and disposal of embryos denies the value of human life.
- There may be a move towards 'designer babies', using pre-implantation screening to only become pregnant with babies that will have particular 'desirable' qualities.
- Many disability rights groups are concerned that this will make negative attitudes towards disability seem acceptable.

Many children have already been born through IVF. While IVF raises some ethical concerns, it is important to understand that the Church does not suggest these children should be seen as different.

> 'Children conceived through this procedure are children of God and are loved by their parents, as they should be. Like all children, regardless of the circumstances of their conception and birth, they should be loved, cherished and cared for.'
>
> Dr Haas, President of the National Catholic Bioethics Center, Boston

Understand

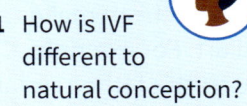

1. How is IVF different to natural conception?
2. What does the Church teach in *Donum Vitae* about using technology to assist conception?
3. Give two further reasons why the Catholic Church is not in favour of IVF.
4. How was the technique of IVF used in the birth of Adam Nash?

Discern

5. Do you think the benefits that a 'saviour sibling' can bring outweigh the risks of any potential harm to that sibling? Give reasons for your answer.

Respond

6. What is your view about the use of IVF?

What are the ethical implications of IVF? 25

1.9 ARTISTIC EXPRESSION OPTION

HOW CAN ART REFLECT HUMAN DIGNITY?

OBJECTIVE
*In this lesson you will consider **how art can be an expression of creation imago Dei**.*

Artistic expression can be found that is thousands of years old. This suggests that beauty and creativity are a fundamental part of being human.

Art as an expression of creation *imago Dei*

The Catechism makes a connection between the creation of human life *imago Dei* and art. For example, Catechism 2501 teaches that art is used by humans to express 'the truth of [their] relationship with God the Creator'. It states that:
- Art comes from the 'talent given by the Creator' to humans and the efforts of human beings themselves.
- Art is a form of 'practical wisdom' which uses skills and knowledge together to express the truth of reality in an accessible way.
- Art is 'inspired by truth and love', just as God's creation was inspired by truth and love. In this it 'bears a certain likeness to God's activity in what he has created.'

The philosopher F. R. Tennant proposed the 'aesthetic argument' as proof of God's existence. Aesthetic means 'to do with beauty'; this argument states that the ability to appreciate beauty and the abundance of beauty in creation are not necessary, but they have been given by God. This can only be, he argued, because God creates beauty and the ability to appreciate beauty as an expression of God's love. Therefore, Catholics believe that art can be an expression of what it is to be human: to be created, known and loved by God.

Sulawesi cave painting

This picture was found in a cave in Indonesia in 2017 and is believed to be 44,000 years old. Many specialists believe it is the oldest picture to have been found and say that it is the oldest example of a story being told through a picture.

Link

You could look back at some examples of artwork from your previous lessons and consider what they express about God's love for humans. For example, Michelangelo's *The Creation of Adam* and Rublev's *Trinity* in *Source to Summit: Year 7* pages 22 and 88; also Köder's *The Jesus Table* in *Source to Summit: Year 8* page 94.

It shows animals, such as a Sulawesi Anoa (a type of buffalo), being hunted by a small number of individuals with human and animal characteristics. These individuals are described as 'therianthropes', which are mythical beings that are part human and part animal. Their presence in the picture causes some people to believe that artists were able to imagine things that did not obviously exist in the material world: they had a sense of something greater than what they could understand in their everyday life – something spiritual.

Creation and Covenant

Cueva de las Manos

This piece of art, which is believed to have been created between 13,000 and 9,500 years ago, is in Argentina. The name *Cueva de las Manos* means 'Cave of the Hands' but just like the Sulawesi art, there are images of animals in the cave as well.

The size of the hand is that of a teenage boy – some people wonder if it's the sign of a rite of passage to mark a boy becoming adult. Others wonder if it is an attempt to leave a reminder about a community of people for generations to come or to record that the group were there. Our handprints are seen by many as the symbol for humanity, to demonstrate the quality of being human and all that this means.

For both examples of cave painting, people question why the art was created in caves. One suggestion was that caves were places of gathering: the community would be together to see the art that emerged from their life experiences. The art told their story, saying something about their experience of the world and the lives that they led. Perhaps it made them feel united, or it was an important part of their culture. It was certainly part of a shared human story.

Catholics see great power in this, that people made *imago Dei* tell their story through art because their lives have meaning. The desire to record this, to leave a record and for those lives to be known (even 10,000 or more years later) suggests to Catholics that art has an ancient origin that comes from a power greater than that of humans themselves.

Understand

1. Identify two ideas from CCC 2501 that connect art and creation *imago Dei*.
2. Explain F. R. Tennant's theory about beauty.
3. How is the idea of creation *imago Dei* shown in a piece of art you have studied previously?
4. Why do some people think the examples of art shown on these pages were specifically created?

Discern

5. Choose one of the two examples of cave art from this lesson and write down your interpretation of it. Do you see the belief in creation *imago Dei* in this piece of art? Explain your answer.
6. 'Art is the best way to understand that humans are created *imago Dei*.' Give a reason for and against this idea.

Respond

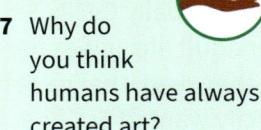

7. Why do you think humans have always created art?

1.10 LIVED RELIGION OPTION

HOW DOES THE HOSPICE MOVEMENT SUPPORT HUMAN DIGNITY?

OBJECTIVE
*In this lesson you will learn **how the hospice movement maintains the dignity and worth of human life.***

When a person has a life-limiting illness (one that can't be cured and is likely to shorten their life) or is reaching the end of their life, they need very particular care. While hospitals provide excellent medical treatments, a hospice can provide a wider variety of specialist care and treatment in a very different environment.

What is the hospice movement?

Hospices are places that provide care for people who are approaching death, or who have life-limiting illnesses. In these cases, medical staff know the person is going to die from their illness or it will greatly reduce the length of their life. The hospice movement is focused on giving end of life and palliative care so that the person who uses the hospice has the best quality of life that they possibly can before they die. Palliative care means treating the symptoms of illness rather than the illness itself. It usually includes using medicine to control a patient's pain and any symptoms that could be uncomfortable or distressing. Other therapies might be used to increase the patient's comfort and this will include talking therapy or counselling, since palliative care focuses on the whole person: the body, mind and soul.

Dame Cecily Saunders

Dame Cecily Saunders (1918–2005) is best remembered for her role in establishing the hospice movement. She believed that it was important to use palliative care in the treatment of people who had life-limiting illnesses, or were dying. Cecily Saunders believed that suffering was formed of four aspects:

- **Physical:** the suffering of the body, for example being in a lot of pain.
- **Spiritual:** the suffering of a person's soul, for example being angry with God for your suffering.
- **Psychological:** the suffering of a person's mind, for example being scared of death.
- **Social:** the suffering of a person in their relationship with others, for example feeling isolated.

While initially Cecily Saunders was not a Christian, she converted to Christianity in her adult life. It was her faith, as well as her experience of caring for friends and family as they died, that gave her the desire to establish St Christopher's Hospice in 1967. Cecily wanted St Christopher's to be a place for people of all faiths and backgrounds to come to be cared for in body, mind and soul.

▲ *Dame Cecily Saunders*

Hospices today

Today there are over 200 hospices in the UK, including hospices for children and young people. Hospices are different to hospitals. Every hospice will have its own character but might include:

- being very homely, with comfortable wards for inpatients, lounge areas and recreation areas, as well as gardens. These are designed to make patients and their families feel at home
- day patient or outpatient facilities. These allow people to come to the hospice to receive care and then go home again
- a chapel or quiet space for prayer and reflection, as well as the support of religious leaders who serve as **chaplains**
- different therapies, such as physiotherapy or occupational therapy, to ensure that the patient is comfortable and gets help with any physical needs
- counselling, both for the patient and their loved ones, to help them to come to terms with what is happening
- activities, such as visits from the hairdresser or time spent in the garden, to help a person to feel good in themselves
- advice on practical arrangements, such as wills and funerals, so that the family can focus on mourning their loved one when they die, rather than worrying about legal issues
- hospices for children and young people will have play areas, sensory rooms and play therapists to support the young patient, as well as their siblings.

▲ Hospice care focuses on the care of the whole person

Useful vocabulary

chaplains: lay people or priests who are appointed to offer spiritual support to people in a particular organisation

Some people associate hospices with death, but the focus of a hospice is on life – however long that life is. Hospices want to ensure that every person receives the care that they need so that they can have a good quality of life and, when their life comes to an end, a good death.

Hospices rely on donations and Christians will often fundraise on their behalf due to their belief in the sanctity of life. Christians believe that hospices recognise the dignity and value of each individual through their loving offer of personalised care. This is, for Christians, a reflection of the belief that all people are created *imago Dei* and that every life has value, from conception to natural death.

Understand

1. Who are hospices for?
2. What is palliative care?
3. What were the four forms of suffering that Dame Cecily Saunders identified?
4. What did Dame Cecily Saunders want St Christopher's Hospice to be like?
5. Name three features that may be found in a hospice.
6. Explain how each feature you identified reflects the dignity of the human person.

Discern

7. Do you think that the hospice movement demonstrates Catholic beliefs about the inalienable dignity of human life? Give reasons for your answer.
8. Investigate the work of a hospice near you. How far could they be seen as a faithful reflection of the Church's teaching on the sanctity of human life?

Respond

9. How could you support and/or fundraise for a hospice near you?

How does the hospice movement support human dignity?

CHAPTER 1

ASSESSMENT

Key vocabulary

Write a definition for these key terms.

imago Dei	inalienable dignity	human person
relational	rational	volitional
sanctity of life	marriage	Sacrament of Matrimony

Knowledge check

1. Which one of the following describes what *imago Dei* means for Catholics?
   a. Humans look like God.
   b. Humans have God's power.
   c. Humans are created with dignity and morality.
   d. Humans have God's wisdom.
2. Complete this sentence: Catholics believe that human life begins at c................. and so they are against a................. (the ending of an unborn baby's life).
3. St Paul said people should honour their human bodies since they:
   a. look like God.
   b. have God's power.
   c. are temples of the Holy Spirit.

4. Give a Bible teaching that shows the importance of marriage.
5. Give an example of how a person might show their belief that all people are created *imago Dei*.
6. What do Catholics mean by 'matrimony'?
7. Give two Catholic teachings about the sanctity of life.

8. Explain what the Genesis creation stories teach Catholics about the value of human life.
9. Explain what the Catholic Church teaches about sexual relationships.
10. Outline three features of a Catholic wedding ceremony.

TIP

Consider the advice given in the Bible and by the Church about when it's right to be in a sexual relationship. Remember that Catholics place high value on sexual relationships.

TIP

Make sure your answer is focused on features that are specific to a Catholic wedding ceremony. Look back at pages 22–23 to help you.

Creation and Covenant

Extended writing activity

This assessment is for you to show what you have learned in this chapter and for you to develop your extended writing skills. Here is a big question:

> 'Getting married is the best way to show the value of human life.' Explain arguments that agree and disagree with this statement. In your answer you should refer to Catholic teaching.

> To answer this question, you'll need to draw on some of the skills you learned about in Year 8:
> - finding arguments for and against (or to agree and disagree with the statement)
> - using specialist religious terminology
> - using evidence and examples to support your points
> - referring to religious texts.

TIP

Using the wording of the statement in your answer can help to keep it focused on the topic. For example, you could start by saying 'Many Catholics would agree that getting married is the best way to show the value of human life, because...'.

TIP

You could also use a spider diagram to plan your answer (for example, see page 59). Choose the method that you think will be the most helpful to you.

1. **Plan your argument.** You could write two headings – 'Agree' and 'Disagree' – and note down some ideas under each one. Here is an example that has been started for you. Can you add in some extra ideas under the 'Disagree' heading?

   <u>Agree</u>
   - In Genesis 2, God saw that it was not good for humans to be alone. God created marriage so that human beings could be in a relationship with each other.
   - Catholics believe that getting married and committing your whole life to someone shows how precious they are.
   - Getting married often involves having children, which Catholics believe is part of God's plan.

   <u>Disagree</u>
   - The call to single life is no lesser in the eyes of God and people can show value in other ways.
   -
   -

2. **Try writing two paragraphs on arguments that agree with the statement.** Choose the ones from your list that you think are the strongest and that you know you'll have lots to say about. Here is an example:

   > Many Catholics would <u>agree</u> that getting married is the best way to show the value of human life <u>because</u> they believe it is part of God's plan for human beings. In <u>Genesis 2</u>, God creates Eve after seeing that it is not good for man to be alone. Later, Genesis 2 explains that this is why a man leaves his parents and is joined in one flesh with his wife. Catholics believe God shows how important human life is by making sure that humans are not lonely and by creating them to be in a relationship with others.

   Using the word 'agree' straightaway shows what the paragraph will be about.

   A clear reason has been given for the argument presented.

   The reason is backed up with evidence, including a reference to a religious text.

3. **Now try writing two more paragraphs explaining arguments that disagree with the statement.** Remember to:
   - Pick the strongest arguments from your list.
   - Develop your points using evidence and examples and referring to religious texts. Remember to use specialist religious terminology where appropriate.

TIP

Use the word 'disagree' at an early stage in each paragraph so you are clear about the opinion you are expressing.

Assessment

CHAPTER 2:
PROPHECY AND PROMISE

Introduction

The Bible contains many important prophets who have shared the messages of God with humanity. Over the centuries, Catholic scholars have come to understand that there are many ways to read and understand the stories they share. This includes how **the story of Adam and Eve can symbolise the lives of Christ and Mary**.

The need for salvation (the process of being saved from sin and returning to God) stems from the story of Adam and Eve and the Fall from God's grace. Adam and Eve became synonymous with sin and death after the Fall of humanity but because God's love for humanity remained, he promised that there would be a second chance for salvation. **Mary carried Jesus to bring that chance to humanity: freedom from sin and the offer of eternal life**.

Many other holy women in the Bible also played important roles in salvation history as prophets, matriarchs and righteous people. **Catholics believe God spoke to and chose these wives, mothers, daughters and sisters as he loved them and recognised their unique value**. Through these women, God unveiled key information about how salvation would come about.

In this chapter we are going to explore the importance of key women in the Old Testament and consider their connection to Mary in the New Testament. Women like Hannah, Sarah, Rebecca and Rachel are 'types' of Mary. They not only foreshadow the coming of Mary, and through her Jesus and salvation, but they also enable salvation through their descendants. **All are faithful women, who trust that the Lord will be there for them. It is this faith and trust in God that brings their personal salvation and enables the universal salvation of humanity**.

We will consider why Catholics believe that Mary is the most important woman in the Bible by looking at key events in her life such as the Annunciation and the Assumption. We will also explore what different titles and teachings connected to Mary reveal about both her and Jesus, and why these are important to understand. Catholics believe the Magnificat, or Mary's prayer, explains that **Mary was a woman of true faith, pure of heart, who delighted in the Lord**. As a result she has become a model for all Catholics everywhere and venerated within the Catholic Church.

The women of the Bible should not be thought of as belonging to the past. **Men and women today take inspiration from their example and work tirelessly to keep their faith alive**. This may be through religious life, as Josephine Bakhita exemplified, or in fighting against oppression as shown by Dietrich Bonhoeffer. As the Mother of the Church, Mary is still believed to work for its mission and carry the prayers of all Catholics to God.

2.1

HOW CAN WE READ THE BIBLE ALLEGORICALLY?

OBJECTIVES
*In this lesson you will learn about **allegory in the Bible and how it can reveal Adam and Eve as types of Christ and Mary.***

As you learned in Year 8, there are many different ways to read or interpret scriptural texts and there are different layers or 'senses' of meaning in a single Bible story. One of these is the **allegorical sense** – this relates to how stories can be symbolic or even predict or hint at events to come. The story of Adam and Eve in Genesis 1–3 is an example of a story that Christians believe symbolises the lives of Christ and **Mary**.

What is allegory?

An allegorical story is one that symbolises or mirrors the events of another time or place. For example, the novel *Animal Farm* is an allegory of the rise of communism in Russia: the characters in the book are animals, but they represent real political figures and do things that mirror real events that took place in Russia. We can draw a particular meaning through the symbolism of allegorical stories.

In Christianity, **typology** is part of the allegorical sense and is the study of Old Testament figures, objects, places or events which foreshadow who or what is to come in the New Testament. This means that certain people or things in the Old Testament are 'types' of things to come in the New Testament. Understanding the allegorical sense of scripture allows Christians to identify these types and come to a deeper understanding of God's word across the whole Bible.

> 'The New Testament lies hidden in the Old, and the Old becomes clear in the New.'
> *St Augustine*

To fully understand the meaning that a particular story is trying to convey, the symbolism behind the people or events in the text needs to be explored. For example, many Christians interpret the story of Noah's Ark as an allegory. The Ark is seen as a type of (or a metaphor for) the Church. The Ark saved people from the great flood, and many Christians understand the allegorical meaning of this to be that the Church Jesus brought can save humanity.

How are Adam and Eve types of Christ and Mary?

In the book of Genesis, God creates the world and the first humans Adam and Eve. Christians believe they are not simply the first man and woman; they are types of Christ and Mary: they are a hint that Christ and Mary are to come in the future. But while Adam and Eve allowed sin and death to enter the world, Christ and Mary bring God's promised offer of redemption.

Useful vocabulary

allegorical sense: the meaning of the text that lies hidden beneath the surface; the actual words are symbolic or foreshadow events to come

Mary: the mother of Jesus

typology: in Christianity, the study of Old Testament figures, objects, places or events which predict or hint at who or what is to come in the New Testament

Link

You can read more about the senses of scripture and interpreting meaning from scripture in *Source to Summit: Year 8*, pages 70–71.

Prophecy and Promise

Genesis 3:15 is known as the **Protoevangelium** or 'first gospel' because it is the first messianic prophecy in the Bible.

> 'I will put enmity [hostile feelings] between you [serpent] and the woman, and between your offspring and her offspring; he shall bruise your head, and you shall bruise his heel.'
>
> *Genesis 3:15*

The Church interprets this prophecy in the following way.
- The words 'her offspring' are a reference to Jesus, who the Catechism refers to as the 'new Adam' (CCC 539).
- The 'woman' mentioned is Mary – also called the '**New Eve**' (CCC 975).
- The offspring bruising the serpent's head means that Jesus will overcome sin (the serpent represents sin); the serpent bruising the offspring's heel means that in order to do this, Jesus will have to suffer (through his crucifixion).
- There is no mention of a father, suggesting that the 'New Adam' has no earthly father, so Catholics interpret this to be a prophecy about the Virgin Birth.

In his first letter to the Corinthians, St Paul links back to this prophecy.

> 'For as by a man came death, by a man has also come the resurrection of the dead. For as in Adam all die, so also in Christ shall all be made alive.'
>
> *1 Corinthians 15:21–22*

For Catholics, this shows how Adam and Jesus almost mirror each other. While Adam gave into temptation, bringing sin and death, Jesus remained faithful, bringing redemption and eternal life.

The Church teaches that the connection between Eve and Mary is similar. Eve was the first mother of the living, but with Adam she brought death; Mary, through her faith, becomes the new 'Mother of all the living' (CCC 2618) and 'Mother of the Church' (CCC 975). She makes redemption possible by willingly carrying Jesus.

▲ *The Annunciation by Fra Angelico, painted around 1445; the angel appears to Mary, announcing she will have a child; in the background, Adam and Eve are being expelled from the Garden of Eden*

Useful vocabulary

Protoevangelium: the 'first gospel'; this refers to Genesis 3:15 because it is the first messianic prophecy in the Bible

New Eve: Eve is the mother of all humans as the first woman; Mary, as the mother of Jesus, who offers redemption and new life to humanity, becomes the New Eve, or mother, for baptised Catholics

Understand

1. Explain what is meant by the allegorical sense of scripture.
2. What does typology mean for Christians?
3. How is Adam a 'type' of Christ?
4. How is Eve a 'type' of Mary?
5. What does the Protoevangelium in Genesis 3:15 prophesise?

Discern

6. 'Understanding the Old Testament is essential to understanding the New Testament.' How far do you agree with this statement? What might a Catholic say to this? Give reasons to explain your ideas.

Respond

7. Do you think it is helpful to interpret biblical texts in different ways? Have you considered new ideas about a Bible story by doing this?

How can we read the Bible allegorically?

2.2

WHO WAS HANNAH?

OBJECTIVES

*In this lesson you will learn about **Hannah and why she is a holy woman of the Old Testament.***

There are many strong and faithful women in the Old Testament. Their stories are an important part of **salvation** history. They contain recurring themes which show God reaching out to these women to offer the hope of salvation, however poor or **humble** they might be. One such woman is Hannah, whose faithfulness to God brings her great joy.

The story of Hannah

Hannah's story can be found in 1 Samuel 1–2. The Church interprets this story, along with other Old Testament stories about faithful women, as pointing to Jesus and preparing the way for him to bring salvation for all people.

> 'Such holy women as Sarah, Rebecca, Rachel, Miriam, Deborah, Hannah, Judith and Esther kept alive the hope of Israel's salvation.'
>
> *Catechism of the Catholic Church 64*

In the story, Hannah faces hardships, but she continues to trust in God despite this.

> '[Elkanah] had two wives. The name of one was Hannah, and the name of the other, Peninnah. And Peninnah had children, but Hannah had no children. … And her rival [Peninnah] used to provoke her grievously to irritate her, because the LORD had closed her womb. So it went on year by year. As often as she went up to the house of the LORD, she used to provoke her. Therefore Hannah wept and would not eat. And Elkanah, her husband, said to her, "Hannah, why do you weep? And why do you not eat? And why is your heart sad? Am I not more to you than ten sons?" …
>
> [Hannah] prayed to the LORD and wept bitterly. And she vowed a **vow** and said, "O LORD of hosts, if you will indeed look on the affliction of your servant and remember me and not forget your servant, but will give to your servant a son, then I will give him to the LORD all the days of his life" … Then the woman went on her way and ate, and her face was no longer sad. …
>
> And in due time Hannah conceived and bore a son, and she called his name Samuel, for she said, "I have asked for him from the LORD." … they brought the child to Eli [the priest]. And [Hannah] said, "Oh, my lord! As you live, my lord, I am the woman who was standing here in your presence, praying to the LORD. For this child I prayed, and the LORD has granted me my petition that I made to him. Therefore I have lent him to the LORD. As long as he lives, he is lent to the LORD."'
>
> *1 Samuel 1: 2, 6–8, 10–11, 18, 20, 25–28*

Useful vocabulary

salvation: the process of being saved from sin and returning to God through God's grace

humble: modest, or not self-centred; for a religious person, this means putting God and other people before oneself

vow: a solemn promise that cannot be broken

Read more…

You can read the full extract about Hannah and the birth of Samuel in 1 Samuel 1:1–28. What is your first reaction to this story?

36 Prophecy and Promise

Why does the Church see Hannah as an example of faith and constancy in God?

Hannah shows complete, unwavering faith in God through her actions following her vow in the Temple. She 'went on her way and ate, and her face was no longer sad' (1 Samuel 1:18) – she seems to trust completely that God will give her a child. This is fulfilled in the birth of her son and she shows her faith again in the name that she gives him, which means 'God has heard'. Hannah recognises the role of God in her blessing of a child.

Why is it important that Hannah was humble?

Hannah is presented in her story as an ordinary woman, married to an ordinary man. She bears the unhappiness of being unable to have children and her existence is a simple and humble one. This may be why Hannah acts in a humble way before God; she does not demand things of him, rather she asks with her whole heart, repeatedly calling herself God's 'servant', and makes promises to God. Catholics believe it is this unselfish behaviour that shows her true faith, which is why God chooses to reward her.

▲ *Hannah is overjoyed by the gift of Samuel from God*

How does Hannah keep the hope of salvation alive?

Hannah's salvation comes when God answers her prayer and gives her Samuel. Her sadness, fear and desperation are lifted, replaced by joy and contentment. Hannah can be seen as a 'type' of Mary, who is also blessed with a child from God.

Catholics believe the salvation of Hannah gives a glimpse of God's greater plan for salvation in Jesus. Hannah was taken from pain to joy, just as Jesus removes pain and fear and replaces it with hope. Here, Catholics believe the following lessons can be learned from Hannah: that God will help people achieve their own personal salvation if they have enough faith, and also that God has a bigger plan for salvation which will come with Jesus.

Samuel goes on to become a priest and a prophet, and helps establish the monarchy in Israel. Samuel will secretly anoint David as king, through whose family line Jesus, the Messiah, is descended. In this way, God's choice of Hannah can be seen to keep alive the hope of salvation.

Understand

1. Where in the Old Testament is Hannah's story found?
2. Describe the story of Hannah.
3. Explain why Catholics believe Hannah's humbleness was a part of why God granted her request.
4. Give one way Hannah shows faith in God.
5. How does Hannah keep alive the hope of salvation?

Discern

6. 'The main reason Hannah's prayer was answered was because she was humble.' How far do you believe the account from 1 Samuel 1:1–28 (on page 36) supports this statement? Give reasons to agree and disagree, using quotations from the account to support your ideas.

Respond

7. Do you think being humble is an important quality in a person? Why, or why not?

2.3

WHY IS HANNAH IMPORTANT?

OBJECTIVE
*In this lesson you will explore **why Hannah is important in the Old Testament**.*

Hannah's story shows her to be a woman of great faith who trusted in God and God's plan for her. For many Catholics, Hannah is also an example of how people should show gratitude to God through praise and exultation (rejoicing) because Hannah's story reveals how God can give people strength and resilience, and bring about remarkable reversals in their lives.

How does Hannah show gratitude, praise and exultation to God?

In Hannah's story, God's glory is revealed through God giving Hannah a son. Hannah recognises this and delights that this honour has been bestowed on her. Hannah's ultimate demonstration of gratitude is to gift her son as a holy man back to God. The beginning of 1 Samuel 2 is a song-like prayer in which Hannah praises God for this miraculous gift to her. 1 Samuel 2:1–10 has become known as Hannah's prayer. For Catholics, Hannah's prayer is a complete confirmation of the power of faith in God.

Read more…
You can read all of Hannah's prayer in 1 Samuel 2:1–10. What emotions can you identify in this prayer?

> 'My heart exults in the LORD;
>   my horn is exalted in the LORD.
> My mouth derides my enemies,
>   because I rejoice in your salvation.

Hannah recognises that she has found favour in God's sight and that this is something to be grateful for. Her life has been transformed by God and she is saved from her sadness and fear.

> There is none holy like the LORD:
>   for there is none besides you;
>   there is no rock like our God.

By referring to God as a rock, Hannah shows that God gives strength and hope to those who need it.

> Talk no more so very proudly,
>   let not arrogance come from your mouth;
> for the LORD is a God of knowledge,
>   and by him actions are weighed …

Hannah recognises the importance of humility in being chosen by God, who judges everyone.

> He raises up the poor from the dust;
>   he lifts the needy from the ash heap
> to make them sit with princes
>   and inherit a seat of honour.
> For the pillars of the earth are the LORD's,
>   and on them he has set the world.

Hannah praises God for valuing every person, however humble their origins.

1 Samuel 2:1–3, 8

Prophecy and Promise

For Catholics, Hannah's story is a lesson. It suggests that those who have similar trust in God will also find joy and have their lives transformed. Many Catholics see her gratitude as confirmation that, through faith in God, everything is possible.

How is Hannah an example of remarkable reversal?

Hannah's story is one of remarkable reversal. This means that there is a great change in Hannah's fortune. Hannah is oppressed by Peninnah and suffers sadness over her lack of children; however, God lifts Hannah up. It is seen as a story of the humble being raised up over the powerful: 'the poor from the dust' (1 Samuel 2:8). This is a common theme in the Old Testament which is echoed in the New Testament through Jesus' treatment of those who were marginalised such as the woman in the story of the Widow's Offering. Jesus teaches that those who are vulnerable or living in poverty will overcome their hardships and overthrow the mighty, through their faith and dedication to God. Hannah willingly offers herself and her son to God to show her faithfulness and, in this act, God raises her up.

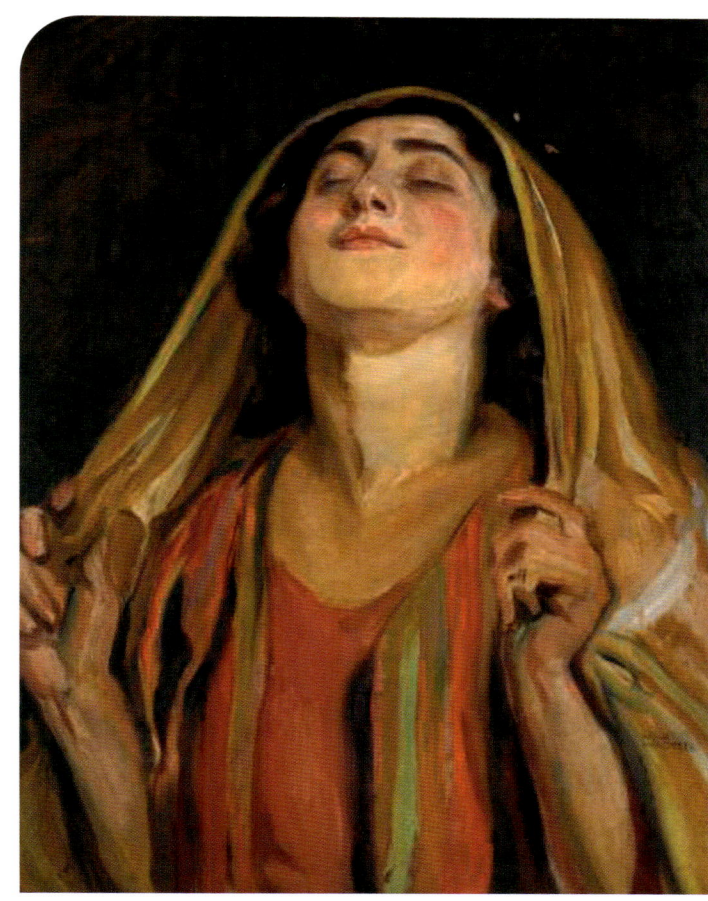

▲ Hannah at Prayer *by Wilhelm Wachtel*

For Catholics, this is important as Hannah gives hope to those who struggle, or are oppressed or suffering. She enables people to believe that they too can experience a remarkable reversal if they have true faith. Many Catholics also see the change in Hannah's fortune as an allegory for the events of the New Testament, foretelling what Jesus will do in the future to save people from sin and death. They believe Hannah is important, therefore, as she is a beacon of hope not just for individuals, but for the whole of humanity.

Understand

1. What is Hannah's prayer about?
2. What does Hannah offer to God to show her gratitude?
3. Choose and explain a quotation that you feel best shows Hannah's exaltation of God.
4. Explain how Hannah's story shows 'remarkable reversal'.
5. How does Hannah's story connect to events in the New Testament?

Discern

6. 'Hannah is a role model for people to follow.' Present arguments for and against this statement, including what a Catholic might say. Evaluate the strengths and weaknesses of the arguments and reach a final judgement.

Respond

7. Do you think it makes a difference if you say 'thank you' for something good that happens to you? Why, or why not?

2.4

WHAT IS THE MAGNIFICAT?

OBJECTIVES
In this lesson you will explore what the Magnificat is and why it is important.

The **Magnificat** is a song of praise that expresses Mary's faith and love of God. Within the Catholic faith, Mary is held as a model of discipleship and faith.

Interpreting the Magnificat

In the Bible, during the **Annunciation**, the angel Gabriel tells Mary that her cousin Elizabeth has also conceived a child. When Elizabeth sees Mary, she recognises her as the **Mother of God**: 'And why is this granted to me that the mother of my Lord should come to me?' (Luke 1:43). Mary answers Elizabeth with the Magnificat, which is Mary's song of praise for God. The title comes from the first word of the song in Latin.

> **Useful vocabulary**
>
> **Magnificat:** Mary's prayer of praise in Luke 1:45–56
>
> **Annunciation:** the announcement of the Incarnation by the angel Gabriel
>
> **Mother of God:** a title given to Mary, because Jesus is God and she is Jesus' mother

Mary shows joy and gratitude to God for all God has done for her.

> 'And Mary said,
> "My soul magnifies the Lord,
>   and my spirit rejoices in God my Saviour,
> for he has looked on the humble estate of his servant.
>   For behold, from now on all generations will call me blessed;
> for he who is mighty has done great things for me,
>   and holy is his name.
> And his mercy is for those who fear him
>   from generation to generation.
> He has shown strength with his arm;
>   he has scattered the proud in the thoughts of their hearts;
> he has brought down the mighty from their thrones
>   and exalted those of humble estate;
> he has filled the hungry with good things,
>   and the rich he has sent away empty.
> He has helped his servant Israel,
>   in remembrance of his mercy,
> as he spoke to our fathers,
>   to Abraham and to his offspring for ever."'
>
> Luke 1:46–55

Mary is humble, showing that she recognises that all that has happened is due to God. When she refers to herself as blessed, she is not boasting but recognising that God has bestowed on her a precious task and that people will recognise this.

Mary says that God will overthrow the powerful and raise up the weak, showing that God recognises the humble for who they truly are: faithful and strong. Those who trust in God and have true faith will be saved.

Mary shows that she trusts God will look after her, as she praises how God looks after those who are vulnerable or living in poverty.

Mary explains that God has fulfilled the promises God made through the prophets, and that by saying yes to God, she has helped bring God's Kingdom to earth in Jesus.

Prophecy and Promise

How does the Magnificat connect Mary and Hannah?

The Magnificat is a clear connection between Mary and Hannah. Many of the themes in Hannah's prayer in 1 Samuel 2:1–10 are repeated within the Magnificat. Both women show great joy in embracing the will of God. The table below shows some key similarities between the two songs.

Hannah's prayer	The Magnificat	Theme and connection
'My heart exults in the LORD; my horn is exalted in the LORD. My mouth derides my enemies, because I rejoice in your salvation.' 1 Samuel 2:1	'My soul magnifies the Lord, and my spirit rejoices in God my Saviour'	**Gratitude and praise:** Both women praise God's greatness and glory and are thankful for the gift God has given them.
'There is none holy like the LORD: for there is none besides you; there is no rock like our God.' 1 Samuel 2:2	'for he who is mighty has done great things for me, and holy is his name.'	**Humility before and exaltation of God:** Both women show God's power and uniqueness.
'The LORD will judge the ends of the earth; he will give strength to his king and exalt the horn of his anointed.' 1 Samuel 2:10	'He has helped his servant Israel, in remembrance of his mercy, as he spoke to our fathers, to Abraham and to his offspring for ever.'	**Salvation:** Both women explain that God will raise up the faithful and fulfil God's promises across the ages.
'He raises up the poor from the dust; he lifts the needy from the ash heap to make them sit with princes and inherit a seat of honour.' 1 Samuel 2:8	'he has brought down the mighty from their thrones and exalted those of humble estate; he has filled the hungry with good things, and the rich he has sent away empty.'	**God's choice of those who are humble or living in poverty:** Both women recognise that God is just and fair, honouring those people who are humble but faithful.

▲ *A painting to represent the Magnificat, by Frank Wesley*

Understand

1. Describe the Magnificat. Try to explain:
   - the circumstances in which Mary says it
   - the different types of things that Mary says
   - why you think Mary says these things.
2. a. Identify two themes that connect the Magnificat and Hannah's prayer.
   b. Explain how each theme is expressed by Mary and Hannah, giving quotations from both songs of praise.

Discern

3. 'The Magnificat reveals important truths about both God and Mary.' To what extent do you agree with this statement?

Respond

4. Do you feel gratitude for anything in your life? Who or what do you feel grateful to?

2.5

HOW DID HOLY WOMEN KEEP ALIVE THE HOPE OF SALVATION?

OBJECTIVE
*In this lesson you will explore **what it means to say that the holy women of the Old Testament kept alive the hope of salvation.***

The Church teaches that faithful women, such as Hannah and later, Mary, played an essential role in keeping 'alive the hope of Israel's salvation' (CCC 64). Other holy women from the Old Testament include Sarah, Rebecca and Rachel. Some of these women are considered **matriarchs** or **prophets** and each has a unique and special story which shows their essential role in the history of salvation.

What does it mean to keep alive the hope of salvation?

Keeping alive the hope of salvation is an important theme in the Old Testament. It means that key people demonstrated that God was close to them and offered signs that God was working to bring salvation. These people were seen as evidence that God had not abandoned humanity. God chose ordinary men and women to do this and they often had to complete difficult tasks in order to fulfil what they understood to be God's will.

What is the Virgin Mary's role in salvation?

The actions of the holy women in the Old Testament lead up to the final promise of salvation that is fulfilled in Mary's willing acceptance to bear Jesus. Mary is therefore called 'the purest figure among them' (CCC 64) for accepting her role as the Mother of God. For Catholics, she links humankind to God completely, but women such as Sarah, Rebecca and Rachel prepared the way for her as matriarchs of the line of David.

The roles of Sarah, Rebecca and Rachel in the hope of salvation

Sarah, Rebecca and Rachel were all women who longed for children. Like Hannah, their prayers were answered by God. They are seen as 'types' of Mary as their sons help to prepare the path to salvation that Mary's son, Jesus, then fulfils. The Church understands each of them in turn to reveal more about salvation. There is a short commentary on each of their stories opposite.

▶ *A mosaic image of Sarah at the St Paul Melkite Cathedral in Harissa, Lebanon*

Useful vocabulary

matriarchs: women who are the head or driving force of their family

prophets: people anointed by God and inspired by God through the Holy Spirit to share God's messages

Prophecy and Promise

Sarah was the wife of Abraham. She is the only woman in the Bible to have her name changed by God, from Sarai to Sarah which means 'princess'. Sarah was unable to have children until God blessed her with a son, Isaac. God said: 'I will bless her, and she shall become nations; kings of peoples shall come from her' (Genesis 17:16).

Through God, Sarah was able to conceive a much-wanted son as part of the covenant God had made with her husband. This covenant would last forever through the line of her son; she would become the mother of the royal line of King David, from whom Jesus is descended.

Rebecca was chosen by God to be Isaac's wife. She had to leave her family and travel alone to a distant land. She showed complete faith and trust in God's plan in doing this. Her family blessed her, saying 'may you become thousands of ten thousands' (Genesis 24:60). Rebecca and Isaac were married for some time but only conceived after Isaac prayed to God and God answered his prayer.

Through God, Rebecca conceived twin sons who she felt struggling within her. When she spoke to God about this, God answered 'Two nations are in your womb' (Genesis 25:23). Jacob was destined to lead God's people but Isaac favoured Esau. Rebecca had to trick Isaac into blessing Jacob instead of Esau in order to fulfil Jacob's destiny.

Jacob's name was later changed to Israel and he became the ancestor of all the people of Israel. As a result of Rebecca's actions, God's covenant with Abraham continued, which helped enable the coming of the Messiah.

Rachel was the favourite wife of Jacob. Like Sarah and Rebecca before her, she struggled to conceive a child. God then 'remembered Rachel, and God listened to her' (Genesis 30:22) and gave her a son, Joseph, who became Jacob's favourite. She went on to have another son, meaning that Jacob had twelve sons in total.

Like Sarah and Rebecca, Rachel's pregnancy was an act of God, and it shows that Isaac, Jacob and Joseph were special. Joseph was destined by God to become the father of the twelve tribes of Israel, formed by the twelve sons of Jacob, from which the Messiah would be born.

Read more…

You could also read the story of Sarah in Genesis 16–18 and 21, and the stories of Rebecca and Rachel in Genesis 24 and 27. Do you agree that these stories show that Sarah, Rebecca and Rachel were faithful women? Why, or why not?

Understand

1. What do Sarah, Rebecca and Rachel have in common?
2. Why was Sarah's son important?
3. How did Rebecca's actions help keep alive the hope of salvation?
4. Why was Rachel's son Joseph important?
5. Explain how Sarah, Rebecca and Rachel connect to the Blessed Virgin Mary's role in salvation.

Discern

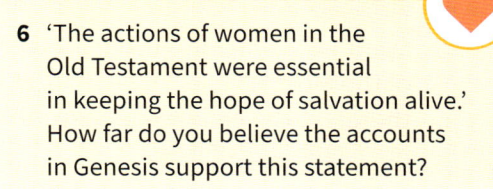

6. 'The actions of women in the Old Testament were essential in keeping the hope of salvation alive.' How far do you believe the accounts in Genesis support this statement?

Respond

7. Have you ever had to make a sacrifice for a greater purpose? How do you feel about what you had to do now?

How did holy women keep alive the hope of salvation?

2.6

HOW IS GOD'S CHOICE OF MARY IMPORTANT?

OBJECTIVE
*In this lesson you will learn **why the Church teaches that the Blessed Virgin Mary is so important.***

The Blessed Virgin Mary is described as the perfect disciple and is **venerated** in the Catholic Church. This reflects the Church's belief that Mary played a very special role in bringing salvation to the world and that through her, much can be learned about Jesus.

Who was Mary?

Little is said about Mary's early life, which means that it is impossible to get a full biography of her. The Catechism says she was 'a daughter of Israel, a young Jewish woman of Nazareth in Galilee' (CCC 488). The Gospels of Matthew and Luke teach that Mary was betrothed to a man called Joseph. Luke also describes how Mary was visited by the angel Gabriel, who told her that she would conceive and bear a son: the Son of God. This is referred to in Christianity as the Annunciation:

▲ The Annunciation – Gabriel and Mary, *from the* Life of Jesus Mafa *project*

> "'Do not be afraid, Mary, for you have found favour with God. And behold, you will conceive in your womb and bear a son, and you shall call his name Jesus. He will be great and will be called the Son of the Most High. And the Lord God will give to him the throne of his father David, and he will reign over the house of Jacob for ever, and of his kingdom there will be no end. … The Holy Spirit will come upon you, and the power of the Most High will overshadow you; therefore the child to be born will be called holy – the Son of God." …
>
> And Mary said, "Behold, I am the servant of the Lord; let it be to me according to your word."'
>
> Luke: 1:30–33, 35, 38

The angel's announcement connects Jesus to the house of David, and connects Mary to the women who enabled this line to survive through the ages, preparing the way.

As the mother of the Son of God, Mary is revered in the Catholic Church as both Mother of God and Mother of the Church.

Mary does not hesitate to accept God's will, showing her trust and faith in God's plan for her.

Prophecy and Promise

Why did God choose Mary?

Mary is sometimes described as having 'singular dignity'; this means she was singled out by God for a unique mission which was supremely important: to bring Jesus the saviour into the world.

The Church teaches that God needed the perfect person to bear Jesus. Catholics have also come to understand that one reason Mary was chosen was that she was born without Original Sin in the **Immaculate Conception**. This means God prevented this inherited sin being passed on to Mary so that she would be pure and sinless, and therefore the only person able to bear the Messiah. Catholics believe God knew Mary's heart and that she would remain sinless throughout her life. The Church reinforces the belief of Mary's purity when it says 'such holy women as Sarah, Rebecca, Rachel … kept alive the hope of Israel's salvation. The purest figure among them is Mary' (CCC 64).

Why is the relationship between Mary and Jesus particularly special?

Mary and Jesus Christ are linked in a special relationship that goes beyond them being mother and son. Catholics believe that Mary played an essential part in God's plan to bring Jesus to earth to offer salvation to all. While this does not give Mary equal status with Jesus, their relationship can help Catholics understand more about Jesus. The Catechism explains the connection between Mary and Jesus in the following way:

> 'What the Catholic faith believes about Mary is based on what it believes about Christ, and what it teaches about Mary illuminates in turn its faith in Christ.'
>
> *Catechism of the Catholic Church 487*

This means that Catholic beliefs about Mary are connected to beliefs about Jesus – Mary is important because of who Jesus was. Catholics can learn things about Mary through what Jesus did and the offer of salvation that he brought to humanity. When the Catholic Church shares teachings about Mary, this allows Catholics to understand more about Jesus, who he was and what he offered.

Therefore Mary can be said to have helped enable Jesus and the promise of salvation, but she is not placed above him, as everything she is comes from him: ultimately he is the Son of God.

Useful vocabulary

venerated: respected and adored

Immaculate Conception: a dogma (teaching) of the Catholic Church that states that Mary, the mother of Jesus, did not inherit the stain of Original Sin when she was conceived by her own mother

Link

You can read more about the Dogma of the Immaculate Conception on pages 46–47.

Discern

6 'Catholics place too much emphasis on Mary.' Present arguments for and against this statement, including what a Catholic might say. Evaluate the strengths and weaknesses of the arguments and reach a final judgement.

Respond

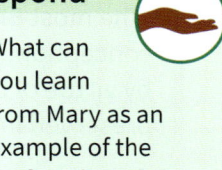

7 What can you learn from Mary as an example of the perfect disciple?

Understand

1 What is the Annunciation?
2 Describe Mary's reaction to the angel Gabriel's announcement.
3 What does it mean to say Mary is the Immaculate Conception?
4 According to Church teaching, why was Mary chosen by God to bear Jesus?
5 How does the Catholic Church explain the relationship between Mary and Jesus?

2.7

HOW DO MARIAN DOGMAS SHOW THE IMPORTANCE OF MARY?

OBJECTIVE
In this lesson you will explore **how Marian dogmas show the importance of Mary.**

There are four Marian dogmas (essential beliefs taught by the Catholic Church about Mary): that Mary is the Mother of God, that she is the Immaculate Conception, that she is Ever Virgin and that she was Assumed into heaven.

What does the dogma 'Mother of God' teach about Mary?

> 'Mary is acclaimed by Elizabeth, at the prompting of the Spirit and even before the birth of her son, as "the mother of my Lord".'
>
> *Catechism of the Catholic Church 495*

The Catholic Church teaches that Mary is the Mother of God. This teaching was confirmed at the Council of Ephesus in AD 431. In Greek, the term for this is Theotokos which means 'Mother of God' or 'God Bearer.' This teaching stems from Elizabeth's words after Mary visits her, but also the account of the Annunciation itself: 'the child to be born will be called holy – the Son of God' (Luke 1:35).

Catholics believe that through Mary, God became **incarnate** in the person of Jesus. They believe Jesus was born human but also divine, meaning that Mary was the person who enabled this when she agreed to bear Jesus and become the Mother of God. This action is said to make her the first and perfect disciple, and also Mother of the Church. As Jesus is the head of the Church and its followers form the body of the Church, as Jesus' mother, Mary becomes the Mother of all those within the Church.

Useful vocabulary

incarnate: embodied in human form; in Christianity, God made human in the person of Jesus, truly human and truly divine

What does the dogma of the Immaculate Conception teach about Mary?

The Immaculate Conception is a dogma that was defined by Pope St Pius IX in 1854 but had been explored by Catholic theologians for centuries before. The term 'immaculate' in this context means without stain:

> 'The most Blessed Virgin Mary was, from the first moment of her conception, by a singular grace and privilege of almighty God and by virtue of the merits of Jesus Christ, Saviour of the human race, preserved immune from all stain of original sin.'
>
> *Catechism of the Catholic Church 491*

Link

This dogma should not be confused with Mary as Ever Virgin. The Immaculate Conception refers to the conception of Mary, not Jesus. You can read more about the dogma of Mary as Ever Virgin on pages 48–49.

Prophecy and Promise

This is an important teaching, as it means that Mary was predestined to be free from the stain of Original Sin due to the role that she would play in salvation. Catholics believe this enabled her to conceive Jesus, and for him to also be born perfect and sinless. Mary is the only person to receive this grace from God, which Catholics believe marks her as uniquely special.

What does the dogma of the Assumption teach about Mary?

The Assumption of Mary is a dogma defined by Pope Pius XII in 1950 but, like the Immaculate Conception, had been explored by Catholic theologians for centuries before. It is a teaching that at the end of Mary's earthly life, she was 'assumed', that is taken body and soul into heaven. The Assumption demonstrates that 'By the grace of God Mary remained free of every personal sin her whole life long' (CCC 493) – only those who are freed from sin can enter heaven.

It confirms the earlier dogma of Mary as the Mother of God and shows her special role in salvation by her being given this honour. It also reflects the belief that due to Jesus' sacrifice, death has lost its power. For Catholics, it shows that through the grace of Christ's sacrifice all people can receive eternal life.

Catholics believe the Assumption allows Mary to intercede on behalf of Catholics as she is eternally close to God and Jesus. Many Catholics also ask Mary to pray with them as a way of drawing closer to God. The Assumption brings joy and hope to all Catholics. It is specifically celebrated in the Feast of the Assumption which takes place every year on 15 August.

▲ Mary is assumed into heaven, her blue cape symbolising her purity and royal status

Understand

1 What does it mean to call Jesus the incarnate Son of God?
2 Explain how Mary is the Mother of God.
3 How does the Marian dogma of the Immaculate Conception show Mary is important?
4 Describe the Catholic teaching of the Assumption.
5 How is the Assumption important in bringing Catholics closer to God?

Discern

6 'Mary as the Mother of God is the most important dogma for explaining why Mary is venerated within the Catholic Church.' How far do you agree that this is true? Explain your ideas with reference to the three dogmas explored in this lesson.

Respond

7 What does Mary mean to you?

How do Marian dogmas show the importance of Mary?

2.8

WHAT DOES IT MEAN TO SAY MARY IS EVER VIRGIN?

OBJECTIVE
In this lesson you will learn what it means to say Mary is Ever Virgin.

As we have seen, there are particular Marian dogmas which explain the nature and importance of Mary in Catholic belief. The final one of these is that Mary was Ever Virgin: a virgin before, during and after Jesus' birth.

What does it mean to say that Mary is Ever Virgin?

Mary as Ever Virgin is also known as the perpetual virginity of Mary. She is believed to have been a virgin before, during and after giving birth to Christ. This Marian dogma was confirmed by the Synod of Milan in AD 389 and is therefore the oldest of the Marian dogmas to be officially verified by the Church. This confirms Jesus' conception and birth as miraculous events.

Virginity before Jesus' birth

> 'Jesus is conceived by the Holy Spirit in the Virgin Mary's womb because he is the New Adam, who inaugurates the new creation: "The first man was from the earth, a man of dust; the second man is from heaven."'
>
> *Catechism of the Catholic Church 504*

This means that Jesus was conceived by the power of the Holy Spirit without the need for the involvement of a man. This demonstrates that Jesus is incarnate: truly God and truly man, and came to atone for the mistake of Adam.

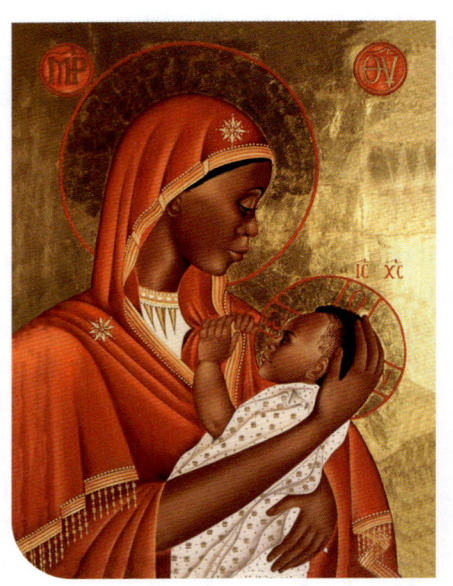

▲ Mary and Jesus; the stars on Mary's forehead and shoulders represent her virginity before, during and after the birth of Jesus

Virginity during and after birth

> 'Christ's birth "did not diminish his mother's virginal integrity but sanctified it."'
>
> *Catechism of the Catholic Church 499*

This means that Mary's virginity remained intact during childbirth. Also, the Catholic Church teaches that 'Jesus is Mary's only son' (CCC 501) and that she abstained from sex with Joseph and remained a virgin as a sign that salvation came through her.

This is an area that is contested between Christian denominations as some scriptural passages contain references to Jesus' 'brothers' and 'sisters' (for example, in Mark 6:3 and Matthew 12:46). Catholics believe that any reference to Jesus' brothers or sisters is interpreted either as meaning not sons or daughters of Mary, but brothers and sisters in a spiritual sense or in the sense of cousins which was a common understanding in the time of Jesus.

Prophecy and Promise

Why is Mary's virginity important?

Her virginity is a sign of her faith in Christ

> 'Mary is a virgin because her virginity is the sign of her faith ... and of her undivided gift of herself to God's will.'
>
> *Catechism of the Catholic Church 506*

The Catechism teaches that Mary's virginity is important because it shows her faith and trust in God. The Church does not consider sex itself to be sinful, so here virginity is symbolic of Mary's dedication to holiness. It indicates her singlemindedness to do God's will as she does not become distracted by earthly things, such as her own personal desire to marry Joseph.

Her virginity is a sign of her purity

> 'By the grace of God, Mary remained free of every personal sin her whole life long.'
>
> *Catechism of the Catholic Church 493*

Mary was totally devoted to Jesus. Her virginity is also seen as a sign of her purity: she was not conceived with Original Sin and the Catechism explains that God prevented her from becoming tainted by any sin throughout her whole life. Her state of perfect sinlessness shows her as the only person worthy of bearing Jesus, the incarnate Son of God.

Her virginity is a sign of salvation and the new creation to come

Mary's virginity is also significant as it is a foreshadowing of heaven, which Catholics understand as the fulfilment of people who, like Mary, say yes to God and follow God's will. This is because in heaven Catholics are told there is no marriage (Matthew 22:30) and all is perfected, so by remaining a virgin Mary shows the fulfilment of life in the new creation.

Her virginity is a sign of Mary as the Bride of Christ

Mary being the Bride of Christ is not meant literally, but that she is the 'type' of his spouse, like she is a 'type' of Eve, Adam's spouse. Just as Eve was Adam's companion during the Fall, Mary is Jesus' companion in the work of redemption. Christ's saving work means Mary becomes the spiritual mother of all believers. Just as she was a virgin in giving birth to Jesus, she is understood as a virgin in mothering members of the Church – a role in which she takes the place of Jesus' spouse.

Understand

1. What does Ever Virgin mean?
2. What are the four signs of Mary's virginity that show her importance?
3. If sex is not sinful, why does the Church teach that Mary's virginity matters?
4. Why was Mary the only person worthy of bearing Jesus?
5. Give two reasons why Mary's perpetual virginity is important to the Church.

Discern

6. 'The belief that Mary is Ever Virgin is essential for understanding why she was chosen by God.' How far do you agree with this statement? What might a Catholic say to this? Give reasons to explain your ideas.

Respond

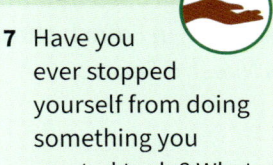

7. Have you ever stopped yourself from doing something you wanted to do? What were your reasons?

2.9

HOW DO MARIAN TITLES FULFIL MARY'S PROPHECY?

OBJECTIVE

In this lesson you will learn **how the different titles of Mary fulfil the prophecy she made in the Magnificat.**

Mary is remembered and venerated within the Catholic Church because she accepted the role God gave her freely and with joy. She is often called **Our Lady** and is seen as a loving role model who many Catholics look to, particularly in times of need. The Church honours Mary through prayers such as **the Rosary**, feast days and religious sites, but particularly through the titles it gives her.

What is Our Lady's prophecy?

Mary realised that bearing Jesus would mean she would be remembered for many years – perhaps for all time. In the Magnificat we see Mary making a prophecy about this when she says 'all generations will call me blessed' (Luke 1:48). In this Mary is not boasting, but thanking God for the blessing of bringing Jesus into the world to fulfil his mission. For her special role, she is remembered and revered within the Catholic Church:

> 'The Church rightly honours "the Blessed Virgin with special devotion" ... The liturgical feasts dedicated to the Mother of God and Marian prayer, such as the rosary, an "epitome of the whole Gospel," express this devotion to the Virgin Mary.'
>
> *Catechism of the Catholic Church 971*

There are many titles used to celebrate Mary; some are taken from the dogmas such as Mother of God, but others show deference for her or praise her qualities.

Useful vocabulary

Our Lady: a title of particular respect for Mary, reflecting her high status within the Church

the Rosary: a set of prayers said in honour of Mary during which Catholics will meditate on particular events in the life of Mary and Jesus

intercession: in Catholicism, praying to God on behalf of humans

How is this prophecy fulfilled through Mary's title 'Our Lady'?

Historically, 'Our Lady' was once a common title of respect and status for a woman. Giving this title to Mary is a mark of her status within the Church. A more literal meaning for Catholics is that the title shows that they belong to her and she to them ('Our') and she is a woman who is venerated above all other creatures ('Lady'). Our Lady is used as a title for Mary throughout the world; for example, in French she is referred to as *Notre Dame* and in Spanish as *Nuestra Señora*.

▶ Madonna of the Magnificat by Botticelli; 'Madonna' is Italian for 'My Lady' and is a name often used to describe Mary

Prophecy and Promise

How is this prophecy fulfilled through Mary's title 'Mother of the Church'?

Catholics celebrate Mary as the Mother of the Church, which was a title given to Mary by St Ambrose around the fourth century AD. This title was reinforced by Pope St Paul VI in 1968:

> 'Blessed Mother of God, the New Eve, Mother of the Church, continues in heaven her maternal role with regard to Christ's members, cooperating with the birth and growth of divine life in the souls of the redeemed'
>
> *Credo of the People of God, 15*

Catholics believe Eve is the mother of all humans as the first woman. Mary becomes the New Eve, or mother, for baptised Catholics.

Catholics believe this teaches that Mary, the Mother of God, also took on the role of being a Mother to the Church. Catholics believe that this is hinted at in a moment in the Bible during Jesus' crucifixion when Jesus places Mary into the care of the apostle John.

> 'When Jesus saw his mother and the disciple whom he loved standing nearby, he said to his mother, "Woman, behold, your son!" Then he said to the disciple, "Behold, your mother!" And from that hour the disciple took her to his own home.'
>
> *John 19:26–27*

The apostle John can be interpreted to represent all of humanity. Catholics believe Mary comes as a mother to help each person of the Church to grow and develop in a personal relationship with Christ.

Catholics believe that they can pray for Mary's **intercession** and that she will help with their prayers as a sign of her motherly love for the members of the Church. Catholics entrust themselves to Mary, knowing that she loves them, and, in their love, they can find grace. The title 'Mother of the Church' fulfils Mary's own prophecy as it represents the deep spiritual connection that members of the Church have to Mary.

Understand

1. What was the prophecy Mary made?
2. How does the Catechism suggest Catholics can honour Mary? How does this fulfil her prophecy?
3. What does the title 'Our Lady' show about how Catholics feel about Mary?
4. How does the title 'Our Lady' fulfil Mary's prophecy?
5. What does the title 'Mother of the Church' show about how Catholics feel about Mary?
6. How does the title 'Mother of the Church' fulfil Mary's prophecy?

Discern

7. 'Mary's titles reflect her relationship with Catholics better than they reflect her relationship with God.' Present arguments to agree and disagree with this statement. Which argument do you think is more persuasive?

Respond

8. How do the titles of Our Lady and Mother of the Church make you feel about Mary?

2.10 ETHICAL OPTION

HOW DOES THE MAGNIFICAT INSPIRE THOSE WHO ARE OPPRESSED?

> **OBJECTIVE**
> In this lesson you will explore why the Magnificat is an inspirational prayer for people who face oppression.

Although the Magnificat is over 2,000 years old, it is not a prayer of the past. Mary's prayer has a long and lasting message of social justice. Many Christians find the message of the Magnificat inspirational, even rebellious, particularly those who are oppressed and suffer under the rule of powerful leaders.

How does the Magnificat show that God cares for the lowly?

The Magnificat is a prayer of praise in which Mary recognises that she is God's humble servant who has been raised up due to God's gift of Jesus. However, the Magnificat is also a revolutionary prayer, with Mary extolling, or rejoicing, that God has done great things for the lowly and ordinary people of the world. This prayer shows that God is on the side of those who are humble, vulnerable or oppressed. Christians believe that it is through Mary that Jesus comes and reveals God to the world, and through him that the lowly will be raised high:

> 'he has filled the hungry with good things,
> and the rich he has sent away empty.'
> *Luke 1:53*

Christians interpret the Magnificat as foretelling what Jesus will do in his ministry. Throughout Luke's Gospel, Jesus shows the importance of social justice for those who have sinned or have been marginalised or oppressed. These people, who others despise and ignore, have a special place in Jesus' work and life, thus showing that the least are the most important. The actions of Jesus underline the message of the Magnificat, showing weakness to be strength and lowliness to be greatness, calling people to change their ideas about who God is closest to. For people who are marginalised or oppressed, the Magnificat can offer inspiration and comfort, but also strength to fight against the persecution they face.

How does the Magnificat show that God judges the mighty?

The Magnificat also praises God's judgement and humbling of the mighty:

> 'he has brought down the mighty from their thrones
> and exalted those of humble estate'
> *Luke 1:52*

This is also a common theme found in the Old Testament, where those with wealth and power take advantage of those who are vulnerable or living in poverty.

> **Link**
> You can explore how the prophet Amos criticised people with power and called for care of those living in poverty in *Source to Summit: Year 8* pages 42–43.

Catholics believe the wealthy and powerful ignore God's commands, but then face punishment for their behaviour. The Magnificat shows God's displeasure with those who hoard power, show arrogance and refuse to help those in need. For people who are being taken advantage of, the Magnificat gives hope that the roles will be reversed and that those with wealth and power will lose these things and those who are living in poverty will gain them.

Why is the Magnificat important for oppressed people?

Through history, particular priests have drawn on Mary's message in their sermons in order to sustain their congregations as they faced great personal danger.

> Dietrich Bonhoeffer was a Lutheran German pastor who lived and worked during the Nazi regime in the Second World War. In 1933 Adolf Hitler gained power in Germany and banned other political parties and trade unions, and began work to eliminate anything 'un-German'. This led to the oppression of Jewish people, gay people, disabled people and minority ethnic groups. In December 1933, Bonhoeffer, who helped found the Confessing Church to stand against Nazi interference by the 'German Christian' group, used the Magnificat in his sermon to inspire his congregation to make the right choices in their daily lives. He referred to the Magnificat as 'the most passionate, the wildest, one might even say the most revolutionary hymn that has ever been sung'. He offered a warning for anyone who believes they have the right to oppress others:
>
> > 'And even if today they think nothing will happen to them, it will come tomorrow or the next day. God puts down the tyrants from their thrones; God raises up the lowly. For this Jesus Christ came into the world as the child in the manger, as the son of Mary.'
> >
> > *Dietrich Bonhoeffer, December 1933*
>
> Bonhoeffer was executed in 1945 for his role in the German resistance, acting against the Nazi regime.

▲ This image of Mary was created by Slovakian artist Mikuláš Klimčák during the collapse of the Soviet Union, when many countries fought for their independence

Understand

1. Why do Catholics believe the Magnificat is still relevant today?
2. What does the Magnificat foretell about Jesus?
3. Explain how the Magnificat praises God's care for the lowly.
4. Explain how the Magnificat praises God's judgement of the mighty.
5. Describe an example of when the Magnificat has been used to inspire those facing persecution.

Discern

6. 'If everyone lived by the message of the Magnificat, the world would be a better place.' Explain how a Catholic might respond to this statement and give a reason why someone might disagree with them. Which argument do you think is more persuasive?

Respond

7. Do you think social justice as described in the Magnificat is important? How do you think others in your community feel about it? Are their ideas the same or different to yours?

2.11 ARTISTIC EXPRESSION OPTION

HOW DO DEVOTIONAL IMAGES SHOW CATHOLIC BELIEFS ABOUT MARY?

OBJECTIVE
In this lesson you will explore how devotional images show Catholic beliefs about Mary.

The Catholic Church teaches that worship is for God alone, however Catholics do show honour and respect to Mary. Devotional images of Mary, including paintings and statues, show Mary's importance within the Catholic Church.

Our Lady of Guadalupe

Our Lady of Guadalupe is a shrine dedicated to Mary in Mexico City. Catholics believe that Mary appeared to St Juan Diego in several visions in 1531. Juan was a man of Aztec descent who had converted to Christianity. His bishop requested a sign to prove that it was actually Mary in his visions. Mary is said to have told Juan to go and pick roses, despite it being winter. When he opened his cloak before the bishop dozens of roses fell out and an image of Mary appeared inside it. The image that remains at the shrine today is believed to be the same one.

Mary's loose hair is an Aztec symbol of virginity. Modern technology has revealed that her eyes contain reflections of many people – this is thought to represent the scene when St Juan Diego opened his cloak.

Her hands are united in prayer, showing Mary's role as one of the **saints** that Catholics pray to.

There are 46 stars on her cloak which form the exact constellations of the sky at the time when Mary first appeared to St Juan Diego.

The crescent moon is a symbol of Revelation 12:1: 'a woman clothed with the sun, with the moon under her feet' who rules over everything. It is covered in black snakeskin which likely represents the Aztec serpent god of human sacrifice. By standing on it, Mary shows that God is above other pagan gods.

The rays are thought to symbolise the Aztec sun god, a malevolent figure. Mary stands in front of him, eclipsing him and protecting the Aztecs.

The high black belt or ribbon shows that she is pregnant with Jesus.

Flowers, like those on her dress, are an Aztec symbol of the presence of God, suggesting God is with her.

The angel has feathered wings and symbolises carrying Mary to the people.

Prophecy and Promise

Our Lady of Walsingham

The Shrine of Our Lady of Walsingham in Norfolk was founded around 1061 after the Saxon noblewoman Richeldis de Faverches had a vision of Mary. Walsingham was one of the most important Marian shrines in medieval times but was destroyed by Henry VIII during the Reformation. It was restored in the late nineteenth century and a new statue of Mary was carved, based on the original. In 1934 the Slipper Chapel at Walsingham was declared the National Shrine of Our Lady for Catholics in England.

Useful vocabulary

saints: people who are officially recognised by the Catholic Church as being very holy because of the way they lived or died; also, anyone who is already in heaven, whether recognised or not

- Mary holds a sceptre, a symbol of royal power, shaped like a white lily. This is a symbol of her fertility and purity and also represents the Immaculate Conception.

- Mary sits on a Saxon-style throne and wears a Saxon crown, reinforcing her royal status in the Church and reflecting the founding of the original shrine in 1061 in Saxon England. The pillars represent the Church and the seven rings represent the seven sacraments.

- Mary's robes are blue, the symbol of royalty, and they are edged with *fleur-de-lis* – lily flowers often used as an emblem on coats of arms by kings and queens.

- Behind Mary the arch of the seat represents a rainbow – a sign of the covenant God made with Noah in Genesis 9:12 to protect 'every living creature'.

- Mary holds her son Jesus on her knee, acting as a throne for him. He also wears a crown and both have haloes – symbols of holiness.

- Mary's feet rest upon the toadstone as a symbol of Revelation 12:1. This is the East Anglian symbol of evil, equivalent of the moon or serpent seen elsewhere in devotional imagery.

Understand

1. Describe the events of Mary's appearance to St Juan Diego.
2. Explain the symbolism of the following in the image of *Our Lady of Guadalupe*: **a)** the crescent moon and **b)** Mary's high belt.
3. Summarise three symbols shown on the statue of *Our Lady of Walsingham*.

Discern

4. Compare and contrast how *Our Lady of Guadalupe* and *Our Lady of Walsingham* present Mary and how well they reflect Catholic beliefs about her. Explain how each representation reflects the local culture in which it was created. Why do you think it is important to Catholics that representations of Mary reflect cultural diversity?

Respond

5. Is there an image of Mary that you find particularly appealing? What meaning does it convey to you?

How do devotional images show Catholic beliefs about Mary?   55

2.12 LIVED RELIGION OPTION

HOW IS JOSEPHINE BAKHITA A WOMAN OF THE MAGNIFICAT?

OBJECTIVES
In this lesson you will explore **who Josephine Bakhita was and why she was a woman of the Magnificat.**

Following in the footsteps of women such as Mary and Hannah are other women who embody their faith and holy qualities. For this, they are recognised by the Catholic Church. One such woman is St Josephine Bakhita, a religious sister who was made a saint in 2000. She was the first Black woman in the modern era to receive this distinction and is seen as a woman of the Magnificat.

Who was St Josephine Bakhita?

Josephine Bakhita was born around 1869 in Sudan and belonged to the Deju people. She had three brothers and three sisters and enjoyed the comfort of her family. However, this all changed in 1877 when Josephine was around seven years old: she was abducted by traders of enslaved people and sold into slavery.

The traders forced Josephine to walk barefoot for 600 miles until she reached the slave market at El-Obeid. Josephine went on to endure 12 years of slavery; she was frequently beaten and even cut with knives so that she would have scars. Finally, as a nanny to the daughter in an Italian family, Josephine and the child were placed in the care of the Canossian Daughters of Charity, a religious order in Venice. It was here that Josephine came to know God and was deeply moved by all the things the sisters taught. In 1890 she was baptised, confirmed and received her first Holy Communion. After the Mother Superior spoke out on her behalf, Josephine was declared free. Josephine chose to become a novice at the convent and in 1896 she became a sister, dedicating her life to God. She spent the rest of her life at the convent, working as a cook and a doorkeeper, welcoming visitors to the convent. She also visited other sisters, telling them of her story.

▲ *St Josephine Bakhita*

How is St Josephine Bakhita seen as a woman of the Magnificat?

To be a woman of the Magnificat means to embrace God's will with humility, to live a life of faith and constancy and to glorify God in gratitude and praise. The suffering that Josephine Bakhita endured during her life was horrific; however, she was a woman of great courage, strength and hope. She saw how violence and suffering could destroy

Prophecy and Promise

Canossian Sisters of Charity attending a meeting with Pope Francis at the Vatican in 2022

people, having experienced it first-hand, yet she never let this destroy her love for God, or her compassion, joy and gentleness towards other people.

> 'If I were to meet the slave-merchants who kidnapped me and even those who tortured me, I would kneel and kiss their hands. If what happened to me had never taken place, how could I become a Christian and a religious?'
>
> *St Josephine Bakhita*

Josephine was grateful to have the opportunity to say 'yes' to God, echoing what Mary herself did. We can see humility and deep forgiveness in her words too; she held no grudge against those who had kidnapped and abused her. Josephine Bakhita can therefore be said to be a woman of the Magnificat as she opened her heart to God and lived her life joyfully and humbly in the service of God. Although she was treated as poor and lowly by those who enslaved her, she is now elevated as someone to be venerated and called blessed.

She was charismatic and well loved and would often be referred to as 'our Black Mother' at the convent in Schio where she lived for 45 years – a title of respect for her which remains today. In this she is also linked to Mary as they both served in the role of mother to others, showing love and kindness to all they met. Towards the end of her life, Josephine suffered illness and great pain, however she did not give up her cheerfulness or faith. Josephine died on 8 February 1947. For three days after her death, Josephine's body lay at rest with thousands coming to see her and pay their respects. She was canonised (declared a saint) by Pope St John Paul II on 1 October 2000 for her great faith, joy and courage. She is venerated as a saint and has been adopted as the patron saint who stands against human trafficking.

Understand

1. What happened to Josephine Bakhita when she was around seven years old?
2. List two examples of suffering that Josephine Bakhita endured in her life.
3. Give a quotation from St Josephine Bakhita showing how she echoes Mary.
4. Give two ways in which St Josephine Bakhita is a woman of the Magnificat.

Discern

5. How far do the life and work of St Josephine Bakhita reflect the Magnificat and the recurring themes in the lives of the holy women of the Old Testament? Use your learning from across this chapter as well as the details in this lesson to explain your ideas.

Respond

6. What do you take away from Josephine Bakhita's life story?

How is Josephine Bakhita a woman of the Magnificat?

CHAPTER 2

ASSESSMENT

Key vocabulary

Write a definition for these key terms.

typology	Protoevangelium	Mary
Mother of God	Immaculate Conception	Our Lady
New Eve	Magnificat	the Rosary

Knowledge check

1. Which one of the following describes an allegorical story?
   a. any story from the Old Testament
   b. a story that symbolises or mirrors the events of another time or place
   c. a story which is intended to be read literally, as word-for-word truth
   d. a Gospel story about the relationship between Jesus and Mary
2. Copy out and complete the following sentence: Catholics believe that Adam is a t................. of C................. which means that he foreshadowed Jesus.
3. God chose Hannah since she was:
   a. humble
   b. boastful
   c. faithless

4. Give a quote from the Bible that shows Hannah's remarkable reversal.
5. Give an example of how Hannah connects with Mary.
6. What do Catholics mean by Mary as the Immaculate Conception?
7. Give two Catholic teachings about Mary.

8. Explain why the Catholic Church teaches that the women of the Old Testament are important.
9. Do you think the Magnificat is still important to Catholics today? Give reasons for your answer.
10. Outline three ways that Mary's prophecies are fulfilled in the Bible.

TIP

Think about the themes that are present in the Magnificat. How are they relevant to Catholics today?

TIP

Make sure your answer is focused on the different titles of Mary and how they show prophecies being fulfilled. Look back at pages 50–51 to help you.

Prophecy and Promise

Extended writing activity

This assessment is for you to show what you have learned in this chapter and for you to develop your extended writing skills. Here is a big question:

> 'Mary is the most important woman in the Bible.' Explain arguments that agree and disagree with this statement and evaluate the strength of each argument. In your answer you should refer to Catholic teaching.

To answer this question, you'll need to draw on some of the skills you learned about in Year 8:
- finding arguments for and against the statement (or to agree and disagree with the statement)
- using specialist religious terminology
- using evidence and examples to support your points
- referring to religious texts
- evaluating your arguments.

TIP

This question is asking you to evaluate the strength of each argument.

- Strong or convincing arguments are usually supported by clear evidence. For example, Catholics see scripture as an authoritative source because it is considered to be the word of God.
- An argument can be seen as weak if it lacks strong evidence, or if it goes against something we have evidence for.

1 **Plan your argument.** You could draw a spider diagram to help you plot out your ideas. Here is an example that has been started for you. Can you add in some more ideas connected to the 'Agree' and 'Disagree' headings?

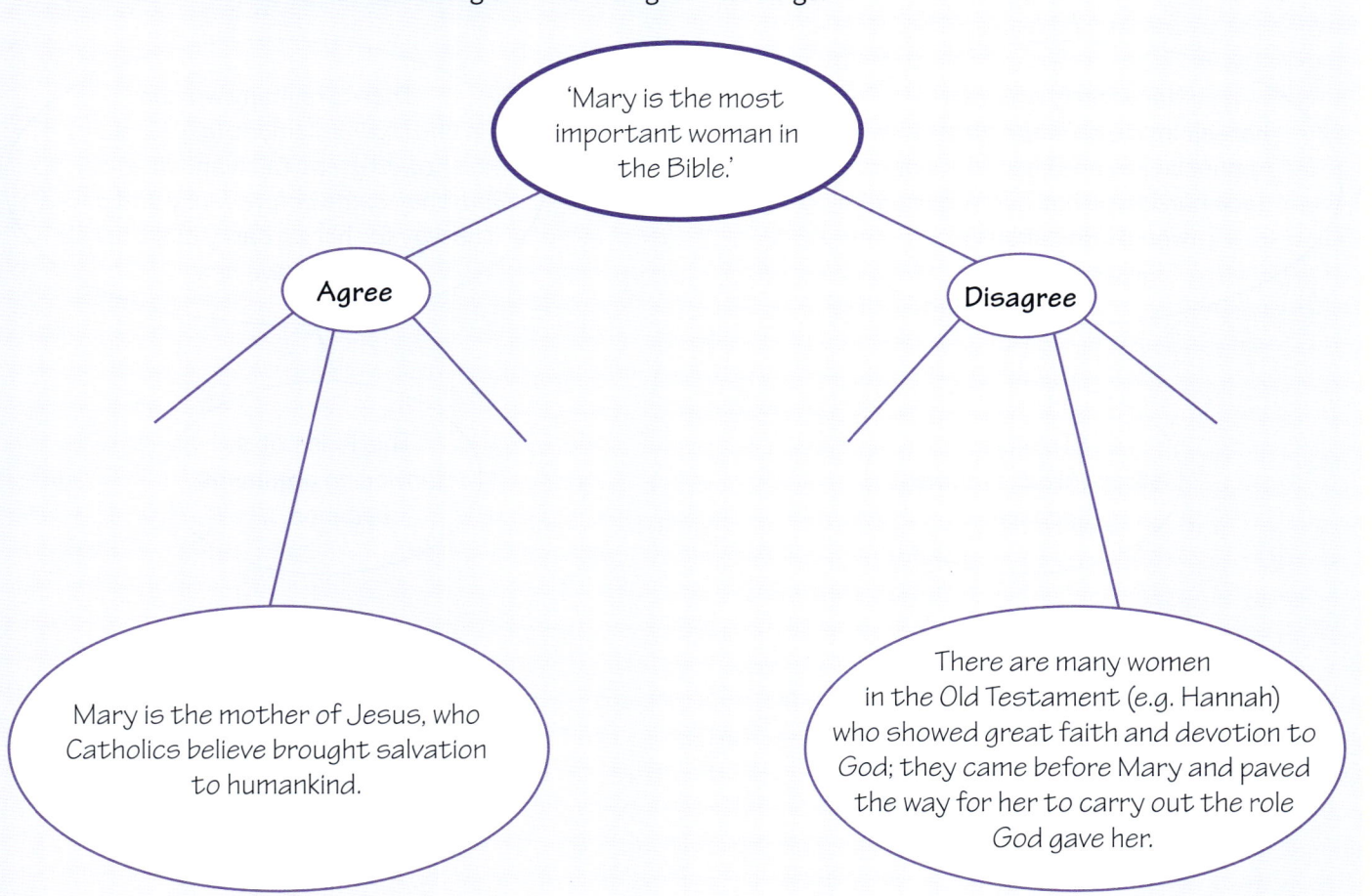

- 'Mary is the most important woman in the Bible.'
  - Agree
    - Mary is the mother of Jesus, who Catholics believe brought salvation to humankind.
  - Disagree
    - There are many women in the Old Testament (e.g. Hannah) who showed great faith and devotion to God; they came before Mary and paved the way for her to carry out the role God gave her.

Assessment 59

The question asks you to 'evaluate' the arguments. Remember this means you need to make a judgement based on reasoning or evidence. It means deciding if you are convinced by an argument based on the evidence used to back it up.

Can you add some ideas to your diagram about how you might evaluate each point? Some example sentence starters have been added below.

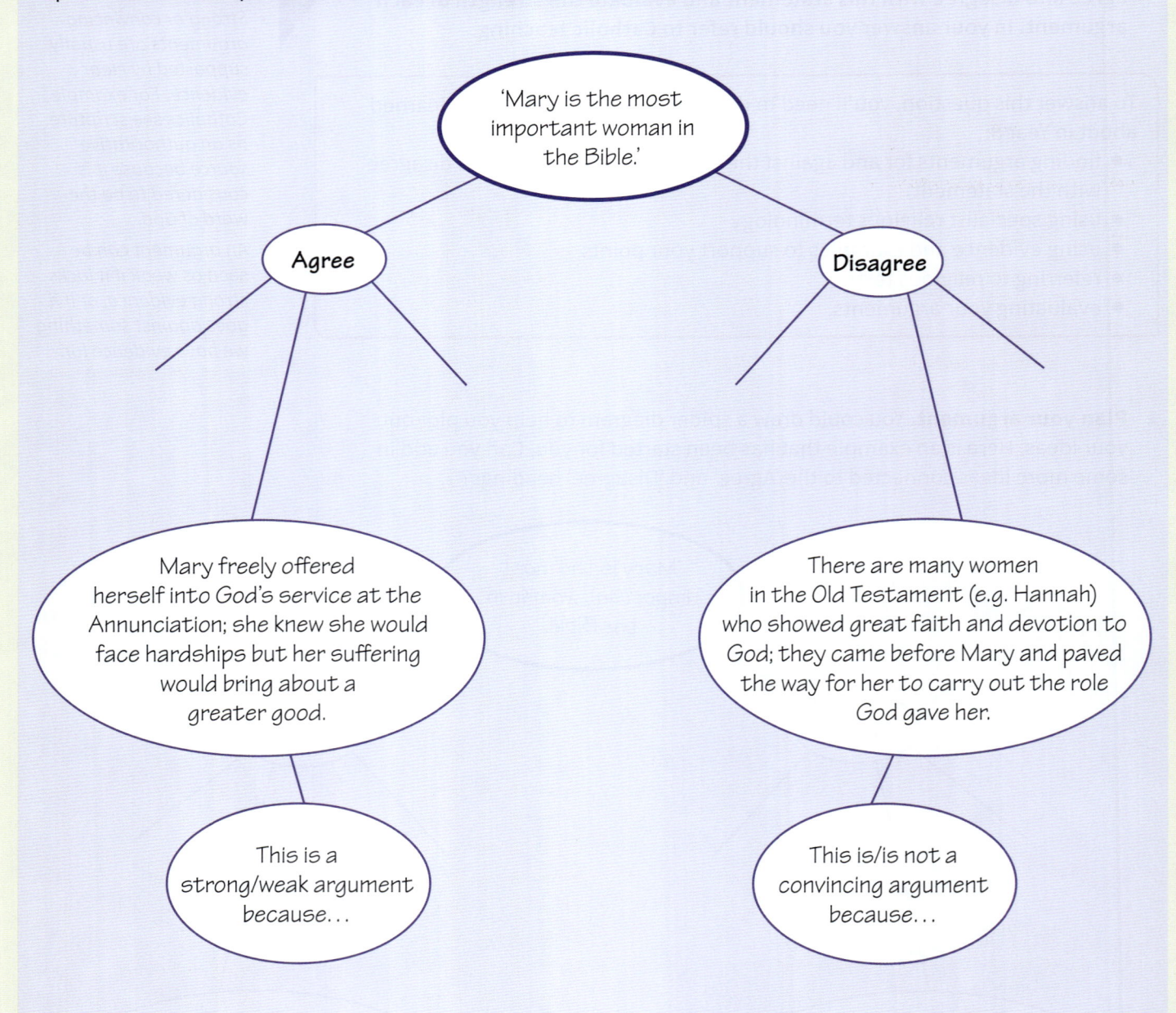

- 'Mary is the most important woman in the Bible.'
  - Agree
    - Mary freely offered herself into God's service at the Annunciation; she knew she would face hardships but her suffering would bring about a greater good.
      - This is a strong/weak argument because...
  - Disagree
    - There are many women in the Old Testament (e.g. Hannah) who showed great faith and devotion to God; they came before Mary and paved the way for her to carry out the role God gave her.
      - This is/is not a convincing argument because...

Prophecy and Promise

2. **Now try writing two paragraphs on arguments that agree with the statement and evaluate your arguments.** Choose the ones from your plan that you think are the strongest and that you know you'll have lots to say about. Here is an example:

> Many Catholics would agree that Mary is <u>the most important woman in the Bible</u> as mother of Jesus. She freely accepted God's will at the Annunciation. <u>She knew that she would face hardships, but she also believed this would bring about a greater good: the opportunity of salvation through Jesus.</u> Mary was humble and accepted her role without hesitation, showing her complete faith and trust in God. This is a <u>strong argument</u> for Mary being the most important woman in the Bible, as Catholics believe that without her faith and acceptance of her role, Jesus would not have come into the world to repair the broken relationship between God and humans.

Using the wording of the question can help to focus your answer.

A clear reason has been given for the argument presented.

The argument has been evaluated and shown to be strong by referencing beliefs about Jesus and Mary that are central to the Catholic faith.

3. **Try writing two more paragraphs explaining arguments that disagree with the statement and evaluate your arguments.** Remember to choose the ones from your list that you have a lot to say about.

Here is an example of an argument that disagrees with the statement. Can you evaluate this argument? Do you think it is convincing? Try to explain your reasoning.

> Some people may disagree and say that there are many women in the Old Testament that paved the way for the coming of Mary. Women like Hannah and Sarah showed great faith and dedication to God throughout their lives and these women could have acted as role models for Mary, helping her to become a woman of faith.

CHAPTER 3:
GALILEE TO JERUSALEM

Introduction

The Gospels show that during Jesus' ministry on earth, he did not work alone. From the beginning, **Jesus called men and women from all parts of society to follow him as disciples**, to learn from his example and his teachings.

Mark's Gospel shows that the call to be a disciple is considerable – it requires an individual to put Christ before all else. This is not always easy and Mark shows the twelve apostles as people who struggle and who often fail. However, **Jesus shows the importance of mercy and forgiveness**, choosing them to be his closest companions in the days leading up to his crucifixion and death.

Many biblical scholars (people who study the Bible closely) believe Mark's Gospel was written especially for an audience of early Jewish Christians who were being persecuted by the Romans for their faith. Stories of flawed disciples who do not always get it right, yet remain close to Christ, may have given Mark's audience hope that **even in difficult times of darkness when it is hard to understand what Jesus wants, he will not abandon them**.

While the twelve apostles are all men, **Mark extends the theme of discipleship to other followers of Jesus, including women**. His gospel emphasises that it is not *just* those twelve men who have been called to follow Jesus. They were chosen to be a positive example for Christians, to inspire them and show them how to be a true disciple of Christ.

Catholics believe that **just as Jesus called the disciples, he calls each person to their own particular mission**. Catholics believe vocations which serve God may be the everyday charitable work they do, or a job which helps the community. Marriage or celibate single life may also be vocations through which a person continues to fulfil Jesus' mission.

Some Catholics will follow a vocation to the religious life, such as monks, sisters and priests, and **are called to live out Christ's mission in the world in the service of others**. This way of life is a calling that requires full commitment to God. In the same way that Jesus chose male apostles, **only men are ordained as priests in the Catholic Church, receiving the sacrament of Holy Orders.**

As well as those who have taken religious vows, **all baptised Catholics are asked to spread Christ's message in the world**. There are many lay apostolate organisations that Catholics can join to do Jesus' work in the world and they are very wide ranging in their aims. One such organisation is the International Young Catholic Students.

63

3.1

WHAT DOES THE GOSPEL OF MARK TEACH ABOUT DISCIPLESHIP?

OBJECTIVE
In this lesson you will explore what the Gospel of Mark teaches about discipleship.

A **disciple** is a person who commits themselves entirely to following the teaching and example of Jesus. This term comes from the Greek word *mathētés*, which means 'one who learns from another' and it is first used in the Bible in the Gospels. The Gospel of Mark teaches important lessons about **discipleship**.

Why did Mark focus on discipleship?

Discipleship is a key focus in the Gospel of Mark. Mark recounts how Jesus begins to call the disciples who would assist him in his mission. The chief disciples of Jesus, known as the twelve **apostles**, acted as early Christian teachers or missionaries and were sent out by him to share his message. However, while the twelve apostles are important, the concept of discipleship actually extends far beyond those twelve individuals. It is significant that Mark tells of other people who were disciples rather than apostles, such as some of the women who were known to Jesus. The Catechism emphasises the idea that discipleship is inclusive: 'Jesus calls all people to come together around him' (CCC 542).

Catholic scholars suggest Mark focused on discipleship for a particular reason. The audience of Mark's Gospel was a community who faced brutal persecution from the non-Christian Roman Empire. However, through the way he presents the disciples, Mark gives this community hope and urges them to persevere.

Useful vocabulary

disciple: someone committed to following the teaching and example of Jesus

discipleship: the condition of being a disciple; the ways of living and actions carried out by them

apostles: the chief supporters of a teaching or cause

Who were the disciples?

The disciples are shown to be very real people who often demonstrate great loyalty to Jesus, but fail in other ways. However, this emphasises that disciples are not perfect, and that surrendering oneself entirely to Jesus is extremely difficult. Jesus frequently called his followers from people who were marginalised by the rest of society in order to show how all people are of equal value to God and God's purposes. When Jesus called Levi, the tax collector, to follow him, the Pharisees were outraged because tax collectors were disliked for working for the Romans. Jesus said, 'Those who are well have no need of a physician, but those who are sick. I came not to call the righteous, but sinners' (Mark 2:17).

▲ *The Calling of the Apostles Peter and Andrew by Duccio di Buoninsegna; Jesus called Peter (formerly Simon) and Andrew while they were working as fishermen*

64 Galilee to Jerusalem

What does Jesus ask of his disciples?

The calling of the first disciples appears quite early in Mark's Gospel and sets a pattern that is repeated when different disciples meet Jesus. For example, those who are called are often working when Jesus approaches them, which shows that the call can come unexpectedly and interrupt their lives.

> 'Passing alongside the Sea of Galilee, he saw Simon and Andrew the brother of Simon casting a net into the sea, for they were fishermen. And Jesus said to them, "Follow me, and I will make you become fishers of men." And immediately they left their nets and followed him.'
>
> *Mark 1:16–18*

The disciples are particularly called on by Jesus not just to believe in him, but to share his mission. Their response is immediate and involves them leaving behind what they were doing at the time, without question. Catholics believe that they too should be prepared to follow the teaching of Jesus wholeheartedly as they are called through Baptism as 'witnesses to Christ' to be priests, prophets and kings (CCC 942).

What does Jesus instruct his disciples to do?

Jesus gives twelve of his disciples special authority when he sends them out to call people to repent. For example, they are given the ability to heal people.

But much of being a disciple of Jesus is to do with following his example and learning from that. Jesus' disciples must also limit their material possessions:

> 'He charged them to take nothing for their journey except a staff – no bread, no bag, no money in their belts'
>
> *Mark 6:8*

There is evidence to suggest that some early Christians gave in to Roman torture, possibly revealing information about their fellow Christians. It might be interpreted, therefore, that Mark is teaching the early Christians that they must have trust in God, and keep faith and hope in spite of considerable challenges. Catholics today share these lessons, and may interpret the lack of material possessions to suggest that disciples should not place their own comfort above sharing the message of God, which is not always an easy path to choose, but is the cost of discipleship.

Understand

1. Who does Jesus call to discipleship in Mark's Gospel?
2. Identify who would have been reading Mark's Gospel originally and describe what was happening in society at that time.
3. What does Jesus instruct his twelve apostles to leave behind when they start following him?
4. How do the audience and historical context of Mark's Gospel influence what Mark writes about discipleship?

Read more…

You can read the full story of Jesus sending out the twelve in Mark 6:7–13. What do you think would have been the most challenging instruction for the apostles to follow?

A staff was used by Moses in Exodus and is symbolic of authority and power. The disciples are instructed to bring nothing except a staff, suggesting that they will need to trust God to provide, but also that they act with God's authority.

Discern

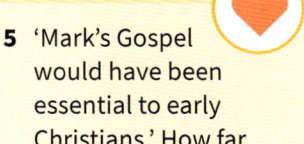

5. 'Mark's Gospel would have been essential to early Christians.' How far do you agree with this statement? What might a Catholic say to this? Give reasons to explain your ideas.

Respond

6. What do you think Jesus might ask of young people today if he called them? Would you respond to the call if he asked you?

What does the Gospel of Mark teach about discipleship?

3.2

WHAT DOES THE STORY OF THE RICH YOUNG MAN TEACH?

OBJECTIVE
*In this lesson you will explore **what the story of the Rich Young Man teaches about discipleship**.*

There are times in Mark's Gospel when Jesus gives a detailed insight into what it means to be his follower. The story of the Rich Young Man is one such example and shows that Jesus did not always give the answers that people expected. In Mark's Gospel, there is an emphasis on radical discipleship: the idea that a half-hearted approach will not do. Radical discipleship suggests that to be a follower of Christ a person must give their all.

What is the story of the Rich Young Man?

While preaching in Judea, Jesus is approached by a rich young man. It is suggested that he is a follower of Jesus who had good intentions and faith in God.

> 'A man ran up and knelt before him and asked him, "Good Teacher, what must I do to inherit eternal life?" And Jesus said to him, "Why do you call me good? No one is good except God alone. You know the commandments …" And he said to him, "Teacher, all these I have kept from my youth." And Jesus, looking at him, loved him, and said to him, "You lack one thing: go, sell all that you have and give to the poor, and you will have treasure in heaven; and come, follow me." Disheartened by the saying, he went away sorrowful, for he had great possessions.'
>
> *Mark 10:17–22*

The events of the story are as follows: a man comes to Jesus eagerly asking for guidance on how to enter the Kingdom of God. Jesus questions him about his life and he answers that he follows all the commandments, but Jesus sees one thing he lacks in his attachment to wealth. Some people suggest the man's question is arrogant because 'Good Teacher' seems forward and Jesus questions whether he really understands what he is calling him. Jesus 'loved him' because of his desire to be holy, but the man goes away disappointed at his guidance. The events of the story, the meaning of the words and what they would have conveyed to Mark's audience are all part of the **literal sense** of the story.

▶ *Christ and the Rich Young Ruler by Heinrich Hofmann*

Useful vocabulary

literal sense: the meaning of the text as the author intended it to be; this is different to reading a passage literally, which means accepting it as word-for-word truth

synoptic: referring to the three Gospels that have many similarities and can be 'read together', i.e. Matthew, Mark and Luke

Galilee to Jerusalem

A spiritual reading of the story might be that even those who uphold religious commandments can, deep down, love material things more than God. Catholics believe there should be no barriers between a person and God. Mark presents the idea that following Jesus requires complete devotion to God, and this can be hampered by weaknesses or distractions such as wealth. Therefore, the man is disappointed because he knows that he does not have the commitment to fully devote himself to Jesus.

Why is the story of the Rich Young Man important in Mark's Gospel?

A similar story to Mark's Rich Young Man appears in the other **synoptic** Gospels. However, it is only in Mark's version of the story that the man is described as 'rich'. The story comes at a point when Jesus begins to talk about the attachment humans have to wealth as an example of why it will not be easy for everyone to be saved. Jesus privately explains to the disciples the difficulty of entering heaven for those who are rich: 'It is easier for a camel to go through the eye of a needle than for a rich person to enter the kingdom of God' (Mark 10:25).

Some Christian scholars believe Jesus uses this analogy to emphasise the burdens which need to be shed in order to be worthy of entering God's Kingdom. The disciples are described as being 'exceedingly astonished' by Jesus' statement, and left wondering who could ever be good enough. Jesus' hopeful response acts as a reminder though that Jesus is not expecting people to act alone: 'For all things are possible with God' (Mark 10:27).

What do Catholics learn from the story of the Rich Young Man today?

In the story of the Rich Young Man, the love of wealth is shown as a barrier to following Jesus fully. The man's reluctance to give up his material possessions gets in the way of his love for God, but this can be true of other things that people value more than God. Vanity (being overly concerned with one's appearance) might act as a barrier for some. For others, refusing to give their time willingly to help others might mean that selfishness will prevent them becoming close to God. Today many people consider consumerism (being preoccupied with buying things) to be a distraction from more important values in life, such as spending time with family, service and generosity to others, and spiritual development. Catholics may use the story of the Rich Young Man to guide their own behaviour and ask what their own personal barrier is to becoming closer to God.

Read more...

You can read the whole story of the Rich Young Man in Mark 10:17–31. Do you think it is important that Mark includes the words 'Jesus… loved him?'

Understand

1. In the story of the Rich Young Man, which of the commandments does the man keep?
2. Suggest why the rich young man appears disappointed with Jesus' response.
3. Explain what you think the events of the story teach about the man's wish to be a disciple.
4. Later, when Jesus explains to the disciples about wealth being a barrier to entering heaven:
    a. What analogy does he use?
    b. What effect does this imagery have for the audience?

Discern

5. 'Many people work hard to be wealthy; the expectation to give all this away is unfair.' Explain how a Catholic might respond to this statement and give a reason why someone might disagree with them. Which argument do you think is more persuasive?

Respond

6. List five things that you have in your life that you need. Now list five things that you have in your life that are a luxury. How would you feel about giving up your luxuries?

3.3

WHAT ARE THE COSTS AND REWARDS OF DISCIPLESHIP?

OBJECTIVE
In this lesson you will explore the costs and rewards of being a disciple of Jesus.

When Mark writes about discipleship in his Gospel, he draws attention to the humanity of the twelve in particular so that his audience can identify with their responses. These may be positive responses like awe and wonder, but they may also be confusion, ignorance or shame. Mark does not hide the difficulty in being a disciple, but he makes clear the promise of reward in the next life.

The costs of being a disciple

Mark's Gospel often shows that it is difficult to be a disciple. Scholars think that Mark hoped his audience would be able to identify with the disciples and learn from them.

In Mark 8:27–38, Jesus talks to his disciples about who they think he is, and what is going to happen to him. It is an example of how the disciples find it difficult to understand the enormity of what Jesus has come to do:

> '[Jesus] asked them, "But who do you say that I am?" Peter answered him, "You are the Christ." ... And he began to teach them that the Son of Man must suffer many things and be rejected by the elders and the chief priests and the scribes and be killed, and after three days rise again. And he said this plainly. And Peter took him aside and began to rebuke him. But turning and seeing his disciples, he rebuked Peter and said, "Get behind me, Satan! For you are not setting your mind on the things of God, but on the things of man."'
>
> *Mark 8:29, 31–33*

Useful vocabulary

martyrs: people who knowingly sacrifice their lives for their religious beliefs

This is one of the costs of discipleship: to learn to think about what God wants and place this above an individual's personal feelings.

Poor Peter! Mark's audience might identify with Peter's reaction to the idea of Jesus' death. However, Jesus' response shows that this is all part of a learning process for Peter, who must change his human way of thinking to place what God wants first. Similarly, this is a learning process for anyone else who hears this message.

Jesus sometimes addresses the disciples as 'children' (Mark 10:24), and they often are like children in need of discipline, or teaching. Jesus goes on to teach them another cost of discipleship in Mark 8:34–36.

▶ *The disciples did not always understand what Jesus was trying to teach them*

Galilee to Jerusalem

To 'deny himself' means a cost of discipleship is to reject selfish impulses and to follow the sacrifice and example of Jesus. The 'cross' foreshadows Jesus' own crucifixion, as well as the persecution that the disciples will face after Jesus' death and resurrection.

Jesus warns that anyone who is not willing to face hardship in his name will not be saved.

> 'If anyone would come after me, let him deny himself and take up his cross and follow me. For whoever would save his life will lose it, but whoever loses his life for my sake and the gospel's will save it. For what does it profit a man to gain the whole world and forfeit his soul?'
>
> Mark 8:34–36

Jesus promises that anyone who is willing to face hardship in his name will be redeemed. Most of the disciples go on to become **martyrs**.

The rewards of discipleship

The costs of discipleship are balanced alongside the considerable rewards of discipleship. Jesus promises the Kingdom of God to those who show loyalty and trust in God:

> 'Jesus said, "Truly, I say to you, there is no one who has left house or brothers or sisters or mother or father or children or lands, for my sake and for the gospel, who will not receive a hundredfold now in this time, houses and brothers and sisters and mothers and children and lands, with persecutions, and in the age to come eternal life. But many who are first will be last, and the last first."'
>
> Mark 10:29–31

This references the community of the early Christians who would have called each other brothers and sisters in Christ. Again, Mark is speaking to the early Christian communities who faced the ultimate test of persecution for their faith but who could find solace in companionship and community.

The rewards will be both eternal life in heaven but also communion in the Church in their life presently.

Jesus promises that those who suffer and are 'last' will be rewarded in the Kingdom of God.

Understand

1. How does Peter fail Jesus in Mark 8:29–33?
2. Describe what Mark 8:29–33 shows about the nature of discipleship when Jesus accuses Peter of worrying too much about 'the things of man'.
3. Explain why Mark may have included this story in his Gospel, with reference to his original audience.
4. What does Jesus mean when he says that a disciple must 'take up [their] cross and follow [him]'?
5. Identify two ways in which true disciples of Jesus will be rewarded.

Discern

6. 'It is much easier to be a disciple today than it was at the time of Jesus.' Present arguments for and against this statement, including what a Catholic might say. Evaluate the strengths and weaknesses of the arguments and reach a final judgement.

Respond

7. If 'taking up your cross' is a metaphor for the hardships disciples face, can you think of a 'cross' you have had to carry? Did it, or does it, bring you closer to God?

3.4

HOW DID THE DISCIPLES SOMETIMES FAIL?

OBJECTIVE
In this lesson you will explore **how the disciples sometimes failed Jesus.**

Mark's Gospel places particular emphasis on the apparent failures of Jesus' disciples. Whether their failures are misunderstanding Jesus or being human in the things they do, there are numerous examples in Mark's Gospel of when the disciples just seem to get it wrong. However, the key message is that, in spite of everything they do wrong, they remain loyal to Jesus and he remains loyal to them.

How do the disciples demonstrate failure at times?

Mark paints a very rounded picture of the disciples in order to communicate that these were ordinary men and women: faithful yet short-sighted, loyal and dedicated yet frequently astonished. They are often shown to be fearful of what they have witnessed simply because they fail to understand the significance of what Jesus was doing. This is then apparently met with frustration by Jesus who questions why they find it so hard to have faith.

In Mark 4:35–41, for example, Jesus performs a miracle of nature by calming a storm:

> 'He said to them, "Why are you so afraid? Have you still no faith?" And they were filled with great fear and said to one another, "Who then is this, that even the wind and the sea obey him?"'
>
> *Mark 4:40–41*

The disciples' fear and lack of faith disappoint Jesus. Despite being his closest friends and followers, they still do not really understand who Jesus is. This story sits in the section of Mark's Gospel that focuses on Jesus' miracles and which reveal Jesus as the Son of God, yet the disciples cannot grasp this. In Jesus Feeds the Four Thousand, which comes at the end of this group of miracle stories, the disciples have just returned from their mission to spread Jesus' teachings. They have cast out demons and healed people who are sick under Jesus' authority yet they *still* do not have faith in God's power and question how Jesus will manage to feed such a crowd: 'How can one feed these people with bread here in this desolate place?' (Mark 8:4).

What can Mark's audience learn from the disciples' failings?

While this continual lack of faith annoys Jesus, he does not turn away from the disciples because they show love and loyalty to him and eagerness to share his ministry. Mark would have known how hard it must have been for the early Christians to keep faith in Jesus when faced with the brutality of the Romans. Through highlighting the humanity of the disciples, Mark is urging his audience to remain loyal to Jesus whatever their journey; if they do then Jesus will not abandon them.

Useful vocabulary

apostolic succession: the teaching that the bishops of the Catholic Church form a direct line of holy authority and leadership that comes from the first apostles of Jesus

Read more...

You can read the full stories of Jesus Calms a Storm in Mark 4:35–41 and Jesus Feeds the Four Thousand in Mark 8:1–9. Which words and phrases tell you more about what the apostles were feeling during these events?

Galilee to Jerusalem

Why are St Peter's failures so significant?

Peter is often the spokesperson on behalf of the disciples. He was renamed 'Peter' by Jesus in the Gospel of Matthew, a name meaning 'rock' in Greek. By doing this, Jesus appoints Peter as the future leader of his Church on earth. Peter, as the first pope, then lays the foundations for **apostolic succession** in the Catholic Church.

As the appointed leader, Peter often argues that he will remain true to Jesus, which makes his failings even more significant when they occur. When, just before Jesus' arrest, Jesus predicts that Peter will deny that he knows him, Peter declares: 'Even though they all fall away, I will not' (Mark 14:29). Shortly after, what Jesus has said comes true and Peter denies Jesus three times. Peter is recognised by the servant of the high priest and, perhaps fearful of what might happen to him if he is associated with Jesus, he allows his fear to rule his actions. He shows weakness and human frailty.

▲ *Peter's Denial by Michael D. O'Brien; perhaps Peter's biggest mistake was to deny that he knew Jesus in Jesus' final hours before his crucifixion*

However, after denying Jesus he is full of remorse: 'he broke down and wept' (Mark 14:72). He knows his disloyalty and cowardice were far from what was needed from him as Jesus' 'rock' (Matthew 16:18).

The Christian community of Rome who Mark wrote for would no doubt find many similarities between their story and Peter's. Questions about their loyalty to Jesus would have been a regular occurrence. At the time of Jesus' arrest, Peter lacks good judgement, courage and understanding, but Christians believe he made amends for this by the end of his life, having led the early Church and been martyred for his faith in Rome around AD 64. If Peter failed to understand who Jesus was during his ministry, he had developed unwavering faith by the end of his own life. For Catholics, Peter's failures are his strengths because only through perseverance and faith in Christ can humans truly see what they can become.

Understand

1. Describe how one of the miracles in Mark's Gospel shows the failings of the disciples.
2. Mark's Gospel suggests that Jesus is frustrated with the disciples at times. Why might this be?
3. What does 'Peter' mean? Explain why Jesus may have chosen this name for him.
4. Explain why Mark's audience would have found it helpful to see the failures of the disciples.

Discern

5. 'The disciples are valuable role models for Christians today, even though they made mistakes.' Explain how a Catholic might respond to this statement and give a reason why someone might disagree with them. Which argument do you think is more persuasive?

Respond

6. Write about a time when you failed at something but you tried again. What made you keep going in the face of failure?

How did the disciples sometimes fail?

3.5

HOW WERE WOMEN IMPORTANT IN JESUS' MINISTRY?

OBJECTIVE
In this lesson you will explore how women in the Bible were shown to possess key qualities that a follower of Christ should demonstrate.

In Christianity, when Jesus sent out the twelve to spread his message, none of his female disciples were among them. However, Mark's Gospel shows that women were not only present during Jesus' ministry, they played an important part in it. It is significant that while we often learn about how the male disciples fall short, in contrast female characters often seem to understand what should be done.

What is the significance of the Syrophoenician woman's faith for discipleship?

Catholics believe the story of the Syrophoenician Woman's Faith is important for many reasons. A literal reading shows it to be a miracle healing story; a spiritual reading teaches that the Kingdom of God is open to everyone. But the story is also about female discipleship.

At this time, it would not be common for men and women who are strangers to have a conversation. The woman has acted decisively in seeking Jesus out.

▶ This painting Crumbs of Love by Michael Cook is based on the story of the Syrophoenician woman

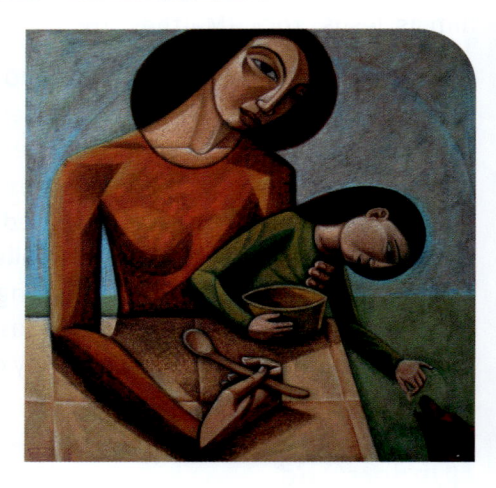

> 'And [Jesus] entered a house and did not want anyone to know, yet he could not be hidden. But immediately a woman whose little daughter had an unclean spirit heard of him and came and fell down at his feet. Now the woman was a Gentile, a Syrophoenician by birth. And she begged him to cast the demon out of her daughter. And he said to her, "Let the children be fed first, for it is not right to take the children's bread and throw it to the dogs." But she answered him, "Yes, Lord; yet even the dogs under the table eat the children's crumbs." And he said to her, "For this statement you may go your way; the demon has left your daughter." And she went home and found the child lying in bed and the demon gone.'
>
> Mark 7:24–30

The woman shows she understands that his message is for everyone.

Discipleship requires humility.

The woman's response to Jesus' question is both intelligent and courageous. One interpretation is that it shows she understands what Jesus has come to do and how he needs to do it.

In recognition of her understanding and faith in God, Jesus grants her request.

Galilee to Jerusalem

Going against social and cultural norms, Jesus allows the woman to have a voice in their conversation, which women were generally never given. Her faith is at the centre of this discussion and this proves to be more important than her gender. This exchange suggests women were prepared to engage with what Jesus said and to ask difficult questions. The story suggests that sometimes disciples need to be brave.

What other qualities do the women of Mark's Gospel demonstrate?

In Mark 14, a woman recognises Jesus as the Messiah and anoints him accordingly to show her faith and respect to him as a king. However, her act is seen to be shocking to Jesus' other followers, as women would not usually come into contact with men they were not married to:

> 'And while he was at Bethany … a woman came with an alabaster flask of ointment of pure nard, very costly, and she broke the flask and poured it over his head. There were some who said to themselves indignantly, "Why was the ointment wasted like that? For this ointment could have been sold for more than three hundred denarii and given to the poor." And they scolded her. But Jesus said, "Leave her alone. Why do you trouble her? She has done a beautiful thing to me. For you always have the poor with you, and whenever you want, you can do good for them. But you will not always have me. She has done what she could; she has anointed my body beforehand for burial. And truly, I say to you, wherever the gospel is proclaimed in the whole world, what she has done will be told in memory of her."'
>
> *Mark 14:3–9*

Neither the Syrophoenician woman nor this woman is given a name; Mark therefore forces the reader to only consider their actions in that moment and nothing else.

This would have been equivalent in price to a whole year's salary for an average worker, which explains why the other followers reacted as they did.

Jesus' words suggest that the woman's action shows she has prophetic insight into his death.

Jesus' final statement is to value the woman's action so highly that it will be remembered by the world even when he has gone. This woman shows that the ultimate act of discipleship is to recognise Jesus for who he is and to value that far above money, material goods or other earthly considerations.

Understand

1. In what ways does the story of the Syrophoenician woman challenge expectations of society at the time?
2. Identify two characteristics demonstrated by women that Jesus appears to value.
3. Give one reason why Mark may not have named the Syrophoenician woman or the woman in Bethany.
4. Explain how women show discipleship in Mark's Gospel.

Discern

5. 'The women of Jesus' ministry show that the first rule of discipleship is absolute faith in Jesus.' How far do you agree with this statement? Refer to the Bible texts in this lesson to explain your answer.

Respond

6. Which quality do you think you possess the most of: faithfulness or willingness to serve? Why?

3.6

HOW DID JESUS' FEMALE FOLLOWERS DEMONSTRATE DISCIPLESHIP?

OBJECTIVE
In this lesson you will explore **the faithfulness of the women in Mark's Gospel in comparison to the twelve.**

The women of Mark's Gospel are mainly portrayed in a positive light: loyal, brave and faithful. The stories of the death and resurrection of Jesus are a particular test of faith, and this is especially poignant given the twelve male apostles are seemingly absent at these crucial moments.

How were women present during Jesus' crucifixion?

The events of Holy Thursday see Jesus betrayed by Judas, one of his twelve apostles, and denied by Peter, one of his closest companions. In this way, Jesus really does seem to have been abandoned by the time he is crucified. However, while the male disciples are nowhere to be seen at this point of the story, Mark makes a clear reference to the women who do not desert Jesus:

> 'There were also women looking on from a distance, among whom were Mary Magdalene, and Mary the mother of James the younger and of Joses, and Salome. When he was in Galilee, they followed him and ministered to him, and there were also many other women who came up with him to Jerusalem.'
>
> *Mark 15:40–41*

This is the first time that Mark names these women as having been closely associated with Jesus over a period of time; some biblical scholars believe he wants his audience to be acutely aware of them. The Greek word that Mark uses here for 'follow' is *akoloutheó* and it is the same word he used when Jesus called Simon and Andrew in Mark 1:17 to become 'fishers of men': disciples. For this reason, Catholics understand that Mark is deliberately recognising the women as disciples of Christ. By pointing this out at this critical time in Jesus' life when the male disciples are markedly absent, he presents the women in a positive light. They show courage and fidelity (faithfulness to a person or cause) when his twelve do not.

▲ Scenes from the Passion of Christ: The Crucifixion *(middle panel)* by Andrea di Vanni; the women who followed Jesus remained near to him at his crucifixion

Galilee to Jerusalem

What role did the women have in the Resurrection story in Mark's Gospel?

The fidelity shown by the women in remaining present during Jesus' crucifixion means that they know where he is buried. They are the first ones to go to Jesus' body on Sunday to carry out the anointing rituals and are therefore the first ones to receive the news of the greatest miracle of all: the Resurrection. The women are then tasked with the job of going to tell the other disciples:

> 'You seek Jesus of Nazareth, who was crucified. He has risen; he is not here. ... But go, tell his disciples and Peter that he is going before you to Galilee. There you will see him, just as he told you.'
>
> *Mark 16:6–7*

The women, who again are named, are centrally important in the Resurrection story. By continuing to serve Jesus by attending his burial site they demonstrate discipleship in the absence of the twelve.

Mark's writing, however, proves to be more complex. Up until this point, the women have always done the right thing from Jesus' perspective: the Syrophoenician woman, the woman who anointed Jesus at Bethany, the women following Jesus at the Crucifixion and now the women here at the tomb. The reader might expect the women to act in the same way again. However, when asked to go and tell the disciples and Peter the news, they no longer remain steadfast; they actually become fearful and show some of the failing characteristics that the twelve have shown before now:

> 'And they went out and fled from the tomb, for trembling and astonishment had seized them, and they said nothing to anyone, for they were afraid.'
>
> *Mark 16:8*

We never know why their courage fails them at this moment. Mark's Gospel is not afraid to show that it is possible to be excellent and then fall short of what God asks; or indeed the other way around. Catholics try to draw inspiration from the positive qualities all the disciples show, but also take comfort in knowing that those closest to Jesus, who so often did the right thing, were also susceptible to human frailty, reflecting how difficult it can be to be a disciple.

Read more…

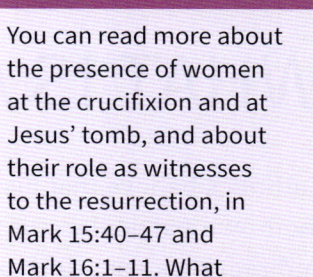

You can read more about the presence of women at the crucifixion and at Jesus' tomb, and about their role as witnesses to the resurrection, in Mark 15:40–47 and Mark 16:1–11. What emotions can you identify in the text?

Discern

5. 'By recording the fearful reaction of the women at the end of his Gospel, Mark undermines the fidelity they showed on many more occasions.' Explain how a Catholic might respond to this statement and give a reason why someone might disagree with them. Which argument do you think is more persuasive?

Understand

1. How is Jesus let down by his twelve apostles not long before his crucifixion?
2. How do the women show themselves to be faithful followers during the death and resurrection of Jesus?
3. Identify two similarities between the actions of the women and the characteristics of a disciple.
4. Explain what Catholics believe is the lesson to be learned from the women's fear after the resurrection of Jesus.

Respond

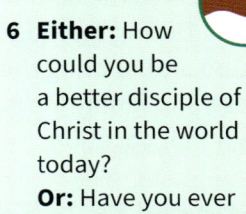

6. **Either:** How could you be a better disciple of Christ in the world today?
   Or: Have you ever been afraid to do something? How did your fear affect your actions?

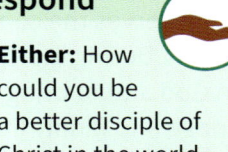

3.7

WHAT IS A VOCATION?

OBJECTIVE
In this lesson you will explore **what is meant by vocation.**

Catholics believe that just as Jesus called the disciples, he calls each person to their own particular mission. Today, people might feel a calling to follow Christ and receive a **vocation** to a particular way of life. This might be a calling to the priesthood or **religious life** or it might be a calling to serve God in other ways.

What is a vocation?

▲ *Some people consider being part of the emergency services or being a teacher to be a vocation*

The word 'vocation' can be used in a religious and a non-religious way. The meaning is quite similar: it means a calling or summoning to a particular role or way of life. What makes vocation distinct for Catholics is that it is to do with serving God. This may be used in connection to serving as a priest, or a religious brother or sister, for example, but vocation can also be used in terms of the lay faithful (baptised Catholics who do not belong to the priesthood or the religious life). These Catholics are called to serve God in other ways, such as through charity work or in working a job that serves the community. Marriage and family life can also be described as a vocation. During marriage vows a Catholic will promise 'to accept children lovingly from God and to bring them up according to the law of Christ and his Church'. Marriage and family life is a calling for some Catholics and a way of serving God through that vocation.

What does St John Henry Newman's prayer say about vocation?

St John Henry Newman (1801–1890) was an English theologian and Catholic cardinal who wrote a prayer that speaks especially about vocation (see next page).

Useful vocabulary

vocation: in Catholicism, a calling from God to love and serve God and the Church in a particular way of life, which leads to holiness

religious life: a consecrated (holy) way of life within the Church in which men or women take vows of chastity, poverty and obedience and live in communities, apart from the lay faithful

Galilee to Jerusalem

> 'God has created me to do Him some definite service. He has committed some work to me which He has not committed to another. I have my mission. I may never know it in this life, but I shall be told it in the next. I am a link in a chain, a bond of connection between persons. He has not created me for naught. I shall do good; I shall do His work. I shall be an angel of peace, a preacher of truth in my own place, while not intending it if I do but keep His commandments.

St John Henry Newman

- God has a unique plan for every person that will allow them to serve God.
- Even if the person is not fully aware of what God wants from them, they still have a particular mission which they will one day understand.
- Every person has a calling which connects them to the rest of humanity. Humans should not see themselves as separate from others: everyone should work together.
- Every person has been created for a purpose.
- By doing good deeds, humans can serve God.
- Bringing about peace and speaking the truth are examples of good deeds that serve God.

What are baptised Catholics called to do?

Through the Sacrament of Baptism, *all* Catholics are called to the 'common priesthood': this means to offer themselves and their gifts as sacrifices to God. Each person has their own mission to serve God in their life and this calling will be different for everyone. St John Henry Newman speaks of 'some definite service', which for some might be the priesthood or religious life, but for others it might be to act as a witness to Christ – to reflect his goodness – in another way. So, a nurse might serve God through caring for those who are sick, while an altar server might serve God through enabling the celebration of Mass.

Catholics believe that Jesus has a mission for every person, even if they do not know it, want it or accept it. In Matthew 28:16–20, Jesus charges the disciples with the mission of calling all people to be followers of Christ: 'Go therefore and make disciples of all nations, baptising them in the name of the Father and of the Son and of the Holy Spirit'. All baptised Catholics have the same mission to serve God as examples of Christ in the world.

Understand

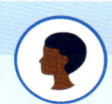

1. Give two examples of religious vocations.
2. Give two examples of how the lay faithful might be called to their own vocation.
3. Identify and explain a quotation from St John Henry Newman's prayer which explains that God has a specific mission for each person.
4. Explain one way St John Henry Newman's prayer about vocation connects to Mark's teachings on discipleship.
5. How do Catholics believe that following a vocation today connects to Jesus' calling of his disciples?

Discern

6. 'If you don't have a clear vocation to the priesthood or religious life, it's difficult to know whether you have a vocation or just a dream.' How far do you agree or disagree with this statement? Do you think it's harder to respond to a vocation in the modern world? Explain your ideas, and how a Catholic might respond to them.

Respond

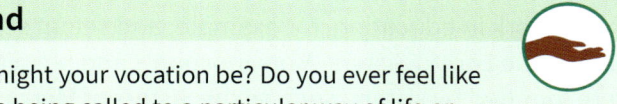

7. What might your vocation be? Do you ever feel like you are being called to a particular way of life or active service?

What is a vocation?

3.8

WHAT IS MEANT BY RELIGIOUS LIFE?

OBJECTIVE
*In this lesson you will explore **what it means to be called to religious life**.*

St John Henry Newman speaks of every Catholic having a calling to 'some definitive service'. For some Catholic men, this may be a calling to the priesthood; for other Catholic men and women, this may be a calling to religious life.

What is religious life?

Religious life refers to the ways in which Catholics might choose to serve God that mean they make binding holy promises called vows, and commit to a whole new way of life as a monk, nun, brother or sister. Religious life is sometimes called consecrated (holy) life and there are many different types of religious life in the Catholic Church for both men and women.

Useful vocabulary

orders: types of religious community that follow particular religious, moral and social rules

Closed orders

Inspired by the Rule of St Benedict, a book of guidance written by the sixth-century monk, some monks and nuns in closed **orders** live separately to the rest of society in a monastery or a convent. Their day is likely to be structured around prayer, meditation, worship and Bible study. Monks and nuns also undertake the everyday chores in running their monastery or convent, such as cooking and cleaning. They may undertake work to generate money for their order, such as through creating artwork or pottery, or selling produce grown in their gardens. Their belongings are very limited and there may be times of the day when monks or nuns are not allowed to speak. They will live a simple and humble life in the service of God.

▲ *Some people choose to join a closed order; here, monks are reciting Gregorian chants at Mass in a Benedictine monastery in Keur Moussa, Senegal*

Community life

Other Catholics who are called to religious life might choose to serve God out in the community. In this case they might be referred to as a friar, or a religious brother or sister. While they would also have some prayer life and worship within their daily structure, the majority of the day would be spent in active service. Some religious orders work in education, for example, and set up schools, such as the Loreto Sisters. Many hospitals and hospices were founded by sisters, such as the Sisters of Mercy. A sister might also live as part of a church community and share many different daily tasks with the parish priest.

▲ *Some religious orders work in the community; this nursery school in Bien Hoa, Vietnam, is run by Dominican Sisters*

What are the evangelical counsels?

Religious life is quite similar to the radical discipleship that Mark writes about in his Gospel because those who enter into religious life must serve God above all else. This involves surrendering earthly possessions and rejecting anything that might distract a person from God. In the story of the Rich Young Man, the man was challenged by Jesus to give up his material possessions. In the same way, those who choose the religious life will also be challenged to give up their material possessions.

Whether a person lives in an enclosed order or an order that focuses on active service, religious life will usually require them to make vows of poverty, chastity and obedience, which are referred to as the **evangelical counsels**.

> By taking the **vow of poverty**, a person is agreeing to live a very simple life and to only possess what is essential; luxury items would not be allowed. Clothes would be basic, and in many cases almost like a uniform, which might include wearing a habit (a long, simple garment).

> The **vow of chastity** means to refrain from having a romantic relationship. A person who takes a vow of chastity is agreeing to not get married or have a partner or any sexual relationship. In a similar way to the vow of poverty, chastity is also to do with remaining focused on God above all else.

> The final **vow of obedience** is taken in relation to the particular order that an individual chooses to become part of. Within any order, there will be individuals who are in charge and who set the boundaries and make decisions. To take the vow of obedience is to agree to follow the rules of that order even when an individual does not want to or even disagrees with that rule. This obedience is ultimately demonstrating faithfulness, commitment and service to God.

Understand

1. Give two examples of actions that a monk or nun in a closed order is likely to carry out as part of their day.
2. What is the main difference between religious life in a closed order and religious life in the community?
3. How does religious life link to the radical discipleship that Mark writes about?
4. What are the evangelical counsels?
5. Explain why the evangelical counsels are important to the vocation of religious life.
6. Which vow links to Jesus' guidance in the story of the Rich Young Man (see pages 66–67)? Explain why the man does not agree to Jesus' guidance.

Useful vocabulary

evangelical counsels: the vows of poverty, chastity and obedience, taught by Jesus in the Bible and taken by individuals wishing to enter religious life

vow of poverty: voluntarily promising to give up all possessions for the common good of a community

vow of chastity: voluntarily promising to abstain from sexual pleasure

vow of obedience: voluntarily promising to follow the authority of a religious order

Discern

7. 'Serving God in a closed order would make you a more faithful Christian.' Present arguments for and against this statement, including what a Catholic might say. Try to explore the strengths of both ways of religious life and then form your overall judgement to explain which argument you find more persuasive.

Respond

8. Find out what your family and friends think about the call to poverty, chastity and obedience that people entering religious life answer. How are their viewpoints different from or similar to your own views?

3.9

WHAT IS THE SACRAMENT OF HOLY ORDERS?

OBJECTIVE
In this lesson you will explore the Sacrament of Holy Orders.

In the Catholic Church only men can receive the Sacrament of **Holy Orders** and become either a **deacon, priest** or **bishop**. Men who take on these roles are called to continue the work of Jesus, just as his disciples were.

What is the Sacrament of Holy Orders?

The Sacrament of Holy Orders is one of the two Sacraments at the Service of Communion; the other is the Sacrament of Matrimony. Both of these sacraments are about building God's Church whether that is in the parish or in family life. There are three degrees or levels of **ordination** in the Sacrament of Holy Orders. All men will first become deacons. Some men become permanent deacons, while others go on to be ordained as priests. Some priests are later ordained as bishops.

Taking Holy Orders is a vocation and these roles are a lifelong commitment. A person must freely choose the path of Holy Orders and prepare by joining a seminary (religious college) so they can be educated, trained and developed spiritually. Men usually spend around six years in the seminary in both study and prayer.

The origins of holy service and leadership in the Church can be traced all the way back to the early Christians – the characteristics of service and commitment were recognised from the time of the twelve apostles.

> 'And when they had appointed elders for them in every church, with prayer and fasting they committed them to the Lord in whom they had believed.'
> Acts 14:23

This idea of Church 'elders' developed over time and the three degrees of ordination we have today were formally established in the second century AD.

Useful vocabulary

Holy Orders: the Sacrament at the Service of Communion in which the grace and spiritual power to sanctify others is conferred by the placing of a bishop's hands on a candidate

deacon, priest, bishop: the three sacramental degrees of Holy Orders

ordination: the ceremony in which a man is granted Holy Orders and becomes a deacon, priest or bishop

celibacy: the state of being entirely consecrated to God and therefore unmarried

What does it mean to be ordained?

Deacon

A deacon might be either permanent or transitional (temporary). A transitional deacon will be ordained on their route to priesthood, whereas a permanent deacon intends to remain as a deacon. Deacons, under the direction of the bishop, assist the priest *in persona Christi servi* – as a servant of Christ. For example, they can baptise people, marry them or read the Gospel during Mass. This is a voluntary role so deacons will likely have another job. A permanent deacon can be married and have a family.

▲ *During one part of an ordination the man being ordained will lie face down on the floor*

Galilee to Jerusalem

Priest

Priesthood is a way of life that involves service to God. A priest must take a lifelong vow of **celibacy**. As a priest stands *in persona Christi* – in the place of Christ – they can consecrate the Eucharist and absolve a person of their sins (whereas a deacon cannot). As a Sacrament at the Service of Communion, an essential part of Holy Orders is being in communion with other people. Some priests belong to a particular religious order such as the Jesuits. However, many priests will work within a parish. A priest must do what he can to bring his congregation closer to God, working directly with people through administering the sacraments, supporting local Catholic schools and saying Mass. A priest's role is wide-ranging: they will care for people in both their happiest and their saddest moments of life.

Bishop

A bishop leads an area called a diocese. His role is also to teach and sanctify, which means bishops hold the fullness of Holy Orders. He will oversee the placements of priests within local churches, as well as directing Catholic schools in their mission and ordaining new deacons and priests. Bishops are appointed by the Pope and can only be ordained by another bishop.

What happens during an ordination?

Feature of the rite	Why is this important?
Promise of obedience (to the bishop and his successors)	The bishop of the diocese will direct and guide the new deacon, priest or bishop; as a symbol of this, the candidate will place his folded hands inside the folded hands of the bishop.
Litany of the saints	This is a reminder that the candidate has been called to this role just as the saints were called to a life of holiness. At this point, deacons and priests lie prostrate on the floor to show their submission to God.
Laying on of hands	The bishop will pray in silence as he lays his hands on the head of the candidate. This is an ancient ritual that was used by the apostles when the first deacons were elected. The action is understood as transmitting the spiritual gifts necessary for the role.
Vesting of stole, chasuble and/or ring	At this point, the candidate has actually been ordained. A new priest or bishop will receive a sign of their new ministry: a new priest will be given a chasuble (a vestment worn for the celebration of the Mass), a bishop will receive a ring.
Anointing of hands with sacred chrism	The bishop will anoint the man's hands as a reminder that he is now to do Jesus' work in the world.

Understand

1. What are men who take the Sacrament of Holy Orders called to do?
2. What are the origins of the Sacrament of Holy Orders?
3. Identify two differences between a deacon and a priest.
4. Explain the role of a bishop.
5. Holy Orders and Matrimony are both Sacraments at the Service of Communion. Can you identify any similarities between them? You could refer back to pages 20–23 to help you.
6. Identify two rituals that a bishop carries out during an ordination.
7. Explain why the laying on of hands is important during the rite.

Discern

8. 'The priest is the most important role to be ordained into.' Present arguments for and against this statement, including what a Catholic might say. Evaluate the strengths and weaknesses of the arguments and reach a final judgement.

Respond

9. Has learning about what is involved in the Sacrament of Holy Orders made you think differently about what it means to follow this path?

What is the Sacrament of Holy Orders?

3.10 ETHICAL OPTION

WHY ARE ONLY MEN ORDAINED AS CATHOLIC PRIESTS?

OBJECTIVE
In this lesson you will explore the arguments presented by the Catholic Church for ordaining only men.

In the Catholic Church the sacrament of Holy Orders is one that only men can receive. The question of why women cannot also become deacons, priests or bishops has been increasingly discussed in recent times. You will explore why the Catholic Church has not taken the same stance as some other Christian **denominations** and changed the requirements for ordination.

Why can only men be ordained in the Catholic Church?

Some believe there may have been women deacons very early on in the Church. Apart from this, women have never been allowed to take the Sacrament of Holy Orders in the Catholic Church. Increasingly, other denominations have moved towards ordaining women. This has not always been greeted positively, with some priests leaving their Churches and joining the Catholic Church instead. In 1994, Pope St John Paul II wrote an apostolic letter called *Ordinatio Sacerdotalis* (Priestly Ordination) to reiterate the position of the Catholic Church. He gave four main reasons why the ordination of women should not take place.

Useful vocabulary

denominations: branches of Christianity

Reasons given in *Ordinatio Sacerdotalis*	Explanation
The twelve apostles chosen by Jesus were all men.	As Jesus chose men to teach, sanctify (make holy) and govern, the Church ought to continue to do the same.
Jesus' choice to have male disciples was made freely and was not simply a product of his society and the culture at the time.	Jesus chose to not follow societal norms at other times, such as speaking directly to women. So had he wanted to, Jesus could have chosen female disciples, but he did not. The Church believes this was a conscious decision.
The Blessed Virgin Mary was not given a mission as the apostles were, nor was she given a ministerial role.	The importance of Mary's role as Mother of God shows that women are valued in the Church in other ways, so only ordaining men is not a matter of discrimination.
	Roles within the Church cannot be ranked in terms of their importance. Pope St John Paul II emphasises it is actually the saints, not men who are ordained, who are the greatest in the Kingdom of God.
The ordination of men alone has been passed on by **tradition**: the Church has no authority to change this.	The Church believes that ordination continues the roles Jesus gave to the apostles. The apostles all did the same as Jesus and chose men when they elected their successors; from such decisions as this, the Church takes its tradition.

Galilee to Jerusalem

The Catechism also summarises the Church's position:

> '"Only a baptized man (vir) validly receives sacred ordination." The Lord Jesus chose men (viri) to form the college of the twelve apostles, and the apostles did the same when they chose collaborators to succeed them in their ministry. ... The Church recognizes herself to be bound by this choice made by the Lord himself. For this reason the ordination of women is not possible.'
>
> *Catechism of the Catholic Church 1577*

Why do some people call for the ordination of women in the modern world?

There are a variety of reasons why some people argue women ought to be ordained into the Catholic Church. For example:

- In Jesus' time, women were not expected to play important roles outside the home: it would have been more difficult for them to be accepted and listened to. However, much of the world is very different now.
- Jesus had female disciples and treated women fairly and respectfully. To refuse to ordain them seems to go against the way Jesus frequently behaved.
- While Jesus didn't choose female apostles, this doesn't mean he was against the idea: there is no direct teaching in the Bible against it.
- Great efforts are made in other areas of society, business and government for women to be treated equally; the Church could be seen to be at odds with this and discriminating against women by refusing to ordain them.
- Some women may have a vocation to the priesthood which is being frustrated by the Church and denying them the chance to fulfil their calling from God.
- Other Christian denominations ordain women and one third of Church of England clergy are now women; this shows large numbers of women want to be involved as ministers.
- Numbers of men wanting to be ordained are dropping; ordaining women would allow there to be more ministers, which would allow Jesus' saving message to be shared further.

Useful vocabulary

tradition: also known as Apostolic Tradition, these are actions and teachings of Jesus faithfully passed on through the sacraments and teachings of the Church

▲ Bishops attending Mass at the Vatican; in the Catholic Church all bishops, priests and deacons are men

▲ Reverend Rose Hudson-Wilkin, Bishop of Dover, speaking at a service in Windsor; women can be ordained in the Church of England

Understand

1. **a** Explain two reasons why the Catholic Church only ordains men.
   b Using CCC 1577, explain why the Catholic Church's position on the ordination of women is unlikely to change.
2. What reason does the Catechism state for not carrying out the ordination of women?
3. Give two reasons why someone might call for the ordination of women.

Discern

4. 'Women should be ordained into the priesthood in this day and age.' Present arguments for and against this statement, including what a Catholic might say. Evaluate the strengths and weaknesses of the arguments and reach a final judgement.

Respond

5. How does the idea of the ordination of women personally affect you? Have you ever thought about this question before today?

3.11 ARTISTIC EXPRESSION OPTION

HOW IS THE CALLING OF THE TWELVE DEPICTED IN ART?

OBJECTIVE
In this lesson you will compare and contrast two pieces of art that depict Jesus calling the apostles.

There is very little detail about the reactions of the twelve in the moments when Jesus calls them. They mostly seem to drop everything and follow him, which reflects the idea of vocation being a calling from God. The Gospel writers leave it to the reader to imagine what these events would have been like in reality. As a result, many artists have explored the different ways in which this may have occurred.

The Calling of St Matthew by Caravaggio

Michelangelo Merisi da Caravaggio (1571–1610) was an Italian artist who created detailed paintings full of light and shadow. He painted *The Calling of St Matthew* around 1599; it hangs in the Contarelli Chapel in Rome. This painting depicts the exact moment that Jesus Christ calls Matthew, the tax collector, to follow him.

Read more…
You can read the story of Jesus Calls Matthew in Matthew 9:9–13.

- Jesus and a figure believed to be St Peter seem to have entered the room abruptly, directly calling Matthew. They do not hesitate or show uncertainty – they point to him directly. It is a reminder of the immediacy of the calling of the disciples; there is no time to spare.

- Matthew seems to lean back in the direction of the money being counted. This is a reminder of the radical discipleship asked of the twelve: a full abandonment of their comfortable, material possessions. This suggests that, for many, the call to vocation is a great test and a difficult choice.

- Matthew's reaction is one of surprise and he seems to question Jesus' choice by pointing at himself. As a tax collector, marginalised by society, Matthew would not have expected to be singled out by Jesus.

- The light on the hands could symbolise a spiritual awakening.

- Matthew and his companions are dressed in sixteenth-century clothing. This reinforces the idea of the divine entering normal life.

Jesus Calls His Disciples by He Qi

Jesus Calls His Disciples is a contemporary painting by Chinese artist He Qi. His work is particularly influenced by Chinese folk art and medieval European painting. In this painting he creates a tableau (a picture that captures a whole story) of the story Jesus Calls the First Disciples.

This is a bright and colourful painting. He Qi is not trying to portray real-life characters; he presents a tableau of the whole Gospel story in a two-dimensional style.

The mood is welcoming and inclusive. He Qi presents a friendly Jesus with a pleasant facial expression, outstretched arms and open palms. These gestures and the number of disciples being called in this painting build a sense that the calling to discipleship is open to everyone.

The final disciple, John or James, is waving to his father Zebedee in the boat, who waves back. He Qi captures this personal moment between them, which could symbolise the sacrifice disciples made in leaving behind their home and loved ones to follow Jesus.

Most of the disciples do not look at Jesus but turn their faces up to heaven, suggesting the divine nature of their call. Their closeness to Jesus suggests they are willing and eager to accept the vocation he calls them to.

Read more...

You can read the whole story of Jesus Calls the First Disciples in Mark 1:16–20.

Understand

1. Explain why artists are drawn to interpret the calling of the disciples in their work in different ways.
2. Explain how Caravaggio has used light in *The Calling of St Matthew*.
3. Identify one typical characteristic of discipleship in Mark's Gospel that is portrayed in *The Calling of St Matthew*.
4. Choose three words to describe what He Qi's Jesus appears to be like and explain your reasons for these.
5. Choose one of the paintings and explain how the cost of discipleship is depicted.

Discern

6. What Catholic ideas about discipleship and vocation do you think stand out most from *The Calling of St Matthew*? Do you think *Jesus Calls His Disciples* explores ideas about discipleship and vocation in a similar or different way?
7. Which painting do you think best communicates Catholic ideas about discipleship and vocation? Give reasons for your opinions.

Respond

8. How do you feel about discipleship when you look at these paintings? What emotions do they create in you?

3.12 LIVED RELIGION OPTION

WHAT IS THE ROLE OF LAY PEOPLE IN THE CATHOLIC CHURCH?

OBJECTIVE
*In this lesson you will explore **how lay people and lay associations support the mission of the Church**.*

The mission of the Church extends beyond those who have taken religious vows to all followers of Christ. The notion of discipleship is lived out by **lay people** today, who can contribute to the Church's mission by supporting or becoming involved in associations that work to strengthen the Church community and spread Jesus' message, such as International Young Catholic Students.

Why do lay people support the mission of the Church?

The Catholic Church teaches that through their baptism, lay people are called to be part of the mission of the Church.

> 'The whole Church is apostolic, in that she remains, through the successors of St. Peter and the other apostles, in communion of faith and life with her origin: and that she is "sent out" into the whole world. All members of the Church share in this mission, though in various ways … "Christ, sent by the Father, is the source of the Church's whole apostolate"; thus the fruitfulness of apostolate for ordained ministers as well as for lay people clearly depends on their vital union with Christ. In keeping with their vocations, the demands of the times and the various gifts of the Holy Spirit, the apostolate assumes the most varied forms.'
>
> *Catechism of the Catholic Church 863–4*

- All baptised Catholics must continue the tradition of St Peter and the apostles.
- The apostles were **commissioned** to spread Jesus' message, and all Catholics (including lay people) are expected to continue the Church's mission today.
- The apostolate is the movement or activity within the Catholic Church to spread the word of God.
- The Church recognises the many different gifts and talents that individuals can contribute to its mission; Catholics are called to many different roles within the Church.
- Catholics believe at Confirmation the gifts that they need to bring Christ into the world are strengthened by the Holy Spirit.

Useful vocabulary

lay people: all Christians who are not ordained as deacons, priests, bishops, or as consecrated members of a religious order

commissioned: given a special task; in Christianity, this task was to spread Jesus' message

We have seen how lay Catholics can be part of the Church's mission through their vocation. Another way they can do this is by becoming involved with a lay apostolate organisation or association: a group that shares in the mission of the Church. Examples include the Legion of Mary, International Young Catholic Students, Worldwide Marriage Encounter, and Teams of Our Lady.

Such groups are varied with wide-ranging aims, but have one shared goal of spreading the message of Jesus. For example, the Legion of Mary is largely based within local parishes, where their focus could be reintroducing lapsed Catholics back into the faith or visiting people in their parish who are sick. Teams of Our Lady supports married couples spiritually, with the aim of helping them to deepen their relationship with each other and with God.

What is International Young Catholic Students?

International Young Catholic Students was established in 1946 after the Second World War to encourage students to build a peaceful future based on justice and freedom. By asking them to 'see, judge and act', it aims to help young people to put their faith into action and to match their life to the Gospel. The IYCS is a membership-based movement that is active in schools, universities and parishes in 86 countries. Each member is given the opportunity to be part of a closely-knit community group in which they are trained to take responsibility for their life as a whole, to deepen their faith and reach out to each other, as well as those in their student world, to help spread Jesus' message. Members are supported by mentors and spiritual advisors.

Among other aims, the IYCS seeks to promote justice, peace, human dignity, humanitarian action, and **sustainable development** – a vision which is rooted in the values of the Gospels. Student members are encouraged to engage with and advocate for this vision, for youth and student rights, and for other important issues linked to student poverty. For example, the IYCS regularly consults with agencies of the United Nations, such as UNICEF (the United Nations International Children's Emergency Fund), and members have a chance to highlight inequalities and make proposals for actions to address these.

In August 2023, ten representatives of IYCS travelled to mark World Youth Day in Lisbon, which involved a week-long celebration of the work and achievements of young Catholics. IYCS members attended workshops exploring how young people could develop a deeper understanding of their faith and commit to creating a more just, peaceful and compassionate world. The event included a Mass celebrated by Pope Francis, which was attended by 1.5 million young Catholics. IYCS provides young Catholics with opportunities to discuss and influence important issues facing the world today as modern disciples of Jesus.

▶ *International Young Catholic Students (IYCS) members participated in World Youth Day in Lisbon*

Useful vocabulary

sustainable development: carefully managing the use of the earth's resources so that they are not destroyed or used up as a result of human activities

Understand

1. What is meant by the term 'lay people'?
2. Give two examples of ways in which baptised Catholics can live out Jesus' mission.
3. How does International Young Catholic Students enable young people to be disciples in a modern world?

Discern

4. Do you think that becoming a member of a lay apostolate organisation (like International Young Catholic Students) is comparable to being a disciple at the time of Jesus? Give reasons for your answer, including what a Catholic might say. You can re-read pages 64–75 to help you.

Respond

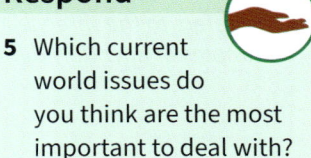

5. Which current world issues do you think are the most important to deal with?

What is the role of lay people in the Catholic Church?

CHAPTER 3

ASSESSMENT

Key vocabulary

Write a definition for these key terms.

discipleship	vocation	Holy Orders	deacon
priest	bishop	religious life	evangelical counsels
vow of poverty	vow of chastity	vow of obedience	celibacy

Knowledge check

1. Which one of the following is thought to have been Mark's main audience?
   a. Jewish women
   b. People who might become Christian
   c. Christians being persecuted by the Romans
   d. People who knew Jesus

2. What did Jesus tell the rich young man that he needed to do?
   a. To fast and abstain from nice food for a day each week.
   b. To learn the scriptures and apply them.
   c. To pray each day.
   d. To go and sell all he had and give to the poor.

3. Copy out and complete the following sentence:
   Mark often shows that it is difficult to be a d................ of Jesus. However, he also shows that it comes with r................. .

4. Write down a quote from the Gospel of Mark that teaches about wealth.
5. State one example of how the disciples failed.
6. Give two ways in which women are shown to be disciples of Jesus.
7. What do Catholics mean by a 'vocation' to the priesthood?

8. Explain why Catholics believe true discipleship is challenging.
9. Explain the importance of the evangelical counsels.
10. Outline the three degrees of ordination in the Catholic Church.

TIP

Think about how the evangelical counsels impact religious life – how do Catholics believe they help a person to become closer to God?

TIP

This refers to the three levels of ordination. Give some examples of how they differ.

Extended writing activity

This assessment is for you to show what you have learned in this chapter and for you to develop your extended writing skills. Here is a big question:

> 'In the story of the Rich Young Man, Jesus shows that wealth is a barrier to becoming close to God, therefore it is wrong that the Church holds on to valuable possessions.' Evaluate this statement.
>
> In your response you should:
> - explain arguments that agree and disagree with the statement
> - refer to Catholic teaching
> - reach a justified conclusion.

> To answer this question, you'll need to draw on some of the skills you learned about in Year 8:
> - finding arguments for and against the statement (or to agree and disagree with the statement)
> - using specialist religious terminology
> - using evidence and examples to support your points
> - referring to religious texts
> - evaluating your arguments.
>
> In addition, you will need to learn how to write a justified conclusion. Your conclusion comes at the end of your piece of extended writing and should make a final decision about the statement. It is a way of drawing together the different arguments being made and highlighting the main points for the reader to consider. It shows the reasoning behind your final judgement.

1. **Plan your argument.** You could write two headings – 'Agree' and 'Disagree' – and note down some ideas under each one. Here is an example that has been started for you. Can you add in some more ideas under each heading?

Agree
- **Argument:** Some Church buildings/artefacts are worth a lot of money; people living in poverty could benefit from that money being used to help them.
-
-
-
-

Disagree
- **Argument:** Church property is open to everyone. Anyone can go inside a Catholic church and appreciate its architecture and beauty.
-
-
-

> **TIP**
>
> *You could also create a spider diagram to plan out your answer. Choose the method you think will be the most helpful to you. And your plan doesn't have to be in full sentences – jotting down quick notes is fine.*

The question asks you to 'evaluate' the arguments. Remember this means deciding if you are convinced by an argument based on the strength of the evidence used to back it up.

Can you add some ideas to your list about how you might evaluate each point? Some examples are shown below.

<u>Agree</u>
- **Argument:** Some Church buildings/artefacts are worth a lot of money; people living in poverty could benefit from that money being used to help them. **Evaluation:** Strong argument; supported by story of the Rich Young Man.
-
-

<u>Disagree</u>
- **Argument:** Church property is open to everyone. Anyone can go inside a Catholic church and appreciate its architecture and beauty. **Evaluation:** Strong argument; Jesus visited the Temple and valued others' efforts to praise God, e.g. woman who anointed him with oil (Mark 14).
-
-

TIP

It can be helpful to use a quotation or a source to explain why an argument is strong.

2. **Now that you have planned your arguments, try to write two paragraphs to agree with the statement, based on your plan.** Here is an example of a first paragraph that you might write.

> Some people would agree that the Church is wrong to hold on to valuable possessions. The Catholic Church owns buildings and artefacts all over the world and many of these are worth a lot of money. If the Church were to sell its possessions, they could use the money to help people who are living in poverty, <u>for example</u> by building homes for those who need them. This is a strong argument because <u>Jesus said to the rich young man</u> that he should sell all that he has and give to those living in poverty, so doing this would be following Jesus' teaching directly.

It is always a good idea to use clear examples to support your points.

Using direct references to the Bible can help make your argument stronger. Referring to the teachings and actions of Jesus is especially helpful as they are regarded as the 'word of God' and an important source of authority for Christians.

3. **Now try writing two more paragraphs explaining arguments that disagree with the statement. Remember to include some evaluation of your argument.**
Here is an example paragraph:

> <u>However</u>, some people might disagree with the statement, arguing that the Church's possessions do not belong to a single individual. Instead, Church property is open to everyone – no matter their circumstances. All people can visit and enjoy the beauty of Church property and, of course, churches provide somewhere for people to practise their faith. This is a convincing argument because Jesus himself frequently visited the Temple and he valued people's efforts to praise God. <u>For example</u>, he praised the woman who anointed him with expensive ointment; in doing this she was making an offering to God. In the same way, grand church buildings filled with beautiful religious objects can be seen as worthy offerings to God.

Words and phrases like 'however', 'on the other hand' and 'yet' can make your writing more sophisticated and help you demonstrate a real grasp of the different perspectives.

Scriptural evidence of Jesus' words and actions supports the point being made here.

Galilee to Jerusalem

4. **Finally, write a conclusion to your answer.** Writing a *justified* conclusion means that the conclusion makes logical sense based on the arguments presented – the reader should be able to understand how you have reached your final judgement about the statement based on what they have read. Construct a paragraph that considers the different arguments that have been put forward, highlights the important points and then evaluates them as a whole.

You could use some of these sentence starters:

- The arguments presented to agree with the statement are weak because…
- Overall, this is the strongest argument because…
- The arguments for are more persuasive than the arguments against because…
- In conclusion, there are some good arguments to support the statement, but the arguments against are the most convincing because…

> **TIP**
>
> *It is good to use comparative language ('strongest', 'more persuasive', 'most convincing') to show that you are weighing up the different arguments against each other.*

Here is an example:

> It is true that Jesus told the rich young man to sell his possessions and give to those living in poverty. While Jesus' words to this man seem to present a strong argument for giving up wealth, this example is about freeing people from distractions so they can be true <u>disciples</u>. Beautiful church buildings do not distract people from following Jesus – they encourage people to follow him. <u>Therefore, I think</u> that the strongest arguments disagree with the statement and suggest that it is acceptable for the Church to hold on to valuable possessions in order to glorify God.

Using key words from the chapter helps to make the answer more precise.

Here, the student makes a personal judgement ('Therefore, I think…') about which argument they consider to be stronger after weighing up both sides. You might reach a different conclusion. The important thing is to explain why you have reached your conclusion, based on evidence and reasoning.

CHAPTER 4:
DESERT TO GARDEN

Introduction

At the heart of the Christian faith is the sacrifice of Jesus. It is upon this that Christian beliefs about sacrifice, salvation and redemption are built. However, the origins of these beliefs have a longer history. We need to look back to the faith and practices of those first called by God – the Jewish people of the Old Testament – in order to fully understand these beliefs. In Christianity, this takes us to a time where animal sacrifice was routinely offered to God to atone for sin and expressed **the human desire for God's forgiveness**, a desire that is still felt by many today.

Catholics believe the Temple in Jerusalem was built to house the Ark of the Covenant, which contained the laws of God. The Temple was the heart of Jewish life and the worship that happened there is a **foretaste of the significance of Jesus' life, death and resurrection**.

Catholics believe the animal sacrifices of old were replaced by the most perfect of all sacrifices: that of Jesus himself. The sacrifices that were made at the Temple were to atone for sin, to repair the broken relationship with God. **Christians believe that Christ's own sacrifice was the fullest and final sacrifice needed for the forgiveness of all sin, for all time**.

For Catholics, Christ *is* the Temple and its High Priest. Christ is the place where God's glory dwells and the place of sacrifice. In Jesus, God's presence goes beyond the confines of a building, and comes to live among humans, as a human, for the sake of humankind. Christians believe **the sacrifice of Jesus brought a New Covenant**. They believe that Christ's death was an act of supreme, divine love but that it was necessary to overcome human sin and to reconcile God and humanity.

This belief is at the heart of Catholic life and worship, from the Liturgy of the Eucharist in Mass through to the Catholic belief in forgiveness. It motivates individual Catholics and organisations, such as Pax Christi, to work for peace and forgiveness in the world, and it inspires artists such as Josefina de Vasconcellos to place reconciliation at the heart of their creative work.

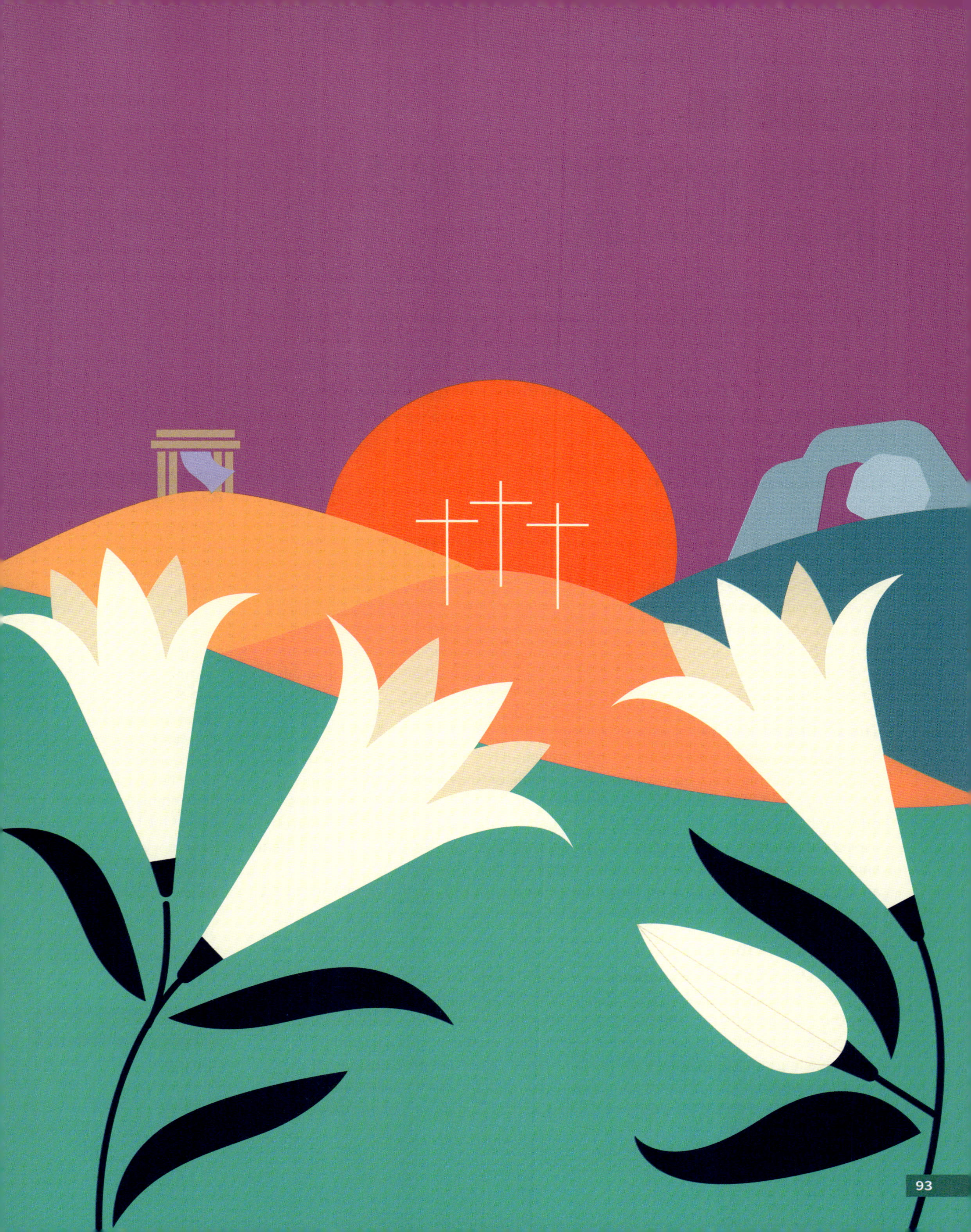

4.1

WHAT WAS THE TEMPLE IN JERUSALEM?

OBJECTIVE
In this lesson you will learn about the Temple, a vital place in the history and identity of the Jewish people.

The **Temple** was the central place of worship in Judaism in ancient Israel. It is of great importance to the Jewish community – today synagogues are orientated towards the place where the Temple used to stand, in Jerusalem. Two different temples were built on this site at different times, and both were destroyed. Today, many Jewish people visit the Western Wall, the only part of the second Temple still standing. They go there to pray, as it is considered to be a very holy place.

The history of the Temple

A covenant to establish a sacred land

To tell the history of the Temple, we need to go back to the **covenants** that God formed with Abraham and Moses. These are recorded in the Torah – the first five books of the Hebrew Bible, which are also part of the Christian Old Testament. In the covenant with Abraham, God promised land, descendants and blessings to Abraham. The land – or 'Promised Land' – was the land of Canaan, which is now called Israel. Genesis tells how Abraham built an altar to worship God when he arrived there and later, at Bethel, he built another one. God tells him 'To your offspring I will give this land' (Genesis 12:7), fulfilling part of the covenant with Abraham.

The sealing of covenants with blood

In the **Sinai covenant** with Moses, God established the Jewish people as God's people by showing them how to live as the people of God, so that in the Promised Land they could live as a nation in their own right. The laws given by God to Moses on Mount Sinai are more than the Ten Commandments – they cover many different aspects of religious and everyday life. To seal this covenant, the Jewish people made animal sacrifices at the altar: 'half of the blood [Moses] threw against the altar' and the remainder he threw 'on the people' (Exodus 24:6–8) to show that they had entered into their covenant agreement with God.

Creating a sanctuary

God told Moses to make a **sanctuary** so that God could dwell among the Jewish people. Exodus 25–40 contains detailed information that God gave to them about how they would construct the sanctuary, about the priests who would lead worship and the items that would be contained within the sanctuary. This was initially to be a travelling sanctuary known as the Tabernacle. The most precious part of the sanctuary would be the Ark of the Covenant, in which the commandments that God had given (carved on stone) would be carried so that God remained with the people at all times.

Useful vocabulary

Temple: the Jewish building for religious worship

covenants: agreements or promises between two or more people; God made covenants with humans such as Abraham and Moses

Sinai covenant: the covenant Moses made with God at Mount Sinai, when he was given the Ten Commandments as part of the Law

sanctuary: a place of great holiness

Holy of Holies: the most sacred part of the Temple, which originally housed the Ark of the Covenant

Read more...

You can read more about the sealing of the Sinai covenant in Exodus 24:1–8.

Establishing the Temple

In roughly 1000 BC, King Solomon had the first Temple built to replace the Tabernacle after King David had conquered Jerusalem. King David had made Jerusalem, at the centre of Israel, his capital. The Temple contained different public areas called courts, then a private sanctuary. Within this area the Ark of the Covenant was placed in a windowless room, at the heart of the construction. This room was called the **Holy of Holies**.

The Temple was a centre for sacrifices made to God by the people. It was used for worship, not just on festivals but for everyday prayer. It was a place of assembly too – for gathering together as a community. It was attacked a number of times by opposing nations, and in 586 BC it was destroyed by King Nebuchadnezzar, the King of Babylon, when he conquered Jerusalem. At this time the Ark of the Covenant was lost; its fate remains uncertain.

Later, a second temple was built on the same site and over time it was developed and expanded. Like the First Temple, it was constructed to closely follow the instructions in the book of Exodus. You will learn more about the Second Temple in the next lesson.

▲ *A reconstruction of the Second Temple*

The sanctuary – the Holy of Holies was at the heart of the Temple.

The Court of Israel and Court of the Priests, where only Jewish men were permitted and where the sacrifices took place.

The Court of the Women was in the outer forecourt, just outside of the Court of Israel.

Gentiles could access the area just outside of the Temple compound, but only Jewish people could go inside.

Understand

1. Where are the covenants with Abraham and Moses recorded?
2. How were some covenants sealed, such as the Sinai covenant with Moses?
3. How does this connect with one of the functions of the Temple?
4. Give two other reasons why the Temple was important to Jewish people.

Discern

5. 'The Temple's most important purpose was to house the Ark of the Covenant.' Do you agree or disagree with this statement? Consider the reasons for your answer, as well as what a Catholic view would be.

Respond

6. Have you ever made a promise and sealed it in some way? Does sealing a promise make it different? Why?

What was the Temple in Jerusalem?

4.2

WHAT WAS HEROD'S TEMPLE?

OBJECTIVE
In this lesson you will learn about the Second Temple, expanded by Herod in the first century BC.

The Second Temple was the Temple that Jesus would have known and that is recorded in stories in the New Testament. It was rebuilt in part by King Herod around 40–4 BC following the exact details set out in the Torah.

The construction of the Second Temple

Following the destruction of the Temple in 586 BC by King Nebuchadnezzar, the Jewish people were exiled to Babylon. When they returned to Jerusalem in 538 BC they began to build the Second Temple on the site of the original Temple. This Temple was simpler than the one built by King Solomon, since the Jewish people returning from exile didn't have great wealth. Nevertheless, the Temple was once more used for gathering and worship, and the sacred room where God's presence was believed to live (the Holy of Holies) was at its centre, although without the Ark of the Covenant.

The Temple and Temple Mount (the land surrounding the Temple) were added to over time, thanks to donations from wealthy benefactors. King Herod, who reigned from 40BC to 4BC, undertook the task of rebuilding and enlarging the Temple. He was not Jewish himself but showed his power and authority through extensive building projects; the Second Temple is sometimes called Herod's Temple. It was rebuilt and developed in accordance with the strict instructions of the book of Exodus.

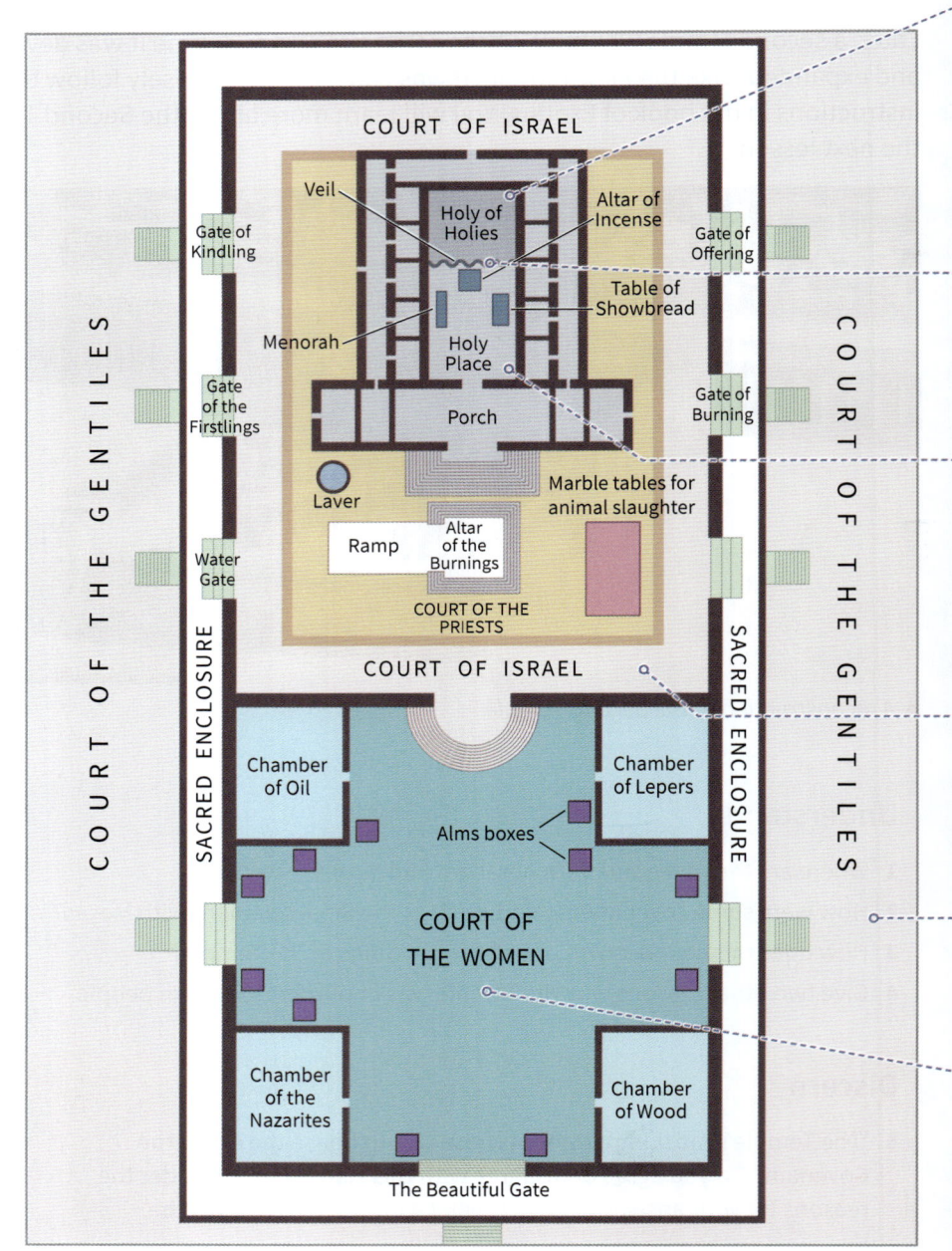

96 Desert to Garden

The specific features of King Herod's Temple are described below. Jesus would have known this Temple, and it is referred to in the Gospels. Herod's Temple was destroyed in AD 70 by the Romans and has not been rebuilt since.

> The most holy place or Holy of Holies was at the back of the sanctuary. According to the Mishnah (the written collection of the Jewish oral traditions), in place of the Ark of the Covenant in Herod's Temple was the Foundation Stone, marking the Ark's original location. Jewish people believe that God's presence was felt most powerfully in this place.
>
> In Exodus, God instructed Moses to add a lid to the original Ark, which has been translated as the 'Mercy Seat'. This was where God would communicate the Law to Moses and where the **atonement** sacrifice offering would be made. In the absence of the Mercy Seat, some claim that the **High Priest** of Herod's Temple treated the Foundation Stone as the resting place of God. The Catechism teaches that 'The mercy seat was the place of God's presence' (CCC 433).

> In Herod's Temple, a veil separated the Holy of Holies from the rest of the Temple – it was hung to mark the separation of heaven and earth and to show the sacredness of this holy place.

> Beyond the porch in the sanctuary, the first room was called 'The Holy Place'. It contained a menorah (seven-branched candlestick), altar of incense (where sweet-smelling herbs were burned to purify the air) and the Table of Showbread (twelve loaves of bread were placed here as an offering to God).

> There was a separate court for men called the Court of Israel. From this court, the priestly offering of sacrifices could be watched. Within this, there was also a separate court for the priests who led worship and offered sacrifices.

> The outer area of the Temple was called the Court of the Gentiles since anyone could enter this place. However, it was strictly forbidden for gentiles or Jewish people who were considered 'ritually impure' to pass any further into the Temple. As King Herod was not Jewish, even he could not move beyond this point.

> The Court of the Women was where Jewish women could worship God, though Jewish men could go there too.

Useful vocabulary

atonement: the action of making up for or repairing the damage done as a result of wrong behaviour

High Priest: the chief priest in historical Judaism; also a name for Jesus due to his role in the New Covenant

Understand

1. Draw out your own floor plan of Herod's Temple and mark on it:
   a) the three courts, b) the sanctuary, c) the Holy of Holies, d) the veil.
2. For each of these items, write a brief description of their role in Temple life and worship.
3. Explain two ways the Mercy Seat was important.

Discern

4. 'The layout of Herod's Temple meant most people were kept far away from God.' How far do you agree with this statement? Use information from this lesson and the previous lesson to assess why the Temple was laid out as it was.

Respond

5. Find a Gospel story where Jesus is shown to be in the Temple. Does knowing about the Temple help you to understand this story better? If so, how?

What was Herod's Temple?

4.3

WHY IS THE DAY OF ATONEMENT RELEVANT FOR CHRISTIANS?

OBJECTIVE
In this lesson you will explore the connection between the Jewish Day of Atonement and Christian beliefs about Jesus.

Christians read about Jesus' own experiences of the Jewish Temple in the Gospels, which helps them to understand the world in which he lived. However, understanding the role of High Priest and the **Day of Atonement** rite in ancient Judaism also allows Christians today to understand how Jesus' sacrifice changed the meaning of these things.

The role of the High Priest

The Holy of Holies was considered the most sacred place in the whole Temple. The only person who could go into the Holy of Holies was the High Priest and this was only permitted once a year. The High Priest was the chief of all the priests in the Temple, and was a man taken from the descendants of Aaron (Moses' brother, and the first High Priest). The High Priest had the role of interceding between humans and God, most notably on the Day of Atonement.

The Day of Atonement

The Day of Atonement (called Yom Kippur in Judaism) is the holiest festival of the whole Jewish calendar. On this day, Jewish people atone or seek forgiveness for their sins in order to become 'at one' with God. They ask for forgiveness, first from the people they have wronged, then from God. In doing this, they believe they can be cleansed of sin and restore their relationship with others and with God.

The High Priest of the Temple played a key role on the Day of Atonement. Some of his tasks included:
- making animal sacrifices for his own sins and the sins of the Jewish people
- transferring the sins of the community onto a goat, which would be sacrificed
- making a burnt offering for himself and the people to make atonement and show devotion to God
- ritually washing to cleanse himself and dressing in clean clothing
- putting incense on the altar of incense in the Holy of Holies to obscure his vision so that he would not see God (because if he did, he would die)
- sprinkling the blood of two sacrifices in the Holy of Holies to purify people from their sin, and to make atonement for the sins of the Jewish people.

Useful vocabulary

Day of Atonement: also known as Yom Kippur; the day when Jewish people seek forgiveness for sins

salvation: the process of being saved from sin and returning to God through God's grace

▲ *The Jewish High Priest is believed to have worn special garments on the Day of Atonement*

Jesus offers a heavenly sanctuary

The Letter to the Hebrews in the New Testament is believed to have been written to the Christians who had previously been Jewish, who were being persecuted in Jerusalem; some were believed to be considering returning to Judaism. Hebrews 9 draws on details from the Old Testament – which would have been very familiar to Jewish Christians – to explain that the old covenants established an earthly sanctuary: the Temple.

> The author reminds the reader that the Old Covenant was not the only covenant.

> Worship was 'earthly' and connected to the Temple, a physical place. It was usually based on the sacrifice of animals, food and drink.

> 'Now even the first covenant had regulations for worship and an earthly place of holiness. For a tent was prepared, the first section, in which were the lampstand and the table and the bread of the Presence. It is called the Holy Place. Behind the second curtain was a second section called the Most Holy Place...'
> *Hebrews 9: 1–3*

Hebrews 9 suggests that Jesus brings 'a new covenant' and a new way to **salvation**.

> The author emphasises that Jesus brings a heavenly (not earthly) sanctuary.

> The author believes that Jesus is the ultimate high priest.

> 'But when Christ appeared as a high priest of the good things that have come, then through the greater and more perfect tent (not made with hands, that is, not of this creation) he entered once for all into the holy places, not by means of the blood of goats and calves but by means of his own blood, thus securing eternal redemption.'
> *Hebrews 9: 11–12*

Many Catholics draw on the anagogical sense of scripture when they read Hebrews 9 – this means they think about the spiritual significance of the words and how they point to the ultimate destiny of humankind, which Catholics believe is salvation and everlasting life with God.

Useful vocabulary

redemption: in the Old Testament, the act of saving a person from sin or suffering, or clearing a debt; in the New Testament, the belief that Jesus paid the 'ransom' to free humans from sin by dying on the cross

Only the High Priest could enter the Most Holy Place. It was believed that only they could truly experience God's holiness.

Read more...

You can read more in Hebrews 9:1–15. What do you think the author wanted to emphasise about the New Covenant?

The author says that Jesus made the ultimate and final sacrifice that brought about eternal redemption. This suggests that he replaces the Atonement rite in the Temple, bringing God's holiness to all people.

Understand

1. What was the role of the High Priest?
2. Explain what Jewish people do on the Day of Atonement.
3. What were the main features of the Day of Atonement rite carried out by the High Priest?
4. How does Hebrews 9 suggest that the Temple is an earthly sanctuary?
5. How does Hebrews 9 suggest that Jesus' sacrifice replaces the Atonement rite in the Temple and offers a heavenly sanctuary?

Discern

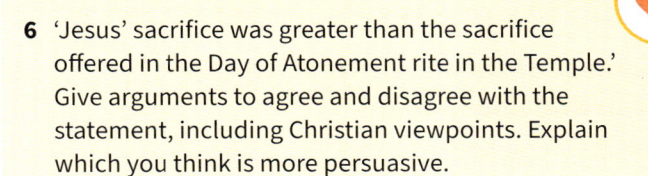

6. 'Jesus' sacrifice was greater than the sacrifice offered in the Day of Atonement rite in the Temple.' Give arguments to agree and disagree with the statement, including Christian viewpoints. Explain which you think is more persuasive.

Respond

7. Have you ever asked forgiveness from a person, or from God? If so, what was the experience like?

Why is the Day of Atonement relevant for Christians?

4.4

WHY WAS JESUS' SACRIFICE NECESSARY?

OBJECTIVE
In this lesson you will explore **why Catholics believe that Jesus' sacrifice was needed to conquer sin and death, and to overcome division.**

Sacrifice was part of the faith in which Jesus was raised. The idea of sacrificing a life for the benefit of others is something many people find hard to understand, yet it is at the heart of the Gospel message – the very core of the Christian faith. Christians place trust in God's plan of redemption to save humanity from sin and to bring all people and God back together.

Why was the mystery of redemption needed?

Redemption is often called the **mystery of redemption**. Catholics believe that humans cannot hope to fully understand exactly *how* Jesus' sacrifice paid the debt of human sin, but they trust that it was needful and part of God's plan.

It was needful because the sin of Adam and Eve in the Fall spoiled God's perfect creation and brought disharmony and disorder into the world. The Catechism teaches that 'By our first parents' sin, the devil has acquired a certain domination over man, even though man remains free' (CCC 407). Sin not only harms the relationship between God and humans; humans find their relationships with others challenged by sin. Catholics believe that God acted through the mystery of redemption to offer the chance to restore this broken relationship: 'all need salvation and that salvation is offered to all through Christ' (CCC 389).

Catholics also believe that human attempts to overcome sin through sacrifice in the Day of Atonement rite were inadequate, as the sacrifice could only cover, not overcome, the sin. In the sacrifice of Christ – a perfect sacrifice – the Church teaches that 'God's saving plan was accomplished "once for all"' (CCC 571) in order to bring salvation.

What did the mystery of redemption achieve?

Forgiveness of sin and restoration of the broken relationship between God and humans

The Catechism makes clear that Jesus completely redeemed people (freed them from sin) through his life, death and resurrection:

> 'Redemption comes to us above all through the blood of his cross, but this mystery is at work throughout Christ's entire life'
> *Catechism of the Catholic Church 517*

Useful vocabulary

mystery of redemption: the truth of how God redeems humanity through Jesus' sacrifice, which can never be fully understood

▲ *Catholics believe that Jesus' death brings redemption*

100 Desert to Garden

Catholics believe that:
- through his words and actions, Jesus showed people how to live in order to be redeemed
- by his death, he overcame sin
- through his resurrection, he conquered death in order to bring eternal life.

Matthew's Gospel recounts how, at the moment of Jesus' death, the veil that set apart the Holy of Holies dramatically rips: 'behold, the curtain of the temple was torn in two, from top to bottom' (Matthew 27:51). This imagery is a reminder that Jesus' death removed the barrier between God and humanity.

Restored harmony between people

When a person sins, they not only harm their relationship with God; their relationship with others is spoiled too. Sin causes division and suffering which in turn can lead to mistrust, disharmony and antagonism. God created people to live in harmony, so in his life, Jesus showed humanity how to act with love, justice and compassion. Through his death and resurrection he overcame sin and death to restore God's creation to harmony.

St Paul reminds Christians that believers are all one in Christ since Christ removes all sin-related divisions. He teaches that:

> Baptism brings people to Jesus.

> 'for in Christ Jesus you are all sons of God, through faith. For as many of you as were baptised into Christ have put on Christ. There is neither Jew nor Greek, there is neither slave nor free, there is no male and female, for you are all one in Christ Jesus.'
>
> *Galatians 3:26–28*

> Through Jesus, differences and divisions no longer matter: people are united through their faith.

Saved people from death and saved them for eternal life

In Genesis 3:3 the result of sin was suffering and death: humans were sent out to live mortal lives on earth. St Paul reinforces this in his letter to the Romans: 'Therefore, just as sin came into the world through one man, and death through sin, and so death spread to all men because all sinned' (Romans 5:12). However, while physical death is an accepted part of being alive, many people believe that St Paul is teaching that sin causes spiritual death. Christians believe that Christ's death and resurrection overcomes physical and spiritual death. Through dying, Jesus paid the price for sin, and through rising, he opened the gates of heaven so that physical death is not the end, but is the beginning of a new, eternal life with God.

Understand

1. What is redemption?
2. Why do Catholics believe the mystery of redemption was needed?
3. What three things does the mystery of redemption achieve?
4. a What does the teaching in Galatians 3:28 mean when it says that believers are 'all one in Christ'?
   b How does the event in Matthew 27:51 show that Jesus' sacrifice overcomes sin-related divisions?
   c How do these two teachings link with each other? What do you think is their shared message?

Discern

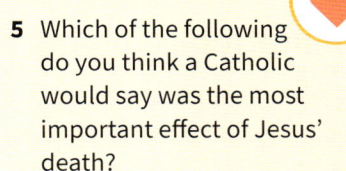

5. Which of the following do you think a Catholic would say was the most important effect of Jesus' death?
   - Repairing the broken relationship between God and humanity
   - Showing humans how much God loved them

   Give reasoned arguments to support your choice.

Respond

6. Do you think that the life, death and resurrection of Jesus was the best way to repair humans' relationship with God?

4.5

WHAT IS REDEMPTION?

> **OBJECTIVE**
> In this lesson you will learn that **the Church has many ways to express the mystery of redemption.**

The mystery of redemption is a difficult idea to comprehend. It can be expressed in different ways, because it has more than one single effect, but they all come back to the belief that Christ brought redemption through his life, death and resurrection.

Redemption is an expression of God's grace

God's **grace** is God's freely given love and help. Catholics believe that God gives this to humans, even though they do not deserve it since they are sinful following the Fall. However, God's grace is believed to be an expression of God's great love and care for humans, as God acts as the heavenly father. St Paul teaches that:

> 'In him we have redemption through his blood, the forgiveness of our trespasses, according to the riches of his grace, which he lavished upon us, in all wisdom and insight'
>
> *Ephesians 1:7–8*

Redemption and forgiveness come through Christ's physical sacrifice and this is because of God's grace.

God's grace is presented as a generous gift.

Redemption is buying back or paying the price

People had historically made animal sacrifices to pay for individual sin. Christians believe there was a price that needed to be paid for the sin of all humanity, and it is this payment that they believe Jesus made for them on the cross. St Peter teaches that the purity and heavenliness of 'the precious blood of Christ' (1 Peter 1:19) makes Jesus' sacrifice worth far more than any earthly thing that could be offered as payment.

Redemption is atonement

The Christian idea of atonement centres on Jesus' action on the cross. Through Jesus' death he reconciled God and humanity or made them 'at one'. Jesus is both the High Priest and the sacrifice made to bring God and humanity back together with no division through sin. St Paul explains: 'in Christ God was reconciling the world to himself' (2 Corinthians 5:19).

Redemption is salvation

Salvation is the act of saving or protecting, a word with connections to salvaging, where something (or in this case someone) is rescued from being lost or harmed. Christians believe that sinfulness obscures what is good in life,

Link
You can read more about the Jewish idea of atonement in the festival of Yom Kippur, the Day of Atonement, on pages 98–99.

Useful vocabulary

grace: a gift of love freely given by God to humankind

reparation: the act of making right a wrong by helping to repair something and restoring it to its original condition

sanctification: the act of making holy

saints: holy and virtuous people whose lives act as an example to other Christians; all people in heaven

Desert to Garden

meaning that people get lost. Humans need to be rescued from this state. Christians believe that they need God's help to be saved, and that God saves them from sin and the consequences of sin through the life, death and resurrection of Jesus.

> 'For God so loved the world, that he gave his only Son, that whoever believes in him should not perish but have eternal life.'
>
> John 3:16

Jesus was given in death, as a sacrifice.

The effect of this sacrifice is salvation, which will be freely offered to all. If a person chooses to accept this gift through faith in Jesus, they will enjoy eternal life.

Redemption is reparation

Reparation is the act of making right a wrong by helping to repair something and restoring it to its original condition. Jesus repaired the damage caused by the first sin (Original Sin) and all human sin that followed from the Fall. The damage was done to the relationship with God and with each other. By repairing this, God and humans could live in harmony once more. The Catechism teaches:

> 'Man's sins, following on original sin, are punishable by death. By sending his own Son in the form of a slave, in the form of a fallen humanity, on account of sin, God "made him to be sin who knew no sin, so that in him we might become the righteousness of God".'
>
> Catechism of the Catholic Church 602

While Jesus was innocent of sin, he was sent by God to right the wrong of sin and to bring humanity back to God.

Redemption is sanctification

Sanctification means being made holy. Catholics believe that through the Church, which is Christ's body, a person can become holy. This happens first at Baptism, where Original Sin is washed from the individual and they are filled with the Holy Spirit. Through the sacraments and God's grace, the individual grows in holiness in this life. The completion of this growth into holiness is when the individual enters into heaven as a **saint** and becomes united with God for eternity.

▲ *The Sacred Heart of Jesus is emphasised in some images to represent his sacrifice*

Link

You can read more about how Jesus was born free of sin due to the Immaculate Conception of Mary on page 45.

Understand

1. Create a table summarising the six expressions of the mystery of redemption. Use the information in this lesson and from pages 100–101 to help you.
   Use the headings:
   - Redemption is …
   - Meaning of this definition
   - How Jesus' life, death and resurrection show this

Discern

2. Which of the expressions about the mystery of redemption do you think are most helpful in understanding the nature of redemption? Give reasons for your answer.

Respond

3. Have you ever tried to right a wrong? If so, how did you go about this?

What is redemption? 103

4.6

WHAT IS THE NEW COVENANT?

OBJECTIVES

In this lesson you will learn what the New Covenant is and why it is important for Catholics.

The covenants in the Bible tell Christians of God's great love for them. Through the covenants, God saves humans by calling them to a relationship. Christians believe that the greatest covenant, which supersedes (or rises above) the covenants of the Old Testament, is the covenant that was sealed with Jesus' blood. This is known as the New Covenant and it is celebrated in particular ways within the Mass.

The Old and the New Covenant

The covenants of the Old Testament with Adam, Noah, Abraham, Moses and David (collectively called the Old Covenant) are important events in the story of the relationship between God and humans. For example, God gave the Law to Moses to share with God's people so that they could live in accordance with God's will.

During his life on earth, Jesus showed that he had come to make real the prophecies and promises of the Old Testament. In the Sermon on the Mount, Jesus taught that he had not come to destroy the Law but to 'fulfil' it (Matthew 5:17). Jesus didn't believe that there was error in the Old Covenant – by fulfilling the Law, Jesus was showing how to live it most fully by living it perfectly; and in dying he ended the need for any other blood sacrifice. His resurrection showed the aim of all sacrifice had been achieved: sin had been forgiven and salvation made possible. For this reason, Jesus is called the New and Everlasting Covenant. Just as the Old Testament covenants were often sealed with blood, so Catholics believe the New Covenant was sealed with Jesus' blood.

At the Last Supper, Jesus spoke of the New Covenant:

> 'This cup that is poured out for you is the new covenant in my blood'
>
> *Luke 22:20*

This helps Christians to understand a little more of the nature of Jesus, and the way in which they should respond to his sacrifice.

Useful vocabulary

Messiah: a Hebrew term meaning 'anointed one'; many Jews interpret the Messiah to be a future leader of the Jewish people who will rule with kindness and justice; for Christians the Messiah is Jesus; the word 'Christ' is the Greek form of the word 'Messiah'

Jesus, the Lamb of God

Lambs were used in animal sacrifice in ancient Judaism. To many, lambs symbolise innocence, purity and peace. Describing Jesus as the Lamb of God reflects that he was a perfect and pure sacrifice.

▲ *Jesus is described as the Lamb of God to emphasise that his death was a sacrifice*

Desert to Garden

Jesus is referred to as the Lamb of God in Mass during the Communion rite. This is the part of the Mass that follows the consecration of the bread and wine, when Catholics believe that the Holy Spirit transforms the bread and wine into Jesus' body and blood. As the priest breaks the host, the congregation join him in saying the *Agnus Dei*:

> 'Lamb of God, you take away the sins of the world, have mercy on us.
> Lamb of God, you take away the sins of the world, have mercy on us.
> Lamb of God, you take away the sins of the world, grant us peace.'
> *Agnus Dei*

Agnus Dei is Latin for Lamb of God. In this prayer, Catholics acknowledge that the sacrifice of Jesus on the cross was made to bring forgiveness of sins.

Someone who shows mercy shows compassion or forgiveness when they have the power to punish instead. In sacrificing Jesus, God chose to show compassion and forgiveness so that sin could be forgiven.

The *Agnus Dei* echoes Revelation 5:6–10, which tells of a Lamb bearing the wounds of slaughter being praised by those assembled, who sing:

> 'for you were slain, and by your blood you ransomed people for God from every tribe and language and people and nation'
> *Revelation 5:9*

Next in the Mass, the priest raises the host and says:

> 'Behold the Lamb of God,
> Behold him who takes away the sins of the world.'
> *Ecce Agnus Dei*

This word is a command to look and see, to notice. In Mass, this is just before Holy Communion is received – it invites the congregation to see who Jesus truly is.

These words are from John 1:29, where John the Baptist says 'Behold, the Lamb of God' to identify Jesus as the **Messiah**. This is at the start of Jesus' ministry on earth and so Catholics believe John the Baptist is foretelling the nature of Jesus as the perfect sacrifice.

Understand

1. What is the difference between the Old Covenant and the New Covenant?
2. What does it mean to say that the Old Covenant is superseded by a New and Everlasting Covenant?
3. What does *Agnus Dei* mean?
4. What does the *Agnus Dei* teach about a) sacrifice, b) mercy?
5. What does the *Ecce Agnus Dei* invite the congregation to do?
6. Summarise how the *Agnus Dei* and *Ecce Agnus Dei* make the nature of the New and Everlasting Covenant clear.

Discern

7. To what extent do you think the image of a lamb is a good representative of the new covenant? Give reasons for your answer.

Respond

8. Does the symbolism of Jesus as the Lamb of God help you to understand Catholic beliefs about Jesus' sacrifice?

What is the New Covenant?

4.7

HOW IS JESUS BOTH HIGH PRIEST AND TEMPLE?

OBJECTIVES
In this lesson you will explore why Catholics believe that Jesus is the High Priest and how he brings a new way of worship as the true Temple.

Catholics believe that Jesus' sacrifice in the New Covenant brings in a new priesthood, where Jesus is the High Priest. They also believe that Jesus' physical sacrifice makes Jesus' body the Temple of God. The Church teaches that this brings a whole new way of worship 'in spirit and truth' (John 4:23).

How is Jesus the High Priest?

Earlier in this chapter, you learned that Catholics believe:
- Jesus came to fulfil the Law given to the Jewish people in the Old Covenant.
- Jesus brought the full and permanent forgiveness from sin, through his life, death and resurrection.
- Jesus is the New High Priest since he *offers* and *is* the sacrifice.

The High Priest had a central role in offering the sacrifices for atonement of sin in the Temple. Catholics believe that Jesus is the new High Priest because he both *offers* the sacrifice and *is* the sacrifice.

What does the Church teach about Jesus' body as the true Temple?

The Catechism teaches that God is alive in Jesus, 'the divine name that alone brings salvation' (CCC 432). As a consequence, the body of Jesus is also described as the Temple of God:

> 'Christ is the true temple of God, "the place where his glory dwells"; by the grace of God, Christians also become temples of the Holy Spirit, living stones out of which the Church is built.'
>
> *Catechism of the Catholic Church 1197*

Catholics believe that the gift of God's grace makes them holy and calls them to be part of a living Church.

In John 2:13–25, Jesus drove the traders out of the Temple and referred to his body as the Temple when he foretold his death and resurrection:

> 'Destroy this temple, and in three days I will raise it up'
>
> *John 2:19*

Desert to Garden

A new way of worship 'in spirit and truth'

In John 4:23, Jesus explained that 'But the hour is coming, and is now here, when the true worshippers will worship the Father in spirit and truth'. Many people believe that here Jesus is referring to the change that his sacrifice will make to prayer and worship. With the Old Covenant, prayer rituals were based in the Temple and were very specific, but in Jesus (the true Temple) worship will be through him.

In fulfilling the Old Covenant, Jesus became the New and Everlasting Covenant for Christians. Hebrews 9 explains that the laws of the Old Covenant were temporary and prepared the way for Jesus – by living, dying and rising, Jesus reformed everything humans understood and established a new way of worship.

▲ Matthew 27:51 says that when Jesus died, 'the curtain of the temple was torn in two'

The Old Covenant:	The New Covenant:
required the Jewish people to keep God's Law so God would protect and bless them	shows that God is the unconditional source of salvation, offered to all people through Jesus
required repeated animal sacrifice to atone for human sin	means that Jesus is the sacrifice that ends all sacrifice. Jesus' death is for the forgiveness of sin
meant only the High Priest could enter the Holy of Holies	reveals that Jesus is the High Priest. The division between God and humans was removed by Jesus' death, symbolised when 'the curtain of the temple was torn in two' (Matthew 27:51)
was 'a shadow of the good things' that were to come (Hebrews 10:1).	is 'much more excellent than the old' (Hebrews 8:6).

John's Gospel explains how God should be worshipped in the following way:

> 'God is spirit, and those who worship him must worship in spirit and truth.'
> John 4:24

The Church teaches that Jesus is the spirit and the truth, so faith in him leads humans back to God. All Catholics are called to become living temples through the presence of the Holy Spirit in their lives. The body of Christ is therefore seen to be a living reality on earth: a Temple that unites God and humanity.

Understand

1. What does Jesus do that shows he is the High Priest?
2. Why is Jesus' body described as a 'true temple' (CCC 1197)?
3. What did Jesus explain about himself in John 2:19?
4. What does the tearing of the curtain in the Temple show?
5. What does John 4:24 say about how to worship God?
6. How does the Church interpret the teaching about worship in John 4:24? How can Catholics become 'living temples'?

Discern

7. 'The New Covenant means that Christians no longer need the Old Covenant.' Present arguments for and against this statement, including what a Catholic might say. Which argument do you think is most persuasive?

Respond

8. Does the description of Jesus as the Temple help you to understand the Christian view of him better?

4.8 ETHICAL OPTION

CAN ALL SINS BE FORGIVEN?

OBJECTIVES
In this lesson you will explore **Catholic teaching on the forgiveness of sins and whether all sins can be forgiven.**

Forgiveness is when one person pardons another for their wrongdoings, or sin. Catholics believe that, despite Jesus' sacrifice for human sin, people must seek forgiveness for the sins they commit and offer forgiveness to others; they cannot rely on Jesus' actions alone.

What does the Church teach about the forgiveness of sin?

The Catholic Church teaches a clear message that all sins can be forgiven by God:

> 'There is no offence, however serious, that the Church cannot forgive. "There is no one, however wicked and guilty, who may not confidently hope for forgiveness, **provided his repentance is honest**." Christ who died for all men desires that in his Church the gates of forgiveness should always be open to anyone who turns away from sin.'
>
> *Catechism of the Catholic Church 982*

There are conditions that must be met, one of which is genuine **repentance** for what the person has done wrong. In order to receive forgiveness, Catholics take part in the Sacrament of Reconciliation through which 'the baptized can be reconciled with God and with the Church' (CCC 980). This sacrament is often called Confession because individuals must confess their sin to a priest. There are four stages which must all be completed: contrition (regretting the sin), confession (admitting the sin aloud), penance (doing something to make amends for the sin) and absolution (being forgiven for the sin).

Useful vocabulary

repentance: showing that you recognise and regret a mistake

Link

You can read more about the Sacrament of Reconciliation in *Source to Summit: Year 8* pages 114–117.

What do Catholics believe about personal forgiveness?

We learned that a key part of the Day of Atonement, when Jewish people seek forgiveness for their sins, is that individuals first ask for forgiveness from the person they have wronged. They then ask for forgiveness from God. Some Catholics today believe that this shows people must be willing to forgive others who have committed sins against them if they expect forgiveness – this holds true for forgiveness from both humans and God. In fact, some Catholics would argue that being unforgiving is a sin, and they would use the words of the Lord's Prayer to support this point:

> 'Our Father … forgive us our trespasses, as we forgive those who trespass against us'

In the parable of the Unmerciful Servant in Matthew 18:21–35, Jesus shows how a servant faces punishment for accepting the mercy of his master, but refusing to show mercy to another man. Many Catholics believe this shows that Jesus taught that everyone should be forgiving.

▲ *Catholics believe that God is a forgiving father and pray to God for forgiveness*

Desert to Garden

Can evil be forgiven?

While the Church teaches that all sins can be forgiven, not all people agree that this is possible. For example, some people may say:

> Some sins are too awful to be forgiven, such as murder or abuse. To forgive them would suggest that they aren't as bad as they are.

> Forgiving a person for hurting someone you love is disloyal to your loved one. It is more important to care for innocent people who behave in the right way than it is to care for people who commit evil.

> Refusing to forgive someone is the best way of punishing them for what they have done wrong.

> Any sin that breaks the Ten Commandments breaks the law of God. Jesus said that 'whoever speaks against the Holy Spirit will not be forgiven' (Matthew 12:32).

Why do Catholics believe it is important to forgive?

Catholics have many reasons why forgiveness is a necessary and positive response to sin:

> In Luke 23:34, Jesus showed the value and importance of forgiveness by willingly being the sacrifice for human sin and forgiving those who executed him.

> Forgiveness is a gift to the person who has sinned, helping them to move on from the shame and regret they feel, and giving them the chance to be a better person.

> Jesus showed that forgiveness should be offered even if others disagree, such as his forgiveness of Zacchaeus (a wealthy tax collector) in Luke 19:1–10 and the woman caught in adultery in John 8:1–11.

> Forgiveness allows the person who forgives to move on from their place of pain and darkness, instead of focusing only on what has happened.

Link
You can read about Margaret and Barry Mizen, who forgave the man who murdered their son Jimmy, in *Source to Summit: Year 8* pages 122–123.

Understand
1. What is forgiveness?
2. What does the Church teach about the forgiveness of sin?
3. What must Catholics do to receive forgiveness from God?
4. Give two examples from the Gospels where Jesus showed the importance of forgiveness.
5. Explain two things Catholics might believe about personal forgiveness.

Discern
6. 'Some deeds are too awful to be forgiven.' Using the ideas presented in this lesson, give arguments for and against this statement including a Catholic response. Evaluate the strengths and weaknesses of each argument before coming to a final judgement.

Respond
7. What is your personal response to the belief that all sin can be forgiven?

4.9 ARTISTIC EXPRESSION OPTION

HOW DOES ART DEPICT RECONCILIATION?

OBJECTIVE
In this lesson you will explore **how Catholic ideas about reconciliation and forgiveness are expressed in artistic representations.**

Reconciliation is such a powerful topic that it is sometimes best expressed in ways that go beyond words. Artwork, sculpture, drama or music can communicate profound beliefs in ways that give humans an emotional connection with the subject. Art can also promote personal reflection and inspiration.

Reconciliation by Josefina de Vasconcellos

The sculpture *Reunion* was first created in 1977 by the English artist Josefina de Vasconcellos in response to the suffering and separation created by the Second World War. It has since been renamed *Reconciliation*. The artist said, 'The sculpture was originally conceived in the aftermath of the War … I read in a newspaper about a woman who crossed Europe on foot to find her husband, and I was so moved that I made the sculpture. Then I thought that it wasn't only about the reunion of two people but hopefully a reunion of nations which had been fighting.'

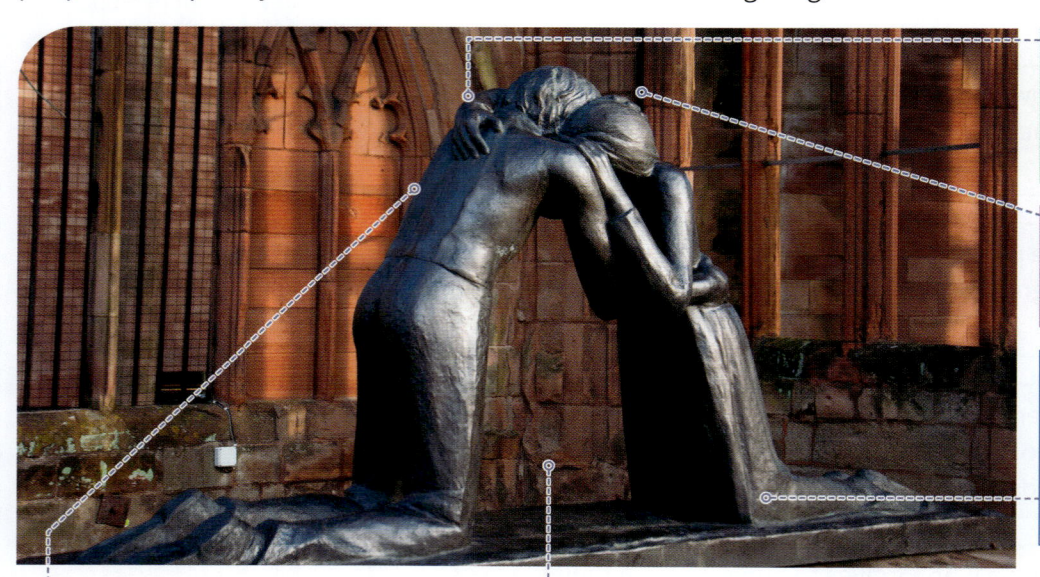

- The woman's arm reaches round to enclose the man's shoulder, suggesting closeness and tenderness.
- The man is cradling the head of the woman, suggesting gentle care.
- They are both in a penitent position, kneeling, as people may kneel before God when confessing their sins.
- The positions of the man and woman mirror one another, showing they are equal in wanting reconciliation and offering forgiveness.
- There is a clear space between them but it is bridged by their embrace, suggesting that forgiveness brings people together and nurtures unity.
- However, the wide space also suggests that reconciliation can be difficult and sometimes there is a great distance that needs to be bridged before it can take place. This suggests that both sides may need to make sacrifices in order for forgiveness to take place, following the teaching of the Lord's Prayer: 'forgive us our sins, as we forgive those who trespass against us'.

Desert to Garden

Life of Jesus Mafa: The Prodigal Son

The Prodigal Son from the *Life of Jesus Mafa* project is a contemporary representation of the parable in which Jesus reminds his followers that God awaits the return of sinners and welcomes with open arms those who come back to God. The prodigal son left home and wasted his share of his father's fortune, while his brother remained at home and worked hard.

The person dressed in orange may be the mother, who is joyful at the son's return. The whole community are coming to welcome the son home. This implies that reconciliation is a positive thing for the whole community and that forgiveness has a ripple effect, bringing peace to more than just the person forgiven. This reminds Catholics of the goodness of God's mercy.

The prodigal son wears tattered garments. He is leaning into his father's embrace, with his forehead on his shoulder. He may be weary and simply thankful for his generous welcome, or hiding his face in shame at his actions. This implies that forgiveness offers both a physical and emotional gift. There is no barrier between the son and his father – on the ground lie the symbols of his absence: the son's staff and sack where he dropped them.

The father is shown dressed in white garments, possibly to show his purity and holiness. His eyes are closed, and he is gently supporting and welcoming his son who has returned.

Understand

1. Give two ways *Reconciliation* suggests what forgiveness can mean to Catholics.
2. Identify one way *Reconciliation* reflects a Catholic practice connected to reconciliation.
3. What does the use of the colour white in *The Prodigal Son* suggest?
4. Why is the community's joy at the son's return significant for Catholics in *The Prodigal Son*?

Discern

5. Which artwork do you think best communicates Catholic ideas about forgiveness and reconciliation? Give reasons for your opinion.
6. Which Catholic ideas about forgiveness and reconciliation do you think stand out most from *Reconciliation*? Do you think *The Prodigal Son* explores ideas about forgiveness and reconciliation in a similar or different way?

Link

The parable of the Prodigal Son is explored in *Source to Summit: Year 8* page 81.

Respond

7. Inspired by these pieces of art, create your own symbol for reconciliation. This can use any artistic form. Write a short explanation of your symbol.

4.10 LIVED RELIGION OPTION

WHAT IS PAX CHRISTI?

OBJECTIVE
In this lesson you will learn about **an organisation that works for justice and peace: Pax Christi.**

Many Catholics believe that it is important to act to bring reconciliation to broken relationships and peace where there is a lack of harmony. While this can be seen in how individual Catholics live their day-to-day lives, there are charities that operate with this aim at the heart of what they do. Pax Christi is a Catholic membership organisation that seeks to bring Christ's peace to a troubled world.

How did Pax Christi begin?

The first half of the twentieth century saw two World Wars, times of enormous conflict and lost life. The murder of over six million Jewish people in the Holocaust showed further what hatred and injustice could do, and the threat of nuclear war began to loom over people, leading them to feel anxious about what lay ahead.

Pax Christi England and Wales, part of Pax Christi International, began in France in 1945 following the end of the Second World War, when a teacher, Marthe Dortel-Claudot, began a campaign of prayer for reconciliation between France and Germany. She was joined by Bishop Pierre Marie Théas, who had been imprisoned for protesting about the persecution of Jewish people. Together they prayed for German people and encouraged other people to do the same, reflecting the Catholic teaching in John 3:16 that all who repent and turn to God can be forgiven and be redeemed through Jesus' sacrifice.

What does Pax Christi do?

The phrase *Pax Christi* is Latin for 'the peace of Christ'. It is a reminder that in Christ's life, death and resurrection, he brought God's peace and love to humanity. Just as Christ showed this through his teachings and his example in the way that he lived, Pax Christi focuses on teaching forgiveness and justice and sharing Jesus' message that all people are loved by God.

> **'Pax Christi – our vision:** The work of Pax Christi – the Peace of Christ – is based on the gospel and inspired by faith. Our vision is of a world where people can live in peace, without fear of violence in any form. Pax Christi is rooted in Catholic Christianity but is open to all who share its values and work.
>
> Pax Christi works for:
> - Peace – based on justice. A world where human rights are respected, basic needs are met and people feel safe and valued in their communities.
> - Reconciliation – a process which begins when people try to mend relationships – between individuals or whole countries after times of violence or dispute.
> - Nonviolence – a way of living and making choices that respects others, challenges what is not fair or just, and offers alternatives to violence and war.'
>
> *www.paxchristi.org.uk*

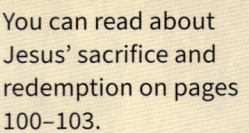

Link
You can read about Jesus' sacrifice and redemption on pages 100–103.

▲ *Bishop Théas is recognised as Righteous Among the Nations, a Jewish honour for people who took great risks to save Jewish people during the Holocaust*

The influence of the Second Vatican Council

Between the years 1962–1965, the Second Vatican Council met with the purpose of reforming some elements of the Catholic Church. Pope St John XXIII published the encyclical *Pacem in Terris* (Peace on Earth) in 1963, setting out the rights and responsibilities of all humans in respect to social justice. It explained that people must 'pardon those who have done them wrong' (PT 171) to keep the hope of peace alive. Pax Christi was inspired by this and developed an objective to help 'further peace by fostering international friendship'.

From this time onwards, Pax Christi has undertaken work to:
- educate people in how to promote a culture of peace, and how to make choices based on Christian values. For example, Pax Christi creates resources that can be used in schools and other settings to share its message and the teachings of Jesus on reconciliation
- develop solidarity between people who are working nonviolently for justice and peace. For example, Pax Christi gives advice on how Christians can pray together, provides information on what is happening in places where violence is taking place, and explains who Christians can write to in order to voice their concerns about achieving peace in the world
- promote an understanding of sustainable security to meet human needs and to protect the environment. This means avoiding weapons and warfare to solve conflict. For example, Pax Christi shares information on nonviolent action, has voiced concern about drone warfare, and campaigns at a global level to ban nuclear weapons.

Pax Christi particularly shares its message of justice and peace every year on Peace Sunday, around the middle of January, which supports the World Day of Peace celebrated on 1 January in the Catholic Church.

▲ *Pax Christi is a Catholic membership organisation that promotes peace and an end to conflict in solidarity with those that suffer as a result of war*

Understand

1. What does Pax Christi mean?
2. Give the three main areas of Pax Christi's work.
3. Explain one way in which Pax Christi **a)** educates people, **b)** develops solidarity, **c)** promotes understanding.
4. Explain how one Catholic teaching from the Second Vatican Council influences the work of Pax Christi.

Discern

5. 'The work of Pax Christi shows how Catholic ideas about forgiveness, reconciliation and redemption can be put into real action.' How far do you agree this is true? Explain your ideas with reference to the work of Pax Christi and the Catholic teachings you have learned about in this chapter.

Respond

6. Choose one thing that Pax Christi does that you would like to support. How could you do this? Explore how they connect with young people to give you some ideas.

CHAPTER 4

ASSESSMENT

Key vocabulary

Write a definition for these key terms.

Sinai covenant	Temple	sanctuary	Holy of Holies
Day of Atonement	High Priest	mystery of redemption	grace
redemption	atonement	salvation	reparation
sanctification			

Knowledge check

1. Which of the following is a religion that used the Temple in ancient Israel?
   a. Judaism
   b. Christianity
   c. Hinduism
   d. Islam
2. Choose the correct ending for this sentence:
   Catholics believe that Jesus' death was necessary…
   a. to repair the damage done by Adam and Eve's sin
   b. to show God's power
   c. as Jesus was causing unrest in Jerusalem.
3. Copy out and complete the following sentence:
   Forgiveness is when a person is pardoned for their s................ .
4. What do Catholics mean by the 'Lamb of God'?
5. Give two features of Herod's Temple.
6. What is the main focus of 'Yom Kippur'?
7. Give two Catholic beliefs about the effects of Jesus' death.
8. Outline three ways in which the Temple was used by Jewish people.
9. Explain Catholic beliefs about Jesus as the New Covenant.
10. Describe Catholic beliefs about redemption.

TIP

Think about the different areas of the Temple, what was found in each area and what these items were used for.

TIP

There are different Catholic beliefs about what redemption achieved – try to include them all. You could re-read pages 102–103 to help you.

Desert to Garden

Extended writing activity

This assessment is for you to show what you have learned in this chapter and to develop your extended writing skills. Here is a big question:

'Jesus should not have been sacrificed.' Evaluate this statement.

In your response you should:
- explain arguments that agree and disagree with the statement
- refer to Catholic teaching
- reach a justified conclusion.

> **TIP**
>
> In this answer you're going to have to think about the morality of Jesus being sacrificed versus the impact that his sacrifice had and continues to have.

To answer this question, you'll need to draw on the following skills:
- finding arguments for and against the statement (or to agree and disagree with the statement)
- using specialist religious terminology
- using evidence and examples to support your points
- referring to religious texts
- evaluating your arguments
- writing a justified conclusion.

1. **Plan your argument.** You could draw a spider diagram to help you plot out your ideas. Here is an example that has been started for you. Can you add in some more ideas connected to the 'Agree' and 'Disagree' headings? Once you have done this, add some notes about how you might evaluate each of the arguments.

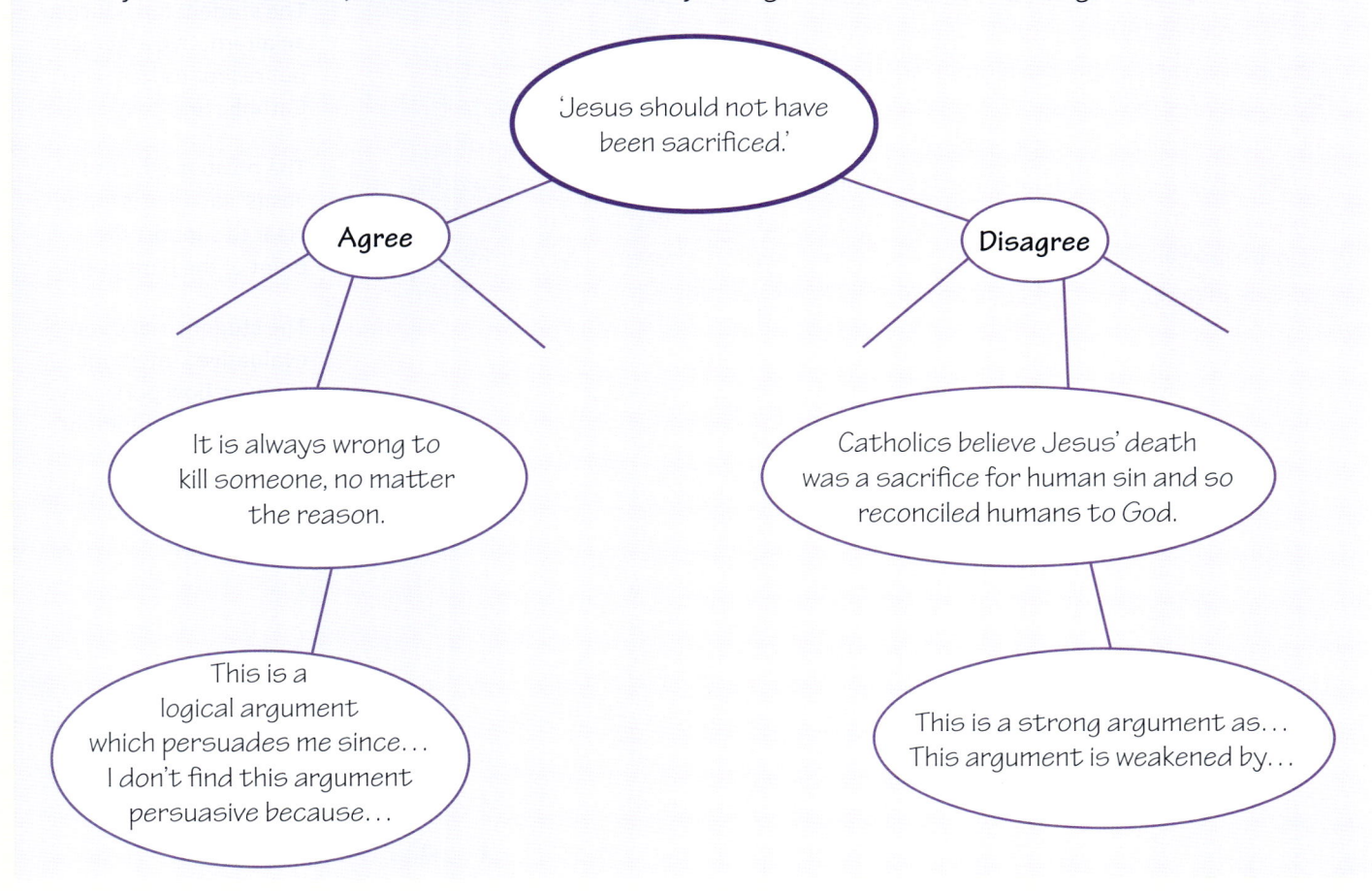

'Jesus should not have been sacrificed.'

Agree
- It is always wrong to kill someone, no matter the reason.
- This is a logical argument which persuades me since... I don't find this argument persuasive because...

Disagree
- Catholics believe Jesus' death was a sacrifice for human sin and so reconciled humans to God.
- This is a strong argument as... This argument is weakened by...

Assessment 115

Try writing two paragraphs on arguments that agree with the statement. Choose the ones from your plan that you think are the strongest and that you know you'll have lots to say about. Here is an example:

> Some people will <u>agree</u> that Jesus should not have been sacrificed <u>since</u> many people, including Christians, believe it is always wrong to kill a person no matter the reason for their death. <u>Catholics believe</u> that Jesus' sacrifice had an important purpose – to bring forgiveness. <u>However,</u> some people might argue that putting Jesus to death is a wrong action in itself and should not have happened or be celebrated today. They might argue that God could have found a way to bring forgiveness without allowing Jesus to die, such as giving Jesus a longer time on earth to teach people how to live.

The student makes clear what they will be arguing and then gives a reason why.

Words and phrases like 'Catholics believe' and 'however' can make your writing more sophisticated and help you demonstrate a clear understanding of the different perspectives.

2. **Now try writing two more paragraphs on arguments that disagree with the statement.** Here is an example:

> Christians would disagree and argue that while it is awful that Jesus was put to death as a sacrifice, <u>the importance of the sacrifice</u> is seen in the impact that it had. It brought about something good – all people being offered salvation from sin. The Bible shows how God had taught people over time about the danger of sin and separation, but people had not heeded this teaching and animal sacrifices in the Temple were not enough to respond to the sin of all human beings. Jesus' sacrifice was therefore the only way for God to show love to all creation and to bring about salvation. Catholics believe this reconciled humans to God and so the sacrifice of Jesus <u>had a good outcome</u> even though the death of Jesus was not a good thing. I would say that <u>this argument is persuasive</u> since the whole of the Christian faith is based on the belief that God was prepared to sacrifice Jesus in order to bring about forgiveness for humankind.

> **TIP**
> *You can draw on a range of ideas here, from Christian beliefs about Jesus' death, as well as the impact that this has on Christian life today. Try to use a variety of ideas in your answer.*

The student introduces an alternative argument but responds to it with Catholic teaching.

The positive effect of Jesus' sacrifice is made clear to support the point of the paragraph.

The student makes an evaluative statement showing how persuasive they find the argument to be. This is backed up by reference to Catholic beliefs.

3 **Write your conclusion.** As you know, your conclusion should make a final decision about the statement.

Look again at the statement to help you to organise your final thoughts:

'Jesus <u>should not</u> have been sacrificed.'

This statement could be interpreted in different ways. It could be seen as a moral judgement (it was wrong to put Jesus to death) or that this action simply wasn't needed (there was another way). Here is an example conclusion:

> <u>I think</u> that sacrificing someone, by putting them to death is wrong. However, in the case of Jesus' sacrifice, I believe that it was a way of God showing great love to humankind in making the ultimate sacrifice to bring about something good – the forgiveness of all people. <u>Therefore</u>, the act of sacrificing someone is wrong, but the goodness that came from Jesus' sacrifice is so beneficial to humankind that it brings a goodness from a wrong action.

By responding with 'I think' it is clear that this is the student's own conclusion to the statement above.

The student weighs up the information, and forms a final conclusion.

TIP

It's acceptable to use the first person ('I think' or 'I conclude') or you can start your paragraph with a phrase like 'To conclude' or 'In conclusion'.

Assessment 117

CHAPTER 5:
TO THE ENDS OF THE EARTH

Introduction

Catholics believe that every human is a unique individual who is loved by God. However, humans are not made to live or act alone: they are created for communion. In this chapter, we will explore the nature of the community that is at the core of Catholicism: the Church.

The letters of St Paul in the Bible provide some of the earliest records of the fledgling Christian communities that emerged following the Ascension. **St Paul teaches Christians key lessons about the nature and purpose of the Church**, and shows how early Christians had many questions about Jesus and faced challenges in living faithfully, just as Catholics today might.

The journey then takes us to a cornerstone of Catholic theology: the Church as the communion of saints. This is the concept that **all Christians on earth, in heaven and in purgatory are united as the Church**. It is not just a theological idea, but a living reality that forms the very heart of the Church. We will explore what it means for Catholics today to be part of this communion and how it is intimately connected to the Sacrament of Eucharist.

The Church teaches that **there are three parts of the Church: the Church on earth, the Church in heaven and the Church being purified (purgatory)**. We will learn more about the structure of the Church on earth, its members and its leadership. We will explore areas of debate among Christian denominations, such as the nature of authority within the Church, the description of the Church on earth as holy and the role of purgatory.

The Catholic Church has always believed **it is important to show honour to saints and angels through veneration in the Mass and other devotional practices**. For Catholics, these are essential ways to connect with their brothers and sisters in the Church in heaven. The Church teaches that **when the Church on earth shows devotion to the Church in heaven and prays for those in the Church being purified, the communion of saints is strengthened in a never-ending circle of faith and community**.

Catholics around the world are united in faith through their diverse celebration of saints and angels. Unique devotional practices, places of pilgrimage and artistic interpretations are ways that the whole Church is enriched by the cultural wealth of the Church on earth.

119

5.1

WHAT DOES THE BIBLE TEACH ABOUT THE EARLY CHURCH?

OBJECTIVE
*In this lesson you will explore **the characteristics of the Church in first-century Corinth.***

The Catechism describes the **Church** as 'the means and the goal of God's plan' for humans (CCC 778). The characteristics and purpose of the Church can be seen from the earliest descriptions of the first Christian communities in the Bible.

What is the Church?

The Church is the community of Jesus' followers and it is known under many names: the People of God, the Body of Christ and the Temple of the Holy Spirit. The Catholic Church teaches that people become members of the Church through Baptism.

The Acts of the Apostles and the many letters of St Paul in the Bible give a good idea of what the early Church looked like, as they describe what early Christians did after the Ascension (when Jesus rose to heaven after his resurrection) and how members of the Church are united with each other and with God:

> The Church is united by a shared faith in the word of God and the teachings of the apostles.

> 'And they devoted themselves to the apostles' teaching and fellowship, to the breaking of bread and the prayers.'
>
> *Acts 2:42*

The Sacrament of Eucharist, also known as Holy Communion, brings together Christian people into one Church community.

Christians form a community through shared practices of prayer and devotion, as Jesus said: 'For where two or three are gathered in my name, there am I among them' (Matthew 18:20).

Useful vocabulary

Church: faithful Christians on earth, in heaven and in purgatory who form a community that can be understood in three ways: as the People of God; as the Body of Christ; as the Temple of the Holy Spirit

Link

You can read more about the Church as the People of God, the Body of Christ and the Temple of the Holy Spirit in *Source to Summit: Year 7* pages 138–139.

The Church in first-century Corinth

In the Acts of the Apostles, we read that the apostle St Paul established many Christian churches across the ancient world during his missionary journeys. St Paul's letters in the New Testament are records of his correspondence with many of those church communities and include some of the challenges and problems they faced.

Based on the biblical account, the Church in Corinth in Greece was in many ways a successful Christian community made of people from many different backgrounds: Jewish and gentile, men and women, those with wealth and those living in poverty, all united together as followers of Jesus.

However, while large and thriving, the Church in Corinth also encountered disagreements and conflicts among its members. It is those disagreements and St Paul's response to them that help teach Catholics today about the nature and role of the Church. They included issues such as:

- **Local practices:** some Corinthian Christians argued about which traditions and personal cultural practices were acceptable, such as whether food sacrificed to idols could be eaten by Christians.
- **Authority:** some argued with each other over which of the apostles they should follow, some calling themselves followers of St Paul, and some followers of other teachers.
- **Gifts of the Holy Spirit:** some debated which gifts of the Holy Spirit, such as the ability to heal or the ability to speak in tongues (communicate in different languages), were most important.
- **Beliefs:** some argued with each other about life after death, with some denying the belief in the resurrection of the body.

What does St Paul tell us about the Church?

In the Bible, St Paul teaches that by joining the community of followers of Christ, every member of the community has to accept the teachings of the apostles, including belief in the resurrection of the body. Furthermore, by becoming followers of Christ, they have to leave behind immoral behaviour and try to live a life inspired by the example of Jesus.

When faced with the conflict over the value of the Holy Spirit's gifts, St Paul used this opportunity to explain how important it was that the Church behaved as one Body of Christ:

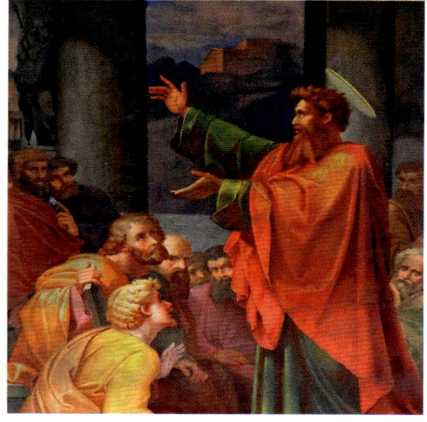

▲ *The letters of St Paul in the Bible reveal how he guided the early Church*

St Paul teaches that although each person within the Church is a unique individual, they all form one Church: one Body of Christ.

Although Jesus is the head of the Church and all people in the Church are valuable, some people are given the responsibility to be leaders and teachers.

> 'Now you are the body of Christ and individually members of it. And God has appointed in the church first apostles, second prophets, third teachers, then miracles, then gifts of healing, helping, administrating, and various kinds of tongues. Are all apostles? Are all prophets? Are all teachers? Do all work miracles? Do all possess gifts of healing? Do all speak with tongues? Do all interpret? But earnestly desire the higher gifts.'
>
> *1 Corinthians 12:27–31*

St Paul underlines that different members of the Church possess different gifts and talents. No gift is more or less important but each has its place in the Church.

St Paul explains that the most important gift that all Christians should strive for is the gift of love.

Understand

1. How are the members of the Church united with each other and with God, according to Acts 2:42?
2. Describe what the congregation of the Church in Corinth was thought to be like.
3. Summarise the key disagreements among Christians in first-century Corinth.
4. What lessons did St Paul try to teach the Corinthian Christians?

Discern

5. 'It is natural that the early Church faced problems and disagreements.' Explain one argument to support and one argument to disagree with this statement. Consider how persuasive you find each of the arguments.

Respond

6. Becoming a Christian in the first century often meant leaving behind familiar customs and practices of the past. How would you feel about making such a big change to your life?

5.2

HOW IS THE CHURCH THE COMMUNION OF SAINTS?

OBJECTIVE
In this lesson you will explore what it means that the Church is the communion of saints.

The Catholic Church teaches that God wants to save all people, not just individually, but as a whole human race. Catholics believe that people cannot return to God by only thinking about themselves, rather they must form a community and work together to fulfil God's plan. All humans are called to participate in this **communion of saints** that is the Church.

The Church as the communion of saints

In the Apostles' Creed, the Christian declaration of faith, Catholics state that they believe in 'the holy catholic Church, the communion of saints' (Article 9). The meaning of this is explained in the Catechism and Youth Catechism of the Catholic Church:

> 'The "communion of saints" is made up of all … who have placed their hope in Christ and belong to him through Baptism, whether they have already died or are still alive. Because in Christ we are one Body; we live in a communion that encompasses heaven and earth.'
>
> *Youth Catechism 146*

Catholics therefore believe that the Catholic Church is made up of those on earth today and those who, while no longer living on earth, continue to be part of the same community, either in heaven or in **purgatory**. These three parts or states of the Church are described in the following way.

> **The Church on earth:** these are Catholics alive on earth today who are answering God's call to sainthood. They continue in their struggle to fulfil their vocation to live a holy life according to the example of Jesus.

> **The Church in heaven:** these are members of the Church that are in heaven, enjoying the eternal presence of God. This is what Catholics believe God ultimately wants for humans. They are called **saints** and continue to offer support and prayers for people on earth. In addition, saints also offer a source of inspiration and example of what it means to live a genuine Christian life, acting as role models and patrons for Christians today.

> **The Church being purified:** these are members of the Body of Christ whose souls are currently in purgatory, assured of their salvation but in the process of being purified. The Catholic Church teaches that the prayers of Catholics on earth can support those in purgatory on their path of purification.

Useful vocabulary

communion of saints: all Christians on earth, in heaven and in purgatory; together they are united as the Church

purgatory: the condition a soul enters when in need of purification before entering the presence of God

Church on earth: Catholics on earth today

Church in heaven: Catholics who have died and whose souls live as saints with the angels in God's presence in heaven

saints: people who are officially recognised by the Catholic Church as being very holy because of the way they lived or died; also, anyone who is already in heaven, whether recognised or not

Church being purified: Catholics who have died and whose souls are in purgatory being prepared for heaven

The universal call to holiness

One of St Paul's most important teachings about the Church can be found in the very beginning of his first letter:

Members of the Church are sanctified (made holy) through their relationship with Jesus.

> 'To the church of God that is in Corinth, to those sanctified in Christ Jesus, called to be saints'
>
> *1 Corinthians 1:2*

Members of the Church share a universal vocation to holiness and sainthood.

▲ *Cloud of Witnesses* by Giusto de' Menabuoi

Inspired by these words of St Paul, the Church teaches that while different Christians have individual vocations and calls from God to answer, they all share one universal call: to be holy and to be a saint.

Catholics believe that God wants all people to be reunited with God in heaven and so wants all people to be saints:

> '"All Christians in any state or walk of life are called to the fullness of Christian life and to the perfection of charity." All are called to holiness: "Be perfect, as your heavenly Father is perfect."'
>
> *Catechism of the Catholic Church 2013*

Living a life of holiness may seem difficult, but Catholics believe that God established the Church as a communion of people that stretches across time and space, supporting each other through prayer, faith and the sacraments: 'The Christian who seeks to purify himself of his sin and to become holy with the help of God's grace is not alone' (CCC 1474). For Catholics the communion of saints is the '"treasury of the Church" … which can never be exhausted' (CCC 1476); it is an unfailing support that allows all people to respond to God's universal call to sainthood.

Understand

1. What does it mean that the Church is a communion of saints?
2. Describe the three states of the Church and explain what the Church teaches about each one.
3. How does 1 Corinthians 1:2 support the idea that all Christians have a shared vocation?
4. Explain what the Catholic Church teaches about the universal call to holiness.
5. Summarise how the communion of saints helps Catholics answer the call to holiness and sainthood.

Discern

6. 'Once you die, you are no longer part of the Church and its mission on earth.' How would a Catholic respond to this statement? How far do you agree? Justify your ideas using quotations from the texts in this lesson.

Respond

7. The Catholic Church teaches that all humans are called to be saints. What does this teaching mean to you?

How is the Church the communion of saints? | 123

5.3

WHAT DO CATHOLICS BELIEVE ABOUT THE CHURCH ON EARTH?

OBJECTIVE
In this lesson you will explore Catholics beliefs about the Church on earth.

The Church on earth is the one state of the Church that Catholics today can see and actively participate in. For that reason it is sometimes referred to as the 'visible Church' and is believed by Catholics to be a sign of Jesus' love and grace in the world.

The Pilgrim Church

Catholics believe the Church, although one whole, exists in three states: the Church on earth, the Church in heaven and the Church being purified. The Church on earth is sometimes also called the Pilgrim Church:

> 'When the Lord comes in glory, and all his angels with him, death will be no more and all things will be subject to him. But at the present time some of his disciples are **pilgrims** on earth.'
>
> *Catechism of the Catholic Church 954*

Useful vocabulary

pilgrims: people on a journey, often travelling for religious reasons and to a sacred place

Catholics believe that the followers and disciples of Jesus who are currently alive on earth are like pilgrims, travelling towards God's Kingdom on a journey that is often filled with challenges and uncertainty. The Pilgrim Church on earth is led by people appointed by God and guided by the teachings Jesus left behind, but it is also in continuous communion with those Christians who are already enjoying the presence of God in the Church in heaven. Catholics believe the saints continue to inspire and pray for their pilgrim brothers and sisters on earth. The Church on earth also has a commitment to its brothers and sisters in the Church being purified, offering prayers to hasten their ascent into heaven.

Who is part of the Church on earth?

The Church on earth is made up of two groups: the laity and the clergy. Each group has an equally important role and responsibility in bringing about God's plan of salvation.

- **The laity:** all baptised Catholics who seek to serve God and the world through the vocation to which they are called by God. This may be to marriage, to family life or to single life, and any role from teacher to sportsperson.
- **Clergy:** those who, like the apostles, are called by God to lead, teach and distribute the sacraments, entrusted to the Church by Jesus. This special assignment is known in the Catholic Church as ecclesial ministry.

To the Ends of the Earth

The Church is the universal Sacrament of Salvation

The Church on earth is the means through which Catholics receive God's grace. Catholics participate in sacraments such as Baptism, Reconciliation and the Eucharist and these sacraments allow God's invisible grace to become visible. The Catechism teaches that the role of the Church in delivering the sacraments makes the Church itself the 'universal Sacrament of Salvation' (CCC 776) and a sign of God's love in the world. When Catholics participate in the Church they participate in the Sacrament of Salvation and help God's love grow.

> The Church on earth is a physical representation of Christians united together.

> 'The Church [is] a **sign** and **instrument** … of communion with God and of unity among all'
> *Catechism of the Catholic Church 775*

> The Church on earth is also a tool for unity – it enables the union between humans and God, and between all humans.

Holy Communion unites the Church on earth

Catholics also believe that the Sacrament of Eucharist plays a particular part in unifying the community of the Church – one of the names of this sacrament is Holy Communion for this very reason. Catholics are united both with God by receiving the body and blood of Jesus, and with each other by sharing the sacrament. For Catholics, the Eucharist has many different fruits, or effects, and the union of people that make up the whole Church is one of them:

> 'The Eucharist makes the Church. Those who receive the Eucharist are united more closely to Christ. Through it Christ unites them to all the faithful in one body – the Church.'
> *Catechism of the Catholic Church 1396*

▲ *Catholics receiving the Eucharist on Palm Sunday in Surabaya, Indonesia in 2019*

Understand

1. What is the Church on earth?
2. Why is the Church on earth sometimes called the Pilgrim Church?
3. How is the Church on earth a sign?
4. How is the Church on earth an instrument?
5. Explain why sacraments are important to the Church.
6. What does it mean to call the visible Church 'the universal Sacrament of Salvation'?
7. Explain the difference between the two groups that make up the Church on earth.

Discern

8. 'If the Church only existed on earth then there would be no motivation to follow Jesus' teachings and example.' Give reasons to agree and disagree with this statement, including a Catholic view.

Respond

9. Do you think of yourself as being part of a community? What do you gain from it? Do you think you lose anything?

What do Catholics believe about the Church on earth?

5.4

IS THE CHURCH ON EARTH HOLY?

OBJECTIVE
In this lesson you will explore ideas about the holiness of the Church on earth.

The Catholic Church teaches that the Church on earth is holy yet always in need of purification. This can seem to be a contradiction: if the Church is holy (sacred and dedicated to God), how can it be right to suggest that it is also a very human institution and needs to be purified?

The Church: human or divine?

Catholics believe that the Church on earth is made holy through the presence and action of God:

> 'The Church is holy, not because all her members are supposedly holy, but rather because God is holy and is at work in her. All the members of the Church are sanctified by Baptism.'
>
> *Youth Catechism 132*

When Catholics recite the Nicene Creed, they state that they 'believe in one, holy, catholic and apostolic Church'. These are known as the four marks of the Church, and mean that there is one true Church that is sacred, offered to all and follows in the footsteps of Jesus (as the apostles did).

However, following the Second Vatican Council, Pope St Paul VI wrote about the mystery of the Church and described it as 'at the same time holy and always in need of being purified' (*Lumen Gentium* 8). He was recognising the idea that although Jesus instituted the Church as a holy thing, people are part of it, and they are not perfect!

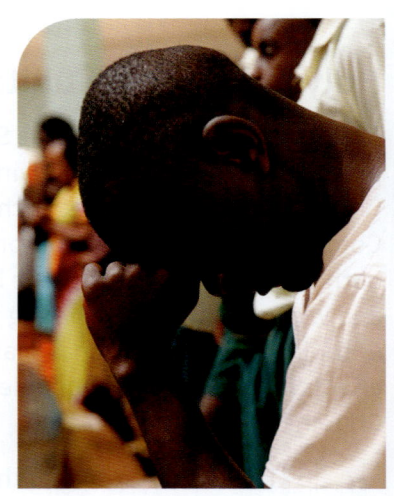

▲ *All people can make mistakes and are in need of divine forgiveness*

Catholics therefore believe that the Church is at once both human and divine. The Youth Catechism teaches this in the following way:

> 'The Church is more than an institution because she is a mystery that is simultaneously human and divine … Viewed from outside, the Church is only a historical institution with historical achievements, but also mistakes and even crimes – a Church of sinners. But that is not looking deep enough. After all, Christ became so involved with us sinners that he never abandons his Church, even if we were to betray him daily. This inseparable union of the human and the divine, this intertwining of sin and grace, is part of the mystery of the Church. Seen with the eyes of faith, the Church is therefore indestructibly holy.'
>
> *Youth Catechism 124*

This means that the Church is made of humans but was established and is led by God.

The Church is made of real people who are fallible (able to fail and sin). Being part of the Church does not make humans perfect.

Jesus continues to faithfully look after the Church and guide it, even when people make mistakes.

To the Ends of the Earth

Is the Church holy or is it always in need of being purified?

Not all Christians believe in purgatory. It also follows that not all Christians agree that the Church is in need of purification.

> Some argue that it is a contradiction to say that the Church is both holy and needs to be purified – it must be one or the other, either the Church is full of sinners and as such is not holy, or the Church was saved by the sacrifice of Jesus and therefore does not need further purification.

> The response to this is clear: there is no contradiction to say that the Church is holy and in need of purification. It is holy as it is led and instituted by God, but it is composed of humans in constant need of reconciliation and purification.

When St Paul wrote letters of guidance to the Church at Corinth, he did this because the Corinthians were making the wrong choices and not living holy lives. They were making distinctions between people and behaving in elitist ways in their celebration of the Eucharist.

> 'For just as the body is one and has many members … so it is with Christ. For in one Spirit we were all baptised into one body – Jews or Greeks, slaves or free – and all were made to drink of one Spirit. … If one member suffers, all suffer together; if one member is honoured, all rejoice together.'
>
> *1 Corinthians 12:12–26*

Link

You can read about the Catholic belief in purgatory in *Source to Summit: Year 8* pages 144–145.

St Paul explains that baptism makes all Christians equally holy and part of the same body of Christ, but their behaviour sometimes undermines this holiness. For Catholics, St Paul teaches how the Church always has been both 'holy' and populated by sinners who imperfectly reflect that holiness. Therefore, the Church is holy not because it is composed of perfect people but because it leads imperfect people on their path to sainthood.

Understand

1. Why do Catholics believe the Church is holy?
2. What role does Baptism play in making the Church holy?
3. What do the four marks in the Nicene Creed teach about the Church?
4. Explain three key points from YC 124 that show how the Church is both human and divine.

Discern

5. 'The belief that the Church is "holy" contradicts the teaching that the same Church is "always in need of being purified".' Present arguments for and against this statement, including a Catholic response, evaluating the strengths and weaknesses of the arguments. Refer to 1 Corinthians 12:12–26 in your answer. Reach a judgement on which argument you feel is the strongest.

Respond

6. How do your strengths help you overcome your weaknesses?

5.5

WHO LEADS THE CHURCH ON EARTH?

OBJECTIVE
*In this lesson you will learn about **authority and structure within the Catholic Church.***

One of the most debated issues among Christians is that of authority within the Church on earth. How should Christians on earth organise themselves and who should lead them? The Catholic Church believes that Christ appointed apostles to continue his mission and intended their successors to be the spiritual leaders of the Church. Therefore Catholics understand the authority of the Pope and bishops to come ultimately from God.

Jesus: the head of the Church

One of the most important descriptions of the Church is the Body of Christ, and one of the most important ideas it communicates is that all Christians are united together, like different parts of the same body, with Jesus as its head. All Christians accept that Jesus is the head of the Church. In the Bible, St Paul writes: 'And he put all things under his feet and gave him as head over all things to the church' (Ephesians 1:22).

Who has spiritual authority on earth?

Catholics believe that Jesus Christ, as the High Priest, is not only the supreme authority over the Church on earth, he is also the source of all other authority within the Church.

> 'This is the one Church of Christ … which our Saviour, after His Resurrection, commissioned Peter to shepherd, and him and the other apostles to extend and direct with authority … the Catholic Church … is governed by the successor of Peter and by the Bishops in communion with him.'
>
> *Lumen Gentium 8*

Link
You can read more about Jesus as the High Priest on pages 106–107.

Catholics believe the responsibility to lead the Church on earth was entrusted by Jesus to the bishops, who are the successors of the apostles. The successor of Peter is the bishop of Rome: the Pope.

The Catholic Church teaches that all the members of the Church, although equal in dignity and value, are ordered hierarchically towards Jesus as the head of the Church. The word 'hierarchy' comes from Greek and its literal meaning is 'holy origin'. To say that the Church is hierarchical means that it has an organised structure of responsibility and authority that is the will of God, under God's ultimate authority. So, in the Church, leaders receive their power and authority from Jesus, who they believe delegates them to lead the Church on earth on Jesus' behalf through Apostolic Tradition.

Some Christians believe that with Jesus as the head of the Church, there is no need for anybody else to act as a leader of the Church. Some Protestant congregations, such as Baptists, believe Churches should be led democratically by the assembly of the congregation, with ministers appointed by the members of the local church. In this view, Jesus can be seen as the only spiritual authority for Christians, with earthly authority being limited to earthly matters.

The structure of the Church: Pope, bishops, priests, deacons

The clergy of the Church on earth, those called by God to the vocation of Holy Orders, are hierarchically divided in the following way:

▲ *Bishops from Spain meet with the Pope at the Vatican in 2021*

Pope: from the Greek word *pappas* meaning 'father', the Pope is the bishop of Rome and the successor of St Peter, who Jesus selected to be the leader of the twelve apostles. The Pope is the head of the Church on earth, and its chief priest and teacher, with supreme authority to govern the entire Church and responsibility for its unity on earth.

Bishops: these are the successors of the apostles, and leaders of particular Church communities. All the bishops together form a college of bishops and are responsible for caring for and leading the whole Church under the guidance of the Pope.

Priests: from the Greek word *presbyteros* meaning 'old' or 'elder', priests support bishops in their task of teaching. They provide care for a local Catholic community and distribute the sacraments to it.

Deacons: deacons support the bishops and priests in the provision of some of the sacraments (specifically Baptism and Matrimony), in preaching and in charitable work. All priests are first deacons, but there are permanent deacons too.

Link

You can explore the Sacrament of Holy Orders on pages 80–81.

Discern

5 'Jesus is the only spiritual authority a Christian can accept.' Present arguments for and against this statement, including Catholic ideas on the authority of the Pope, bishops, priests and deacons. Evaluate the strengths and weaknesses of the arguments and reach a final judgement.

Understand

1 What does it mean that Jesus is the head of the Church?
2 What does 'hierarchy' mean?
3 Explain how the Catholic Church is hierarchical.
4 Describe the structure of the Church on earth:
   a Explain who holds authority and how they have this authority.
   b Describe the roles of the Pope, bishops, priests and deacons.

Respond

6 How important is it to you that your voice is heard in any organisation you belong to? Do you think the voice of all Catholics should be heard more in the Church?

Who leads the Church on earth?

5.6

WHAT DO CATHOLICS BELIEVE ABOUT THE CHURCH IN HEAVEN?

OBJECTIVE
In this lesson you will explore **Catholic beliefs about the Church in heaven.**

Catholics believe that the Church is not only composed of the baptised Christians on earth but also those who are already enjoying the presence of God in heaven. All those in heaven are called saints and, together with the **angels**, are referred to as the Church in heaven. Catholics believe that saints continue to play active roles in the life of the Church today.

The Church Triumphant

Catholics believe the second state of the Church is the Church in heaven.

The Church in heaven is also called the Church Triumphant because Catholics believe it is composed of people who are already enjoying the triumphant and joyful reward of heaven and participating in Christ's victory over sin and death. It was described in the following way by Pope St Paul VI:

> 'We believe that the multitude of those gathered around Jesus and Mary in paradise forms the Church of Heaven where in eternal beatitude they see God as He is, and where they also, in different degrees, are associated with the holy angels … interceding for us and helping our weakness by their brotherly care.'
>
> *Credo of the People of God 29*

Useful vocabulary

angels: pure, intelligent, spiritual beings created by God as servants and messengers; they live with God in heaven

The joy of heaven for saints is the eternal blessing of being in God's presence: 'They will see his face' (Revelation 22:4).

Catholics believe in the existence of angels, who are joined by the saints in the eternal praise of God as part of the Church in heaven.

Angels and saints in heaven offer prayers of intercession to God. These are prayers on behalf of those still living on earth. Catholics believe they 'can and should ask them to intercede for us and for the whole world' (CCC 2683).

Saints and angels

The Church in heaven is composed of two groups: saints and angels.

Saints

In Christianity, saints are men and women who, through their faith and actions, followed Christ faithfully and reflected the power of God's grace for others.

To the Ends of the Earth

The Catholic Church believes there are a great number of saints in heaven, coming from all walks of life. Some are known by name through the study of their earthly lives, the power of their intercessions or due to the great works they did for the Church during their lives. The Pope may **canonise** an individual to recognise that a person has lived a holy life, is in heaven and can serve as a particular example as a saint for other Christians. A patron saint is a named saint who is believed to be a particular advocate, such as for an activity or place. Mary, Mother of God, is the first among the saints, and the only one who Catholics believe was assumed to heaven body and soul.

Angels

In Christianity, angels are spiritual beings created by God as 'servants and messengers' of God's will (CCC 329). The word 'angel' comes from the Greek *angelos* which means messenger. 'Angel' is a description of their role rather than their nature. Angels are pure spirits with 'intelligence and will' (CCC 330); they live in heaven in the constant presence of God.

What are prayers of intercession?

Catholics believe that all the angels and saints play an active and inspirational role in the Church. This includes being role models of saintly behaviour and faith, and through prayers of intercession.

Intercessory prayers are prayers a person makes on behalf of others. They are a common part of Christianity, and indeed of many religions. Catholics may ask other Catholics to pray for them, or individuals may choose to offer prayers on behalf of people they are concerned about. Catholics believe that saints, being in the very presence of God and in a state of grace, can offer particularly effective prayers. Many Catholics ask saints to pray for them to God. Different saints acts as 'patrons', showing particular attention to people from certain professions or in specific situations. So, a Catholic facing a crisis of faith might ask St Teresa of Calcutta (Mother Teresa) to pray for them, as she also struggled with faith during her lifetime. A Catholic worried about a journey might ask St Christopher, the patron saint of travellers, for his protection and prayers.

Catholics believe that saints intercede for them and for the whole world, and as such they continue to participate in the life and mission of the Church.

Useful vocabulary

canonise: to make an infallible statement that a person is a saint in heaven

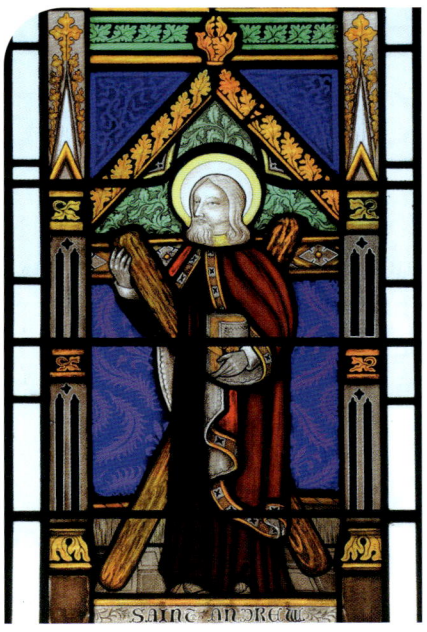

▲ *St Andrew is the patron saint of Scotland*

Understand

1. Which two distinct groups make up the Church in heaven?
2. Explain what is meant by the Church in heaven.
3. What three things does Pope St Paul VI teach about the Church in heaven?
4. Describe the nature and role of an angel according to the Catholic Church.
5. What are prayers of intercession?
6. What do Catholics believe about the intercession of the saints?

Discern

7. 'The Church is an invisible, spiritual bond between Christians, in which visible structures and hierarchies are irrelevant.' Using what you have learned about the Church on earth and the communion of saints, present arguments for and against this statement, including a Catholic response. Evaluate the strengths and weaknesses of the arguments and arrive at a judgement.

Respond

8. Do you ever pray on behalf of someone else? What motivates you to do this?

What do Catholics believe about the Church in heaven?

5.7

WHAT DO CATHOLICS BELIEVE ABOUT THE CHURCH BEING PURIFIED?

OBJECTIVES

In this lesson you will learn what Catholics believe about the Church being purified and the significance of praying for the dead.

Catholics believe the Church is composed of faithful Christians living on earth and those who are saints in the Church in heaven. However, they do not believe that all who die and are saved go directly to heaven to enjoy the beatific vision – the Church is also made up of those Catholics who are going through purification in purgatory.

What is purgatory?

In the previous lessons you saw that Catholics believe that the Church is made of faithful Christians living on earth and the angels and saints in heaven. Those who die and who fully and purposefully reject God's grace and salvation condemn themselves to the state of eternal separation from God that is commonly known as hell. However, as well as heaven and hell, Catholics believe there is a third possible outcome for people when they die: purgatory.

The Catechism of the Catholic Church teaches that:

> 'All who die in God's grace and friendship, but still imperfectly purified, are indeed assured of their eternal salvation; but after death they undergo purification, so as to achieve the holiness necessary to enter the joy of heaven.'
>
> *Catechism of the Catholic Church 1030*

Link

Non-Catholic Christians do not believe in purgatory. You can read *Source to Summit: Year 8* pages 144–145 to learn why.

Catholics believe purgatory therefore is the state of purposeful 'purifying punishments' (*Indulgentiarum Doctrina* 2), where faithful souls are cleansed so that they are ready for the beatific vision in heaven. The Church makes it clear that purgatory is not a test that can be failed; it 'is entirely different from the punishment of the damned' (CCC 1031). The Church teaches that the state of purgatory is temporary and lasts only until the soul is ready to enter heaven. As such, Catholics believe that souls which are in purgatory remain part of the Church.

> 'When the Lord comes in glory, and all his angels with him, death will be no more and all things will be subject to him. But at the present time some of his disciples are pilgrims on earth. Others have died and are being purified, while still others are in glory, contemplating "in full light, God himself triune and one, exactly as he is"'
>
> *Catechism of the Catholic Church 954*

To the Ends of the Earth

What is the Church Penitent?

Just as the Church on earth is known as the Pilgrim Church, and the Church in heaven as the Church Triumphant, those Christians who are in purgatory are known as the Church being purified, or Church Penitent.

A penitent is a person who is humble and regrets their sins. Catholics do not believe that those in purgatory are bad people; they are ordinary people who committed sins in the course of their lives. For Catholics, purgatory is a loving opportunity to be cleansed.

Praying for Christians in purgatory

Catholics believe the Church is a communion of all Christians. Communion is not merely a gathering of people, rather it is a union where all members of the community support each other through faith, prayer and charity. The Catholic Church refers to this as the communion in spiritual goods – a sharing of gifts provided by God for the benefit of all.

Saints share their heavenly reward with other members of the Church through their prayers of intercession. The Church on earth undertakes 'fasting, prayers, and good works, but especially through the celebration of Holy Eucharist' (YC 160) to connect with all Christians who have died, in the belief that those prayers and works can ease and support them in their time in purgatory.

> 'From the beginning the Church has honoured the memory of the dead and offered prayers in suffrage for them … so that, thus purified, they may attain the beatific vision of God.'
>
> *Catechism of the Catholic Church 1032*

Catholics believe that praying for the dead is not just a way to mourn their loved ones, but it is a way to share their gifts and to help them on their path towards God.

▲ *The artwork* When we pray at Mass we are united with Christ in Glory and with the gathering of His saints and the souls of Purgatory *by Elizabeth Wang*

Understand

1. What is meant by 'the Church being purified'?
2. Why do Catholics believe purgatory is necessary?
3. What does the communion in spiritual goods mean?
4. How can Catholics on earth connect with Christians in purgatory?
5. Give two reasons why Catholics pray for the dead.

Discern

6. 'There is no point in praying for the dead.' How would a Catholic respond to this statement? Explain their viewpoint using quotations from the Catechism as support.

Respond

7. How do you honour people who have passed away?

5.8

HOW DO CATHOLICS SHOW DEVOTION TO SAINTS AND ANGELS IN THE LITURGY?

OBJECTIVE
In this lesson you will explore **different ways in which Catholics connect with saints and angels during the liturgy.**

Catholics around the world believe it is important to show their devotion to the saints of the Church in heaven. They also recognise and celebrate angels, in particular the **archangels** who are named in the Bible. Feast days are devoted to particular saints and angels and direct the liturgy of the Church on those days. Devotion to saints is also incorporated into the most important form of Catholic worship: the Mass.

The significance of angels

Just as with saints, the Catholic Church believes there is an uncounted multitude of angels in the Church in heaven, but some of them are named and are of particular importance as archangels:

Archangel Michael: defender of the Church and divine warrior in the fight for good against evil. According to Catholic tradition, he is the leader of God's heavenly army, the angel of death and judgement, and the protector of the Church. Archangel Michael has an important place in traditional Catholic devotion.

Archangel Gabriel: God's special messenger, the angel of mercy and incarnation. He is mentioned four times in the Bible, most notably as the angel who brought the message of the Incarnation to the Virgin Mary.

Archangel Raphael: the last of the angels mentioned by name in the Bible, Raphael is mentioned once in the Old Testament. Catholics believe that he is one of the seven archangels, an angel of healing and a patron of travellers and medical workers.

Useful vocabulary

archangels: angels of particular importance who are named in the Bible and given key tasks to perform by God

Catholics also believe that angels offer watchful care over Christians on earth as guardian angels: 'Beside each believer stands an angel as protector and shepherd' (CCC 336).

▲ The archangels Michael, Gabriel and Raphael

How do saints and angels belong in the liturgy?

Both saints and angels are celebrated within the liturgy of the Church. As such, Catholics believe that during liturgical worship, especially Mass, they are united as the Church on earth with the Church in heaven and the Church being purified. This is evident in many parts of the Mass, especially during the Eucharistic Prayer, the heart of the Liturgy of the Eucharist.

At the end of the preface of this prayer, the priest invites all people attending the Mass to join together in a joyful acclamation known as the *Sanctus*:

> 'And so, with the Angels and all the Saints
> we declare your glory,
> as with one voice we acclaim:
> Holy, Holy, Holy Lord God of hosts.
> Heaven and earth are full of your glory.
> Hosanna in the highest.'
>
> *Eucharistic Prayer II, Preface I for Sundays in Ordinary Time*

Sanctoral cycle

Catholics also show devotion to saints and angels by celebrating feast days for many of the great Catholic saints throughout the **liturgical year**. The Catholic liturgical year is divided into two cycles or series of events: temporal and sanctoral. The temporal cycle follows the key events in the life of Jesus and is divided by 'seasons' such as Lent and Advent. The sanctoral cycle follows the feast days of the many saints and angels of the Church.

Many days of the year mark either a feast or a memorial of a saint or angel and their intercessory prayers will be called upon. Some of these days are known as solemnities and some particularly significant ones remember Mary Mother of God, St Joseph and St John the Baptist. On the Feast of St Peter and St Paul, Catholics remember the lives of these two apostles. It is a Holy Day of Obligation when all Catholics are expected to attend Mass.

Michaelmas is the feast day of the archangels Michael, Gabriel and Raphael. On the Feast of the Holy Guardian Angels, Catholics show honour to the angels who watch over them in their daily lives.

Understand

1. Who are the three named angels in the Bible, and what are their responsibilities?
2. What are guardian angels?
3. Describe how Catholics on earth are united with saints and angels in heaven during the Eucharist.
4. How does the sanctoral cycle allow devotion to be shown to saints and angels?
5. Give two examples of feast days dedicated to saints and angels.

Link

You can read more about the Liturgy of the Eucharist in *Source to Summit: Year 7* pages 110–111.

Catholics believe that at this point of the Mass, the Church on earth and the Church in heaven are united in singing praise to God.

Useful vocabulary

liturgical year: the Church's calendar, which consists of specific liturgical seasons and directs the public worship (liturgy) that takes place

Discern

6. 'Celebrating saints and angels in heaven makes the Church on earth a richer and stronger place.' What would a Catholic say to this? What is your viewpoint? You can refer to your learning in lesson 5.6 to support your ideas.

Respond

7. What does the Catholic belief that each person has their own guardian angel through life mean to you?

5.9

HOW DO CATHOLICS SHOW DEVOTION TO SAINTS AND ANGELS IN PRAYER?

OBJECTIVE
In this lesson you will explore **how Catholics show devotion to saints and angels in prayer.**

The veneration (or deep respect) of saints and angels is one of the most important and well-known Catholic traditions and practices. Many of the ways Catholics show their devotion to the Church in heaven date back to the very early years of the Church. Prayer is the main way in which Catholics show devotion, but they may also sing hymns and take part in processions or other practices.

Why do Catholics show devotion to saints and angels?

Just as Catholics believe that praying for those in purgatory is important for the unity of the Church, they also believe that remembering those in heaven strengthens the Church community and brings all Christians closer to God:

> 'Exactly as Christian communion among our fellow pilgrims brings us closer to Christ, so our communion with the saints joins us to Christ, from whom as from its fountain and head issues all grace, and the life of the People of God itself.'
> *Catechism of the Catholic Church 957*

The Catholic veneration of saints is not the same as praise: praise and worship are reserved for God; veneration is deep respect.

Devotion to saints and angels in prayer

Catholics believe that asking for help from saints and angels shows both love for and respect to them. Prayers of intercession can take many forms, for example the Litany of the Saints and the Angelus.

Litany of the Saints

Litanies are formal prayers consisting of a series of petitions, or requests, made by a priest or deacon, followed by fixed responses from the congregation. The Litany of the Saints is considered the oldest litany of the Church, prescribed by Pope St Gregory the Great in AD 590. It is often used during important Catholic liturgies, including the Easter Vigil and All Saints Day. In the second part of the litany, Catholics call for the intervention of great saints and angels of the Church in heaven.

▲ *A procession of saints in Sicily, Italy to honour three local patron saints*

Link

You can explore how the Rosary is used as a Marian devotion of prayer in *Source to Summit: Year 7* pages 58–59.

To the Ends of the Earth

> '... Holy Mary, Mother of God, *pray for us*.
> Saint Michael, *pray for us*.
> Holy Angels of God, *pray for us*.
> Saint John the Baptist, *pray for us*.
> Saint Joseph, *pray for us*. ...'
> *Litany of the Saints*

According to the Church's tradition, saints are called upon in different important groups: first, the Virgin Mary, the most important of all saints; second, angels; third, St John the Baptist and St Joseph, Mary's husband. The prayer goes on to list other saints by name or by group.

The Angelus

The Angelus is a prayer dating back to the Middle Ages. It focuses on the Incarnation (the belief that Jesus is truly God and truly human). It also shows devotion to Mary, Mother of God, and the archangel Gabriel, messenger of the Annunciation.

> 'The Angel of the Lord declared to Mary: *And she conceived of the Holy Spirit.*
>
> Hail Mary, full of grace, the Lord is with thee; blessed art thou among women and blessed is the fruit of thy womb, Jesus. Holy Mary, Mother of God, pray for us sinners, now and at the hour of our death. Amen.
>
> Behold the handmaid of the Lord. *Be it done unto me according to thy word.*
> Hail Mary...
>
> And the Word was made flesh. *And dwelt among us.*
> Hail Mary...
>
> Pray for us, O holy Mother of God. *That we may be made worthy of the promises of Christ.*
>
> Let us pray;
> Pour forth, we beseech thee, O Lord, thy grace into our hearts; that we, to whom the Incarnation of Christ, thy Son, was made known by the message of an angel, may by his Passion and Cross be brought to the glory of his Resurrection, through the same Christ our Lord. Amen.'
> *The Angelus*

The main part of the Angelus reflects on the Annunciation.

The central part of the Angelus is one of the most well-known Catholic prayers, the Hail Mary, which uses words spoken to Mary by the archangel Gabriel in the Annunciation in the Gospel of Luke.

Just as Mary learned about the true nature of Jesus through the angel, so do all Catholics today.

Understand

1. Why do Catholics show devotion to saints and angels?
2. What is a litany?
3. How does the Litany of Saints connect Catholics with the Church in Heaven?
4. What is the Angelus?
5. How does the Angelus show devotion to Mary?

Discern

6. 'Praying to saints is the same as worshipping saints.' Present arguments for and against this statement, including a Catholic response. Evaluate the strengths and weaknesses of the arguments and reach a final judgement on which argument you think is more persuasive.

Respond

7. Are there any saints that are of particular importance to you? If so, why are they important to you?

5.10 ETHICAL OPTION

SHOULD CATHOLICS USE SHRINES AND RELICS IN WORSHIP?

OBJECTIVE
In this lesson you will evaluate **arguments for and against the Catholic veneration of saints using shrines and relics.**

Showing devotion to saints and angels through the liturgy and prayer is one of the oldest practices of the Catholic Church. Other ancient practices are the creation of shrines (places with religious significance for special veneration) and the veneration of relics (physical objects believed to be associated with saints).

How do Catholics venerate saints and angels?

As you have learned, saints and angels are remembered in the Liturgy of the Eucharist in the Catholic Church and through particular prayers such as the Angelus. Feast days for saints and angels are regularly celebrated during the liturgical year, during which special Masses, processions and celebratory events might take place. Catholics also undertake personal acts of devotion to saints, such as using the Rosary for private prayer, or creating a Mary garden at home or a personal shrine to honour a saint with whom they feel a special connection.

Many shrines also exist to celebrate the places where key events or miracles associated with particular saints are believed to have taken place. Shrines are special places which play a role in the Catholic practice of spiritual pilgrimage. Some of the most famous shrines contain relics associated with Jesus, Mary or one of the saints. The Catholic Church continues to prescribe that every consecrated altar in the Church should contain in it a small piece of a relic associated with a saint. These could be fragments of cloth or other belongings of the saint, or even parts of their bodies. Some of the most famous relics in Catholic history are associated with Jesus, for example a piece of the cross on which he died.

▲ *A vial of blood from St Jean Vianney, sitting inside a glass container, known as a reliquary*

Objections to the veneration of saints and angels

Many Protestant denominations reject the veneration of saints and angels. Their objections to shrines and relics may include the following reasons:
- Catholic devotions to saints and angels amount to worship. The Bible states that 'You shall worship the Lord your God and him only shall you serve' (Matthew 4:10).
- Even if Catholics are not directly worshipping saints, veneration implicitly treats saints as divine beings. Creating statues and shrines to which people pray elevates saints and angels to a level of importance that should be reserved for God.

- Showing devotion to statues and relics is a form of idolatry (worship of something other than God). There is nothing special about the belongings of saints or their bodily remains and such objects should not be treated as having special significance.
- The veneration of relics appears to resemble belief in magic or pagan practices and not genuine Christian worship.
- The authenticity of relics can be questioned, as there is no way of knowing if a particular object is what some people claim it to be. In the Middle Ages, the sale of relics was commercial and profitable. Some unscrupulous people, including clergy, made a great deal of money from the faith of other Christians.

▲ *This crown of thorns, displayed at Notre Dame Cathedral in Paris, is believed to be the same one that was worn by Jesus during the Passion*

Catholic responses to objections

Catholic responses to objections include the following:
- The Catholic Church is clear that worship is due to God alone. It does not agree that traditional Christian veneration of saints, which dates back to the very beginning of the Church, is the same practice as worship. The Catholic Church teaches that veneration is showing 'devotion and respect to [those] who were viewed as faithful witnesses to faith in Jesus Christ' (*Glossary of the Catechism of the Catholic Church*). It believes respectful veneration shown to saints and angels can be clearly contrasted with worship and adoration, which are directed at God alone.
- Catholics do not pray to statues and shrines at all. Instead, statues and holy places can inspire Catholics to reflect on the lives of saints and are an opportunity to contemplate the word of God. Furthermore, Catholics would argue that in the Bible, there are many instances of God encouraging the creation of visual symbols and statues. For example, in Numbers 21:8–9 God commands Moses to create a statue of a bronze serpent so that the people of Israel can be healed from poison.
- The Catholic Church teaches that relics themselves have no special power. Relics are reminders of the lives of saints and should be respected, particularly because the Church teaches that human bodies are 'the living temple of the Holy Spirit' (*Instruction 'Relics in the Church: Authenticity and Preservation'*, 2017).
- The Church does believe that sometimes God works miracles through relics or other physical objects, such as the miracles associated with the water at Lourdes, but that this has a biblical basis. In the books of Kings, the remains of the prophet Elijah are associated with the miracle of healing.
- The Catholic Church has careful procedures to ensure all relics displayed in churches and recognised Catholic shrines have been carefully authenticated, often using independent advice such as carbon dating or research by archaeologists.

Discern

5 'Shrines and relics distract Christians from worshipping God.' Present arguments for and against this statement, including a Catholic response.

Respond

6 How do you show respect and admiration to people who inspire you? Do you think we should show the same kind of respect to people we admire after they die?

Understand

1 How might a Catholic undertake a personal act of devotion to a saint?
2 Explain the purpose of a shrine.
3 Describe three key objections presented by some Protestants to the veneration of saints using shrines and/or relics.
4 Summarise the Catholic responses to each objection given in question 3.

5.11 ARTISTIC EXPRESSION OPTION

HOW ARE SAINTS REPRESENTED IN ART?

OBJECTIVE
*In this lesson you will explore **how the belief in the Church as the communion of saints inspires Catholic art around the world.***

Angels and saints are a central Catholic art motif. They feature as part of larger biblical and religious scenes, and also on their own in paintings, statues, mosaics and icons. However, the presentation of them as the communion of saints allows artists to create particularly impressive pieces of art.

The communion of saints in art

Catholic churches worldwide are decorated with images and statues of saints and angels. For Catholics, this shows love and respect to important individuals within the history of the Church, who offer inspiration as models of faithful service following God's will.

The belief in the communion of saints is one of the most important and popular Catholic artistic themes. One of the most common scenes depicted is the gathering of saints around the throne of God, with Jesus enthroned as the King of heaven.

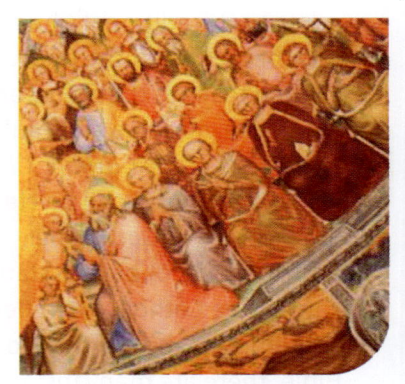

Cloud of Witnesses by Giusto de' Menabuoi

On page 123 you can see *Cloud of Witnesses* by Giusto de' Menabuoi. He painted this around 1375 on the ceiling of Padua Baptistery in Italy.

▲ *A close-up of some of the saints surrounding Jesus; the man holding the key is St Peter*

Look at the image on page 123 and consider the following points.
- At the centre of the painting, Jesus is shown as *Christ Pantocrator*, meaning 'ruler of all'. He is surrounded by the circle of saints, representing the eternity of the Church with Christ at its centre.
- Christ is holding a book which says, 'I am the alpha and omega'. Alpha and omega are the first and last letters of the Greek alphabet; it symbolises that Jesus is God, the beginning and the end.
- The image of the Virgin Mary (see close-up, right) demonstrates the role of the Mother of God. She is painted as part of the communion of saints, but much larger, showing her significance as the Queen of heaven and the most important of all saints.
- This image is a good example of how artistic representations of the communion of saints are used to remind people of the union between earth and heaven in the Church. The placement of the image on the ceiling of a chapel where new Catholics are baptised suggests that all those in heaven are with them at the moment when they join the communion of saints.

▲ *A close-up of the Virgin Mary*

To the Ends of the Earth

The Church Militant and the Church Triumphant by Andrea di Bonaiuto da Firenze

The Church Militant and the Church Triumphant was painted by Andrea di Bonaiuto da Firenze around 1365 in a **Dominican** church in Florence. This painting is sometimes also called *The Church as the Path to Salvation*. It reminds Catholics of the unbroken relationship between the Church on earth and the Church in heaven, and of the role that the work of the Church on earth and all its living members plays in bringing people around the world to eternal life.

Useful vocabulary

Dominican: belonging to a religious mendicant order known for their preaching and teaching

The communion of saints is shown with the Church Triumphant (angels and saints in heaven) gathered around the throne of Christ. The Church Militant, Christians on earth below, are guided by the clergy up towards God.

Those who respond to the message of salvation are shown walking upwards towards St Peter at the gates of the Church in heaven.

Bishops and priests, including Pope Innocent VI, preside over the congregation of the faithful.

St Dominic and the Dominican brothers are preaching to people.

Understand

1. Why are images of saints and angels present in Catholic churches?
2. How is the belief in the communion of saints commonly depicted in art?
3. In *Cloud of Witnesses*, which saint is painted the largest and why?
4. Why do you think Andrea di Bonaiuto's painting is sometimes called *The Church as the Path to Salvation*?

Discern

5. a Which Catholic ideas about the communion of saints do you think stand out most from *Cloud of Witnesses*?
   b Do you think *The Church Militant and the Church Triumphant* explores this subject in a similar or different way?
   c Which painting do you think best communicates Catholic ideas about the communion of saints? Give reasons for your opinions.

Respond

6. Have you ever noticed artwork of a saint in a church or in your school? Did it help you understand the saint better? Explain why.

How are saints represented in art? 141

5.12 LIVED RELIGION OPTION

HOW DO CATHOLICS AROUND THE WORLD SHOW DEVOTION TO MARY?

OBJECTIVE
In this lesson you will explore **two examples of devotion to Mary in different parts of the world.**

To say that the Church is 'catholic' means that it is universal and worldwide. The practices of Catholics around the world share the same central core and are rooted in the same shared faith, even when local culture and history dramatically influence liturgical traditions. This is particularly true of the various ways in which Catholics around the world show their devotion to Mary.

Catholics around the world show devotion to saints

The veneration of saints remains one of the most widespread practices among Catholics worldwide. There is a multitude of Catholic saints, with many representing individual cultures and ways of life. This reflects the diversity within the 24 Catholic Churches that operate in different parts of the world and evolved in unique and special ways. Catholics often feel a very personal connection to saints, which explains why devotions to saints present some of the most diverse and culturally distinct forms of worship in the Church today.

The same saint will often be celebrated in different ways in different countries and represented differently too. A great example of this is the veneration of Mary, Mother of God. She is often shown as a member of the local cultural or ethnic group and, as the Virgin Mary is the most venerated of all the saints, Catholics in every country have their own particular ways of showing their devotion to her.

The Most Holy Virgin Mary, Queen of Poland

The veneration of the Virgin Mary is a very important part of Catholic tradition in Poland and Mary is one of the nation's patron saints. Local tradition says that a member of the religious order of Jesuits called Giulio Mancinelli had a vision of Mary, who told him to call her the Queen of Poland. His experience led other Catholics to increased devotion to the Mother of God in sixteenth-century Poland, which has continued to this day.

The most important Catholic shrine and place of pilgrimage in Poland is the Marian shrine in Częstochowa, which is home to the ancient icon *Our Lady of Częstochowa*. The icon's origin is shrouded in mystery, but there are many legends surrounding it – including one that it was painted by St Luke the Evangelist. The icon is associated with many miracles; millions of pilgrims

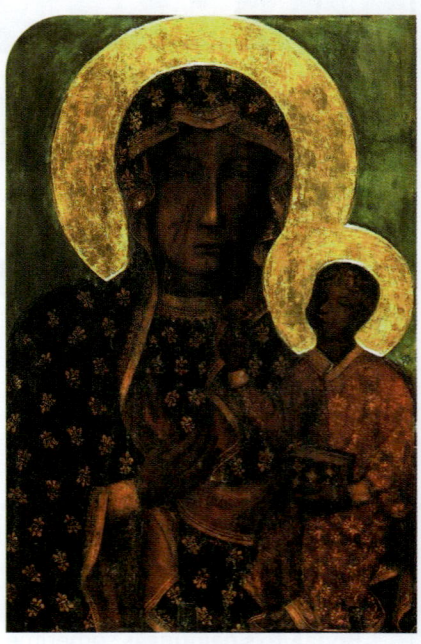

▲ *Our Lady of Częstochowa is believed to be the most venerated Catholic icon in Poland*

142 To the Ends of the Earth

visit it every year. It is one of the traditions in Poland for students preparing for their final high school exams to go on a pilgrimage to Częstochowa.

Marian devotion in Poland is often associated with images of *Our Lady of Częstochowa* and the feast of Mary, the Queen of Poland, celebrated on 3 May. Furthermore, the very first national anthem of Poland (and the oldest song to combine a religious hymn and patriotic themes in the Polish language) is a hymn to Mary, Mother of God called 'Bogurodzica'.

Our Lady of Lourdes

For Catholics, the town of Lourdes in France is associated with the Virgin Mary's apparitions to a young woman named Bernadette Soubirous in the nineteenth century. Bernadette reported that a woman in white appeared to her 18 times and asked her for a chapel, and also instructed her to wash and drink from the spring. A shrine was built and Lourdes has become one of the most important places of pilgrimage for Catholics. Many forms of devotion to the Virgin Mary take place there. Pilgrims can visit the cave, or grotto, where Mary appeared to Bernadette. The Sanctuary of Our Lady of Lourdes is also a common pilgrimage destination for many people who have serious illnesses or health conditions. Waters sprang out of the grotto where Bernadette had her visions. Pilgrims today can wash their hands and faces at special fountains, which take water from the spring, or take water home in containers for their loved ones. Mary also requested pilgrims to process, and many miracles have also happened at the Blessed Sacrament procession.

As a result of the believed healing nature of Lourdes, much of the devotion that takes place centres around service to those who are ill and suffering. For example, one form of pilgrimage and devotion for Catholics is to volunteer to help pilgrims who have serious illnesses or health conditions, for example by helping them to travel around the town, supporting them with their basic needs and sometimes offering companionship. Catholics believe this service to other people is a form of veneration of the Virgin Mary and a form of worship of God.

A communal form of veneration is the daily procession at Lourdes, where thousands of pilgrims walk together from the grotto of the apparition to the entrance of the basilica. A statue of the Virgin Mary is carried at the front of the procession. During this procession, participants pray the Rosary. Each decade is introduced in a different language (from French, German, English, Spanish, Italian and Dutch) and participants each use their own language to say the 'Hail Mary' and 'Our Father'.

▲ *The grotto of Our Lady of Lourdes in France*

Understand

1. Why are saints depicted by Catholics in different ways around the world?
2. What title is given to Mary as a form of devotion in Poland?
3. What is the most significant place of Marian adoration in Poland and why?
4. Give two ways Catholics may show devotion to Mary in Poland.
5. Explain two ways the shrine at Lourdes is important to Catholics.
6. Give two ways Catholics may show devotion to Mary when visiting Lourdes.

Discern

7. The ways in which saints are venerated around the world can differ according to the culture and traditions of local communities. Which do you think is more important, expressing beliefs, culture, or both? Explain your view.

Respond

8. Would you be interested to visit a shrine to Mary? Explain your answer.

How do Catholics around the world show devotion to Mary?

CHAPTER 5

ASSESSMENT

Key vocabulary

Write a definition for these key terms.

Church	communion of saints	Church on earth
Church in heaven	Church being purified	saints
angels	archangels	purgatory

Knowledge check

1. Which one of the following is a teaching from St Paul about the Church?
   a. The Church is the 'Body of God'.
   b. The Church is the 'Body of Christ'.
   c. The Church is the 'Head of Christ'.
   d. The Church is the 'Head of God'.
2. Who is the head of the Church, according to Ephesians 1:22?
   a. The bishops
   b. Jesus
   c. The Pope
   d. St Paul
3. Copy and complete the following quote from the Catechism: Catholics believe the Sacrament of E................. unites the community of the C................. .

4. Name the two groups that make up the Church on earth.
5. What do Catholics mean by the prayers of intercession?
6. State two reasons why the Archangel Michael is significant for Catholics.
7. Give two ways in which Catholics consider the Church on earth to be holy.

8. Explain why Catholics pray for those who have passed away and may be in purgatory.
9. Outline three Catholic beliefs about the communion of saints.
10. Explain why the Church on earth is sometimes called the Pilgrim Church and how this idea might influence Catholics in their daily lives.

> **TIP**
> You could refer to beliefs about what the communion of saints is made up of, or how Catholics are united with other members of the communion of saints.

> **TIP**
> Think about the meaning of the word 'pilgrim'. How might Catholics be seen as pilgrims in their everyday lives?

Extended writing activity

This assessment is for you to show what you have learned in this chapter and to develop your extended writing skills. Here is a big question:

> 'The Church on earth plays a significant role in leading Catholics to salvation.' Evaluate this statement.
>
> In your response you should:
> - explain arguments that agree and disagree with the statement
> - refer to Catholic teaching
> - reach a justified conclusion.

TIP

When you're looking for arguments to disagree with this statement, you don't necessarily need to argue that the Church on earth isn't significant. You could argue that there are other factors that are more significant.

To answer this question, you'll need to draw on the following skills.
- finding arguments for and against the statement (or to agree and disagree with the statement)
- using specialist religious terminology
- using evidence and examples to support your points
- referring to religious texts
- evaluating your arguments
- writing a justified conclusion.

1. **Plan your argument.** You might want to plot your ideas on a mind-map or note them down as a list. Once you've come up with some arguments that agree and disagree with the statement, don't forget to add ideas for how you might evaluate them.

TIP

Remember, you will need to decide how convincing each of the arguments you write about is, so think carefully about the evidence or reasoning you would use to back each one up.

2. **Now try writing two paragraphs on arguments that agree with the statement and evaluate your arguments.** Choose the ones from your plan that you think are the strongest and that you know you'll have lots to say about. Here is one example – can you improve it?

   Some Christians, including most Catholics, would argue that the Church on Earth plays a very significant role in leading Catholics to salvation because of the sacraments. The Catholic Church teaches that the sacraments allow God's invisible grace to become visible. In delivering the sacraments, the Church is considered 'the universal Sacrament of Salvation' and a sign of God's love in the world.

The student has given a reason for their argument, but it could be improved by adding more detail or explanation. They haven't explained how what they've written shows that the Church plays a significant role in leading Catholics to salvation.

TIP

Make sure you evaluate the strength of the argument overall. Is this answer as persuasive as it could be?

3. **Next, try writing two paragraphs on arguments that disagree with the statement and evaluate your arguments.** Remember that you need to explain your reasoning for why you think an argument is strong or weak.

4. **Finally, write a conclusion to your answer.** Remember, your conclusion should make logical sense and show the reasoning behind your final judgement about the statement.

   | This supports… | This implies… | Consequently… | Therefore… |

Assessment **145**

CHAPTER 6:
DIALOGUE AND ENCOUNTER

Introduction

The Second Vatican Council was an opportunity for the Catholic Church to look outwards and embrace the changing world. Since that time, **Catholic organisations around the world have been inspired to work more closely with the communities they serve and the different groups within them**.

New methods of communication, a growing world population and growing challenges mean that there has never been more work for the Church to do to fulfil Jesus' mission, and never a greater opportunity to work with others outside the Catholic faith in order to make the world a better place.

The Catholic Bishops' Conference of England and Wales expressed the importance of interreligious and intercultural dialogue in *Meeting God in Friend and Stranger*. This document draws on the Catechism and papal encyclicals to emphasise important ideas about how dialogue should engage those taking part in a balanced way.

Participants must listen to one another and find shared experiences and common ground in order to show commitment to the common good in the 'dialogue of action'. **Catholics believe there are three essential elements of the common good: respect for the person, social wellbeing and development of society, and peace and security**.

We will explore what each of these elements of the common good means, and how Catholics are embracing the call to support people around them, whatever their religion or worldview. The Caritas Social Action Network (CSAN) shows how charities can support each other across the UK and show **respect for the individual person** in projects that have a national impact. The St Vincent de Paul Society works to support individuals and communities at a local level, **building social wellbeing by appreciating each person for their unique worth**. Finally, the Catholic Agency for Overseas Development (CAFOD) shows how its **compassion and energy can transform the lives of those abroad facing poverty and fear** from both natural and human-made disasters.

Catholics believe their faith calls them to share the light of Jesus in all corners of the world, wherever difficulty persists. Both words and action are needed, but the responsibility to make the world a place without fear, poverty and prejudice falls to every living person.

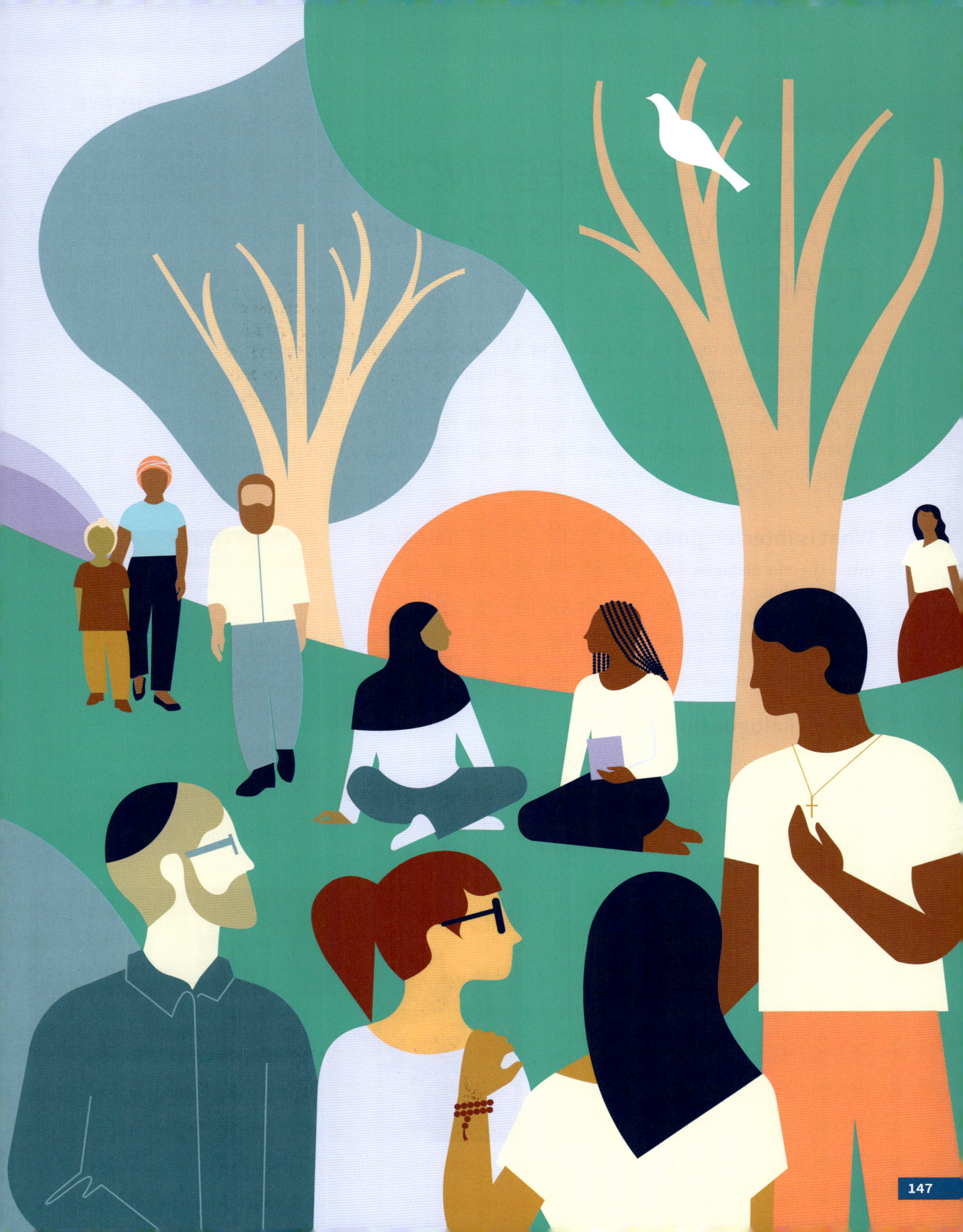

6.1

WHAT DOES *MEETING GOD IN FRIEND AND STRANGER* TEACH?

OBJECTIVE
In this lesson you will explore **what the document *Meeting God in Friend and Stranger* teaches about interreligious and intercultural dialogue.**

Britain is a place of many cultures, religions and **worldviews**. In the document *Meeting God in Friend and Stranger*, the Catholic Bishops' Conference of England and Wales expressed that life is 'greatly enriched by this diversity'. The document explains why using dialogue to foster respect and mutual understanding between different religions and cultures is not only important, but the duty of Catholics everywhere.

What is interreligious and intercultural dialogue?

Interreligious dialogue is explained by the Church as 'not only discussion, but … all positive and constructive interreligious relations with individuals and communities of other faiths which are directed at mutual understanding and enrichment' (*Reflections and Orientations on Dialogue and Mission* 3). **Intercultural dialogue** expands this to include individuals and communities with **non-religious worldviews**.

Why is dialogue important?

Catholics are encouraged to try to live as good neighbours with all people and work together in shared areas of concern, such as justice, peace or the inalienable dignity of the human person. By trying to understand different religions, Catholics believe that they can share the genuine love and respect of their own faith and be open to 'unexpected truth and goodness' (MGFS 9).

Catholics believe they should come to dialogue with an open mind and be ready to learn new things. *Meeting God in Friend and Stranger* also advises that they 'enter into it aware of their Christian identity' – dialogue should not lead them to doubt or forget their own faith, but to use their new knowledge to draw closer to God.

▶ *Pope Francis speaking with religious leaders from Muslim, Orthodox Christian and Catholic communities in Albania*

Useful vocabulary

worldview (religious or non-religious): an overall vision or attitude towards life and the purpose of life, which directs how a person lives and acts in the world; a religious worldview would be based on the teaching of a particular religion, whereas non-religious worldviews would be shaped by beliefs and ideas that are not connected to religion

interreligious dialogue: positive interactions between individuals and communities of other faiths which aim to encourage mutual understanding and enrichment

Dialogue and Encounter

How can we meet God in friend and stranger?

Meeting God in Friend and Stranger suggests four ways in which Catholics can engage in dialogue and collaboration with people from other religions.

Useful vocabulary

intercultural dialogue: positive interactions between individuals and communities of religious and non-religious worldviews which aim to encourage mutual understanding and enrichment

Form of dialogue	Description	What does it teach about interreligious dialogue?
The dialogue of life	'This is when people of different religions simply try to live in an open and neighbourly way with one another' (MGFS 110).	Dialogue can be as simple as a person sharing how they live their life according to their faith so that others can understand why they hold certain beliefs and carry out certain practices. This allows for respectful questions and discussion.
The dialogue of action	'This is where those of different religions collaborate in working for greater human freedom and development, such as in matters of peace, justice and the integrity of creation' (MGFS 111).	All religions have a responsibility to express their faith through action by working together to improve the world for the benefit of all humans. This recognises that humans have a special dignity and are precious.
The dialogue of theological exchange	'Here specialists and scholars seek to deepen their understanding of one another's religious heritage, and their appreciation of one another's spiritual values' (MGFS 112).	This is often a more formal form of dialogue. It allows for deep discussion to understand the history of a religion, and the values and beliefs within it. This is a way to find common ground and enable collaboration.
The dialogue of religious experience	'In this dialogue believers who are well grounded and formed in their own religious tradition share their spiritual riches, e.g. regarding prayer and contemplation, faith, and ways of searching for God' (MGFS 113).	When people of different faiths fully understand the faiths of others and can find common ground or shared values, they are able to pray together, share their faith and share their path to God, which deepens their religious life.

Understand

1. What is **a)** interreligious dialogue and **b)** intercultural dialogue?
2. Why do Catholics believe that dialogue is important?
3. Outline what is meant in *Meeting God in Friend and Stranger* by:
   a. the dialogue of life
   b. the dialogue of religious experience
   c. the dialogue of action
   d. the dialogue of theological exchange.
4. For each form of dialogue, explain one thing it teaches about the value of interreligious dialogue.

Discern

5. 'Interreligious and intercultural dialogue is needed today more than ever.' How far do you agree with this statement? Explain your ideas, including how a Catholic might respond to this statement and why.

Respond

6. Do you think interreligious dialogue could make a positive impact on the future of your community? Why, or why not? Consider where there might be opportunities for dialogue to flourish and whether there might be barriers to this happening.

6.2

WHAT DOES A COMMITMENT TO THE COMMON GOOD MEAN?

OBJECTIVE
*In this lesson you will explore **how dialogue can bring about the common good.***

The Catholic Church teaches that every human on earth is unique and loved by God. Many Catholics therefore believe they should work to ensure that all people around the world are treated with dignity and respect and have access to the essential things that they need. This is also described as the idea of the **common good**.

What does the Church teach about the common good?

The Catholic Church's teaching on the common good is rooted in Catholic Social Teaching, which tries to reduce human suffering caused by injustice, and increase cooperation and friendship between all people. The Catechism identifies three elements within the idea of the common good:

1. **Respect for the person**
2. **Social wellbeing** and **development of society**
3. **Peace and security**

> 'The common good consists of three essential elements: respect for and promotion of the fundamental rights of the person; prosperity, or the development of the spiritual and and temporal [physical] goods of society; the peace and security of the group and its members.'
>
> Catechism of the Catholic Church 1925

The Catechism teaches that this is the work of all people, and the common good is an idea that many people of different faiths and worldviews also share. Consequently, a commitment to the common good is a way to unite people through what is most important to them. When people feel they are working towards a common goal, this helps break down barriers, which can then lead to better communication and other opportunities to work together and make a difference in the world.

Useful vocabulary

common good: the belief that if all people work together to improve the wellbeing of others, all of society will thrive

respect for the person: ensuring that every person is treated with dignity and valued for the unique contribution they can make to life

social wellbeing: building and maintaining healthy relationships and engaging in meaningful interaction with others in a community

development of society: improving the wellbeing of every person in a community as well as the services used by all so society as a whole can flourish

peace and security: a safe environment in which people live without fear and are treated equally, justly and fairly, where disagreements are resolved through non-violent means such as dialogue

Element of the common good	Summary of what the Catechism says
Respect for the person (CCC 1907) 	• Those in authority must ensure that people's rights are upheld. • People should be allowed to fulfil their potential and follow their chosen vocation. This could be aided, for example, by removing any obstacles of discrimination and ensuring fair access to education and training whatever a person's financial circumstances. • People should be allowed to think and act freely, guided by their conscience. For example, people should have a free choice of religion and be allowed free speech.
Social wellbeing and development of society (CCC 1908) 	• Those in authority must make sure that all people in society have access to food, clean water, clothing, healthcare, work, education and culture. • People also have the right to be kept informed about what is going on in society and have their personal rights protected, such as the right to have a family.
Peace and security (CCC 1909) 	• Those in authority have a responsibility to ensure that society has 'just order'. This means that it should be safe and secure for its members. • Only morally acceptable means should be used to keep the peace, such as only using a reasonable amount of force when arresting individuals, establishing a fair and just legal system, and caring for prisoners in a dignified and humane way.

We will explore in detail how Catholics support and work towards these elements of the common good in the next three lessons.

Understand

1. What is the common good?
2. Explain why a commitment to the common good can unite people of different faiths and worldviews.
3. Summarise the three essential elements of the common good.
4. Give one way the Church teaches how each element of the common good might be demonstrated.

Discern

5. 'The most important effect of the common good is that it brings people together.' How far do you agree with this idea? What might a Catholic think?

Respond

6. Do you think working towards the common good is important? Are there ways in which you do this in your life?

What does a commitment to the common good mean?

6.3

HOW DOES CSAN SUPPORT RESPECT FOR THE PERSON?

OBJECTIVE
In this lesson you will explore **how the Catholic charity CSAN demonstrates respect for the person as part of its belief in the common good.**

The first element of the common good is respect for the person. For Catholics, the common good is not simply an idea, it is something that can be put into action and an important way this is done is through the charitable work of Catholic organisations. The work of the Caritas Social Action Network (CSAN) demonstrates and upholds respect for the person. As Catholics believe all humans are created ***imago Dei***, this work connects ideas about the common good with essential Catholic teachings.

What does it mean to show respect for the person?

The Catholic Church teaches that each human person has 'fundamental and inalienable rights' (CCC 1907) which must be respected. By showing respect for the person, the Church suggests that this allows each person to fulfil their vocation and enjoy freedoms which allow them to flourish. Therefore, by ensuring that each person is treated with the dignity and respect that they deserve, this will naturally lead to bringing about the common good.

Catholics believe it is important to live life in relation to other people; this means not being individualistic or selfish but considering how each person connects to another. Failure to do this leads to a lack of respect for others and being forgetful of their needs. Remembering that all people are made in the image of God and therefore deserve respect means people are more likely to see and respond to injustice, which helps everyone to move towards the common good.

> **Useful vocabulary**
>
> ***imago Dei:*** a Latin phrase meaning 'in the image of God', the idea that humans reflect God's nature

What is the dialogue of action?

'Dialogue of action' is one form of dialogue discussed in *Meeting God in Friend and Stranger*. Catholics believe that dialogue that leads to action is an important tool in actually getting people what they need to live well. Discussing problems at a national level allows people from different backgrounds and non-religious and religious viewpoints to have a voice in finding solutions. Talking and listening encourages people to see the bigger picture of what is happening in their country and respond. The Catechism states that 'it is the role of the state to defend and promote the common good of civil society, its citizens and intermediate bodies' (CCC 1910). This means governments should be open to dialogue from all people so that they can support the people they govern. For example, groups such as the Catholic Bishops' Conference of England and Wales, the Church of England, the Board of Deputies of British Jews, the Muslim Council of Britain, the Hindu Council UK, Humanists UK and organisations representing other faiths and worldviews have valuable things to say so that all people in the UK are represented in government policies and decisions.

What is CSAN?

CSAN is the Caritas Social Action Network. It is a charity and an agency of the Catholic Bishops' Conference which helps to support and raise the profile and voice of Catholic organisations involved in social justice. It is inspired by the life and work of Jesus and works to develop social action across England and Wales in order to ensure that 'every person can be fulfilled in their families and communities, living with peace and human dignity'.

CSAN helps coordinate and promote local Catholic charitable activities so they can work together more effectively on common causes, which then helps to bring about the common good at a national level.

▲ Raymond Friel, Chief Executive of CSAN, speaking at the launch of the 'Do Justice' campaign in London

How does CSAN support respect for the person?

CSAN supports respect for the person in many ways. As it works closely with different local charities, it is able to connect people so they can support one another. It offers training and communicates what its members are doing, which brings greater awareness of social issues and what needs to be done to overcome them.

Human rights: the Jesuit Refugee Service UK (JRS UK) published the report 'Being Human in the Asylum System', which aimed to draw people's attention to the way that asylum seekers have been poorly treated and to urge those in power to take action. The report challenged politicians and policy makers to think about how they had previously responded to those in need and to change their approach by putting 'human dignity and a culture of protection at the heart of the asylum system'. CSAN issued a joint statement with JRS UK to promote the report's suggestions, which aim to help bring about the common good.

Social justice: CSAN launched a campaign called 'Do Justice' which aims to remind the Catholic community of the call from Baptism to work for a more just world. It encourages Catholic parishes, schools, individuals and communities to take action to respond to the needs of their communities. The campaign is also intended to be a celebration of the inspiring and varied work being carried out by CSAN's member charities.

Understand

1. What central Catholic teaching supports the idea that respect for the person is essential?
2. Why do Catholics believe it is important to remember all people are made in the image of God when thinking about the common good?
3. Give an example of what the 'dialogue of action' might look like.
4. How does CSAN help Catholic organisations involved in social justice?
5. Give two examples of how the actions of CSAN show its desire to promote the common good.

Discern

6. 'Talking about the common good doesn't mean anything unless you are also taking action to make it happen.' How far do you agree with this statement? What might a Catholic think?

Respond

7. What can you learn from the social action that CSAN promotes?

6.4

HOW DOES SVP SUPPORT SOCIAL WELLBEING AND DEVELOPMENT OF SOCIETY?

OBJECTIVE
In this lesson you will explore **how the SVP supports social wellbeing and development of society as part of its belief in the common good.**

The second element of the common good is to support social wellbeing and the development of society. This means taking care of individuals in a larger context: as a group. Catholics believe that all humans have a special dignity and place in the community. The St Vincent de Paul Society (SVP) works with some of the most in-need and vulnerable people to improve their quality of their lives and relationships, which therefore strengthens the wellbeing of society as a whole.

What does it mean to work for social wellbeing and development of society?

The Catholic Church describes development of society as 'a social duty' which means that each person should have 'what is needed to lead a truly human life' (CCC 1908). The three elements of the common good are therefore closely connected; caring for and respecting individuals is a key part of social wellbeing. Catholics believe that supporting social wellbeing means actively participating in activities that improve people's quality of life. In turn, this improves and develops society.

Ideally those in authority should make sure every person has what they need, but this can be difficult. Individuals make mistakes and sometimes society fails to show enough care for those in need. This situation weakens society because social wellbeing means that every person matters: if one person is suffering then all of society is impacted.

Working for the common good means that by helping the vulnerable person who is suffering, not only is the life of that person changed, but other problems in society are reduced. Charities that work for social wellbeing try to find positive solutions through improving education, improving access to healthcare and reducing poverty. These kinds of changes enable individuals to live happier and more fulfilled lives, which can help avoid problems in the first place, but also mean support is available when it is most needed. This helps to create a more equal society that cares about the needs of all people.

▲ *St Vincent's Furniture Store in Sheffield, where recycled furniture is repaired so it can then be given to someone who needs it*

What is SVP?

SVP is the St Vincent de Paul Society. It operates mainly in England and Wales and is part of an international Christian voluntary network which is dedicated to tackling poverty by giving practical help to those who need it. The SVP reaches out to those

▲ *St Vincent's Furniture Store also has essential items ready for people who are given a home*

Dialogue and Encounter

in need to 'provide support and fellowship in a spirit of justice, while tackling the cause of poverty'. It aims to give hope and to remind each person of their dignity and worth. The SVP works in local communities with the most vulnerable people in order to help them achieve the best quality of life, while trying to end the cycle of poverty that people can find themselves trapped within.

How does SVP support social wellbeing and the development of society?

The volunteers of SVP offer friendship and practical support in different ways.
- Visiting and befriending develops personal contact with people who are living in poverty or who may be vulnerable or isolated in some way.
- Community projects include St Vincent's community shops, furniture stores, support centres, supported accommodation for people who are homeless and accommodation to help ex-offenders who are adapting to life outside prison.
- Vinnie camps give children who may be experiencing family problems such as unemployment, illness or bereavement a week of fun and friendship.

SVP also organises events to bring older people together and supports projects such as signed Masses for people with hearing loss. Together, these actions reflect the Catholic belief that humans must show concern for social wellbeing as part of a commitment to the common good. Dialogue is a key part of how SVP cares for the dignity of those it works with:

> 'The essence of our work is person-to-person contact and spending time with people is our greatest gift.'
>
> www.svp.org.uk

How recycled furniture can mean a fresh start

One form of practical support offered by SVP is their stores that take donations of furniture and appliances and give these to people who are in need. People may experience financial hardship or need to be rehoused for lots of different reasons, including having been homeless, losing their job or having to leave an abusive relationship. But when people are rehoused, they often find the place is stripped bare: no carpets, no curtains, no furniture. SVP has urged councils and social services not to do this, as it can give more stress to those who have often already suffered a great deal in life.

By stepping in to provide these essential things, SVP helps houses and flats become homes, reducing anxiety and financial stress and creating wellbeing and a feeling of dignity. SVP helps create stability for individuals and families, which supports them in moving back into society and making their own contribution to the common good. One volunteer explained he gives his time to help now because the same store supported him when he faced poverty and was rehoused. In this way, SVP shows how working for social wellbeing supports the development of society by creating the desire to help others in those who themselves receive help.

Understand

1. Why do Catholics believe it is important to improve the quality of life of individuals?
2. Give two areas that charities that work for social wellbeing might focus on to improve social wellbeing.
3. Describe how SVP works in local communities to strengthen social wellbeing.
4. Explain one example of how SVP's commitment to the common good has had a direct impact on society.

Discern

5. SVP supports people from every part of society, including people facing personal challenges such as addiction or homelessness. Its volunteers believe Jesus calls them to love all people as their neighbour. Do you agree that all people are our neighbour and that those who need it should be supported? Do you think others would agree with you? Explain your ideas.

Respond

6. How could you help to promote the common good in your area? Explain your answer, giving examples of what you could do.

6.5

HOW DOES CAFOD WORK FOR PEACE AND SECURITY?

OBJECTIVE
In this lesson you will explore **how the Catholic charity CAFOD works for peace and security as part of its belief in the common good.**

The third element of the common good is peace and security. The Catholic Church believes that peace, together with a stable and secure justice system, is essential for the common good to exist. However, millions of people live in war zones and face the threat of death or injury daily. When justice is absent, it is often the most vulnerable people who suffer and live in fear, and without the protection of their essential human rights. The Catholic charity CAFOD works for peace and security at an international level, giving both support and a voice to those most in need.

What does it mean to work for peace and security?

One of the main aims of Catholic Social Teaching is solidarity. Solidarity means showing support for each other and working for the common good as neighbours. The Catholic Church believes that neighbours are beyond local and national communities, and that people all over the world are brothers and sisters. The Church sees the need for Catholic action to be present in any and all places of need.

While governments have a vital role in helping to bring about the common good at an international level, charities are very important too, as they can put dialogue into action and work in direct contact with the people who are most vulnerable and have the greatest need.

What is CAFOD?

CAFOD is the Catholic Agency for Overseas Development. One of its primary aims is to ensure that the common good is achieved for all people. CAFOD works in places where there have been natural disasters, war, hate and discrimination. It delivers aid but also works for peace and security to try and bring global justice that will last.

▶ *CAFOD's partners provide safe activities for children.*

How does CAFOD work for peace and security?

CAFOD works for peace and security by asking people to:
- donate money to help the organisation reach people in need
- take action by participating in its campaigns
- pray for people living in poverty.

CAFOD believes peacebuilding requires a long-term and relational approach, saying: 'We seek to enable the culture of encounter that [Pope Francis] calls for'. Some of the ways CAFOD works for peace include:
- supporting processes that enable dialogue between different groups of people, such as families, impacted by intra-community fighting
- aiming to nurture a 'culture of encounter' between citizens living in conflicting nations, exploring questions around belonging and a shared future
- providing urgent humanitarian support and seeking to provide protection to those at risk
- prioritising support to young people to develop their talents, placing importance on hope and building their futures
- working with like-minded organisations to ensure those in power are upholding international law and taking actions that bring peace closer.

CAFOD's work in the Middle East

CAFOD has been working in the Middle East since the mid-1980s and works with Christian, Jewish, Muslim and secular partner organisations 'with the aim of protecting human rights and contributing towards building more peaceful communities'. CAFOD works with partners across the Middle East to support those impacted by conflict and crisis. Together, they aim to:
- advocate to policy makers and decision makers to protect human rights and build communities where people can live in dignity and peace
- enable women and young people to be active citizens and work together for a better future
- ensure people have legal aid to challenge violations of their rights
- support people to escape poverty through fairly paid and sustainable jobs, businesses and farming
- provide urgent humanitarian assistance for those directly affected by conflict and natural disasters, offering help to rebuild communities.

The future of the common good

Catholics believe earth is our common home; every person in every nation has an equal share in it and the resources it provides. Some countries struggle more than others due to their location, history or economic situation, or as a result of conflict between religious worldviews or non-religious worldviews. Catholics are driven to challenge this by working for the common good and the saving message that they believe Jesus offers. Catholics believe that they can play a part in making the world a better place and realising the Kingdom of God on earth. They feel that this is not only their duty, but part of what makes them human, as they are made in the image of God.

Understand

1. Give two ways that a lack of peace and security impacts people and communities.
2. What does solidarity mean in the context of Catholic Social Teaching?
3. Why do you think peace and security are an essential element of the common good?
4. Describe the role that CAFOD plays in working for the common good.
5. Give two examples of how CAFOD has taken action to promote peace and shown commitment to the common good.

Discern

6. 'The earth is our common home; we have a responsibility to help everyone.' Explain how a Catholic might respond to this statement and give a reason why someone might disagree with them. Which argument is more persuasive?

Respond

7. Do you think you can make a difference for the common good? Come up with some ideas about how you could work with people towards a common goal.

CHAPTER 6

ASSESSMENT

Key vocabulary

Write a definition for these key terms.

intercultural dialogue	common good	respect for the person
social wellbeing	development of society	peace and security
worldview	religious worldview	non-religious worldview

Knowledge check

1. Copy out and complete the following sentence: Interreligious dialogue aims to encourage mutual u................. and e................... .
2. Which one of the following shows what the name CSAN stands for?
   a. Catholic Social Action Network
   b. Christian Social Action Network
   c. Caritas Social Action Network
   d. Charity Social Action Network
3. Copy and complete the following sentence: The Catholic Church teaches that a commitment to the common good is a way to u................. people through what is most important to them, which can then lead to better c................. .
4. Write a sentence to summarise one form of interreligious dialogue found in *Meeting God in Friend and Stranger*.
5. Give two Catholic teachings about the common good.
6. What do Catholics mean by 'respect for the person'?
7. State one example of how CSAN's work supports respect for the person.
8. Describe the three elements of the common good.
9. Choose one of the charities mentioned in this chapter and explain how the work it does aims to bring about the common good.
10. Outline three ways in which the Church teaches that dialogue can bring about the common good.

TIP

Remember you have studied three charities. Pick one and give examples of what it does and how this helps to bring about the common good.

TIP

Focus on key teachings of the Church about dialogue. Show what these teach about the common good. Look back at pages 148–151 to help you.

GLOSSARY

The words in **red** are Key Vocabulary terms from the Religious Education Directory.

A

allegorical sense: the meaning of the text that lies hidden beneath the surface; the actual words are symbolic or foreshadow events to come

angels: pure, intelligent, spiritual beings created by God as servants and messengers; they live with God in heaven

Annunciation: the announcement of the Incarnation by the angel Gabriel

apostles: the chief supporters of a teaching or cause

apostolic succession: the teaching that the bishops of the Catholic Church form a direct line of holy authority and leadership that comes from the first apostles of Jesus

archangels: angels of particular importance who are named in the Bible and given key tasks to perform by God

atonement: the action of making up for or repairing the damage done as a result of wrong behaviour

B

bishop: one of the three sacramental degrees of Holy Orders; this is the third degree, in which a man is ordained *in persona Christi* (to stand in the place of Christ), and is said to hold the fullness of holy orders

C

canonise: to make an infallible statement that a person is a saint in heaven

celibacy: the state of being entirely consecrated to God and therefore unmarried

chaplains: lay people or priests who are appointed to offer spiritual support to people in a particular organisation

Church: faithful Christians on earth, in heaven and in purgatory who form a community that can be understood in three ways: as the People of God; as the Body of Christ; as the Temple of the Holy Spirit

Church being purified: Catholics who have died and whose souls are in purgatory being prepared for heaven

Church in heaven: Catholics who have died and whose souls live as saints with the angels in God's presence in heaven

Church on earth: Catholics on earth today

commissioned: given a special task; in Christianity, this task was to spread Jesus' message

common good: the belief that if all people work together to improve the wellbeing of others, all of society will thrive

communion of saints: all Christians on earth, in heaven and in purgatory; together they are united as the Church

covenants: agreements or promises between two or more people; God made covenants with humans such as Abraham and Moses

D

Day of Atonement: also known as Yom Kippur; the day when Jewish people seek forgiveness for sins

deacon: one of the three sacramental degrees of Holy Orders; this is the first degree, in which a man is ordained *in persona Christi servi* (as a servant of Christ)

denominations: branches of Christianity

development of society: improving the wellbeing of every person in a community as well as the services used by all so society as a whole can flourish

disciple: someone committed to following the teaching and example of Jesus

discipleship: the condition of being a disciple; the ways of living and actions carried out by them

Dominican: belonging to a religious mendicant order known for their preaching and teaching

E

ethic: principles or beliefs about what is right and wrong

evangelical counsels: the vows of poverty, chastity and obedience, taught by Jesus in the Bible and taken by individuals wishing to enter religious life

G

grace: a gift of love freely given by God to humankind

H

High Priest: the chief priest in historical Judaism; also a name for Jesus due to his role in the New Covenant

Holy of Holies: the most sacred part of the Temple, which originally housed the Ark of the Covenant

Holy Orders: the Sacrament at the Service of Communion in which the grace and spiritual power to sanctify others is conferred by the placing of a bishop's hands on a candidate

human person: for Catholics, a living being possessing both a physical body and spiritual soul

humble: modest, or not self-centred; for a religious person, this means putting God and other people before oneself

I

imago Dei: a Latin phrase meaning 'in the image of God', the idea that humans reflect God's nature

Immaculate Conception: a dogma (teaching) of the Catholic Church that states that Mary, the mother of Jesus, did not inherit the stain of Original Sin when she was conceived by her own mother

inalienable dignity: a state of value attached to human life that cannot be challenged or removed

incarnate: embodied in human form; in Christianity, God made human in the person of Jesus, truly human and truly divine

intercession: in Catholicism, praying to God on behalf of humans

intercultural dialogue: positive interactions between individuals and communities of religious and non-religious worldviews which aim to encourage mutual understanding and enrichment

interreligious dialogue: positive interactions between individuals and communities of other faiths which aim to encourage mutual understanding and enrichment

L

lay people: all Christians who are not ordained as deacons, priests, bishops, or as consecrated members of a religious order

literal sense: the meaning of the text as the author intended it to be; this is different to reading a passage literally, which means accepting it as word-for-word truth

liturgical year: the Church's calendar, which consists of specific liturgical seasons and directs the public worship (liturgy) that takes place

M

Magnificat: Mary's prayer of praise in Luke 1:45–56

marriage: in Catholicism, a binding life-long relationship in which a man and a woman live by promises made to each other and to God

martyrs: people who knowingly sacrifice their lives for their religious beliefs

Mary: the mother of Jesus

matriarchs: women who are the head or driving force of their family

Messiah: a Hebrew term meaning 'anointed one'; many Jews interpret the Messiah to be a future leader of the Jewish people who will rule with kindness and justice; for Christians the Messiah is Jesus; the word 'Christ' is the Greek form of the word 'Messiah'

moral: concerned with right and wrong behaviour

Mother of God: a title given to Mary because Jesus is God and she is Jesus' mother

mystery of redemption: the truth of how God redeems humanity through Jesus' sacrifice, which can never be fully understood

N

New Eve: Eve is the mother of all humans as the first woman; Mary, as the mother of Jesus, who offers redemption and new life to humanity, becomes the New Eve, or mother, for baptised Catholics

O

orders: types of religious community that follow particular religious, moral and social rules

ordination: the ceremony in which a man is granted Holy Orders and becomes a deacon, priest or bishop

Our Lady: a title of particular respect for Mary, reflecting her high status within the Church

P

peace and security: a safe environment in which people live without fear and are treated equally, justly and fairly, where disagreements are resolved through non-violent means such as dialogue

pilgrims: people on a journey, often travelling for religious reasons and to a sacred place

priest: one of the three sacramental degrees of Holy Orders; this is the second degree, in which a man is ordained *in persona Christi* – to stand in the place of Christ

prophets: people anointed by God and inspired by God through the Holy Spirit to share God's messages

Protoevangelium: the 'first gospel'; this refers to Genesis 3:15 because it is the first messianic prophecy in the Bible

purgatory: the condition a soul enters when in need of purification before entering the presence of God

R

rational: based on reason or logic

redemption: in the Old Testament, the act of saving a person from sin or suffering, or clearing a debt; in the New Testament, the belief that Jesus paid the 'ransom' to free humans from sin by dying on the cross

relational: concerning the way in which two or more people are connected; in Catholicism this is the relationship between humans, and between humans and God

religious life: a consecrated (holy) way of life within the Church in which men or women take vows of chastity, poverty and obedience and live in communities, apart from the lay faithful

reparation: the act of making right a wrong by helping to repair something and restoring it to its original condition

repentance: showing that you recognise and regret a mistake

respect for the person: ensuring that every person is treated with dignity and valued for the unique contribution they can make to life

the Rosary: a set of prayers said in honour of Mary during which Catholics will meditate on particular events in the life of Mary and Jesus

S

Sacrament of Matrimony: the Sacrament at the Service of Communion in which a man and woman make the lasting commitment of marriage

saints: people who are officially recognised by the Catholic Church as being very holy because of the way they lived or died; also, anyone who is already in heaven, whether recognised or not

salvation: the process of being saved from sin and returning to God through God's grace

sanctity of life: the idea that human life is a holy gift from God

sanctification: the act of making holy

sanctuary: a place of great holiness

Sinai covenant: the covenant Moses made with God at Mount Sinai, when he was given the Ten Commandments as part of the Law

social wellbeing: building and maintaining healthy relationships and engaging in meaningful interaction with others in a community

synoptic: referring to the three Gospels that have many similarities and can be 'read together', i.e. Matthew, Mark and Luke

T

Temple: the Jewish building for religious worship

tradition: also known as Apostolic Tradition, these are actions and teachings of Jesus faithfully passed on through the sacraments and teachings of the Church

typology: in Christianity, the study of Old Testament figures, objects, places or events which predict or hint at who or what is to come in the New Testament

V

venerated: respected and adored

vocation: in Catholicism, a calling from God to love and serve God and the Church in a particular way of life, which leads to holiness

volitional: based on free choice or free will

vow of chastity: voluntarily promising to abstain from sexual pleasure

vow of obedience: voluntarily promising to follow the authority of a religious order

vow of poverty: voluntarily promising to give up all possessions for the common good of a community

vows: solemn promises that cannot be broken

W

worldview (religious or non-religious): an overall vision or attitude towards life and the purpose of life, which directs how a person lives and acts in the world; a religious worldview would be based on the teaching of a particular religion, whereas non-religious worldviews would be shaped by beliefs and ideas that are not connected to religion

INDEX

abortion 17
Abraham 94
action, dialogue of 149
Acts of the Apostles (St Luke the Evangelist) 120
Adam and Eve 11, 32, 34–5, 100
'aesthetic argument', for God's existence 26
Agnus Dei (Lamb of God) 105
allegorical sense 34–5
Andrea de Bonaiuto da Firenze 141
angels
    archangels 134, 135
    in art 140–1
    Church in heaven 130, 131
    guardian angels 134, 135
    significance of 134
    veneration of 118, 136–9
    within liturgy 135
Angelus (prayer) 137
animal sacrifices 92, 94, 97, 98, 99
Annunciation 40, 44
anointing 73
apostles 62, 64, 121
apostolic succession 71
Apostolic Tradition 82, 83, 128
archangels 134, 135
Ark of the Covenant 94, 95, 97
art
    and creation *imago Dei* 26–7
    devotional images of Mary 54–5
    disciples, depiction of 84–5
    reconciliation, depiction of 110–11
    saints and angels, depiction of 140–1
assessment, types of 7
Assumption of Mary 47
asylum seekers 153
atonement 97, 98, 100, 102, 106

Baptism, Sacrament of 77
Bethany, Jesus' anointing at 73
Bible 5
    allegorical sense 34–5
    early Church 120–1
    see also New Testament; Old Testament

bishops 80, 81, 83, 129
Bonhoeffer, Dietrich 53
Bride of Christ 49

CAFOD (Catholic Agency for Overseas Development) 146, 156–7
The Calling of St Matthew (Caravaggio) 84
canonise 131
Canossian Daughters of Charity 56
Caravaggio 84
care, palliative 28
Caritas Social Action Network (CSAN) 146, 152, 153
Catechism of the Catholic Church (CCC) 5
    call to holiness 123
    common good 150, 152
    Eucharist 125
    faithful women 36
    imago Dei 12
    Mary and Jesus 45
    Mary's virginity 48
    morality 14–15
    ordination 83
    purgatory 132
    redemption 100
    sanctity of life 16
    sin 103
Catholic Agency for Overseas Development (CAFOD) 146, 156–7
Catholic Bishops' Conference of England and Wales 148
Catholic Church
    apostolic succession 71
    authority within 128–9
    charities 87
    common good 146, 150–7
    communion of saints 118, 122–3, 140
    dignity of human body 18
    early Christians/Church 69, 70, 71, 80, 120–1
    'elders' of the Church 80
    forgiveness of sin 108

    holiness of 126–7
    Holy Orders 80–1
    interreligious dialogue 148–9
    and IVF 24–5
    leadership of 128–9
    liturgical year 135
    marriage 20–1
    Mary, veneration of 50–1
    religious life 78–9
    right to life 16–17
    Second Vatican Council 113, 146
    structure of 129
    veneration of saints and angels 54, 118, 136–9, 142
    what the Church is 120
    see also Catechism of the Catholic Church; Church...
cave paintings 26–7
CCC *see* Catechism of the Catholic Church
celibacy 80, 81
    see also chastity, vow of
chaplains 29
charities 87, 146, 153, 156
chastity, vow of 79
    see also celibacy
chosen object 14, 15
Church 120
Church being purified 122, 132–3
Church on earth 118, 122, 124–9
Church 'elders' 80
Church in heaven 118, 122, 130–1, 136
The Church Militant and the Church Triumphant (Andrea di Bonaiuto da Firenze) 141
Church Penitent 133
Church Triumphant 130, 141
clergy 124, 129
closed orders 78
Cloud of Witnesses (Giusto de' Menabuoi) 123, 140
common good 146, 150–7
    commitment to 150–1
    peace and security 156–7
    respect for the person 150, 151, 152–3

social wellbeing 150, 151, 154–5
'common priesthood' 77
communion 133, 155
    see also Holy Communion
communion of saints 118, 122–3, 140
communities 69, 78, 120, 121, 146
    and moral choices 14–15
    social wellbeing 150, 151, 154–5
conception 16–17, 24, 25
Confession 108
conflict, military 112, 113, 156, 157
consumerism 67
Corinthian Christians 120–1
Corinthians, first letter to (St Paul) 121, 123, 127
covenants 43, 94, 99, 104, 107
    see also Ark of the Covenant
creation 8–13
    biblical accounts 8, 10–11, 34
    imago Dei 8, 10, 12–13, 26–7
crown of thorns 139
crucifixion 74
CSAN see Caritas Social Action Network
Cueva de los Manos 27

David, King 95
Day of Atonement 98, 100
de Vasconcellos, Josefina 110
deacons 80, 81, 82, 129
dead, prayers for 133
death, overcoming of 101
denominations 82
'designer babies' 25
development of society 150, 151, 154–5
devotion
    Marian devotion 54–5, 142–3
    to saints and angels 136–9
dialogue 146, 148–9
dignity, human 8, 12, 18–19, 28–9
dioceses 81
disciples 62, 64–71
    in art 84–5
    failings of 70–1
    female disciples 72–5
    mission 77
discipleship 62, 64–71
    barriers to 66–7

costs and rewards of 68–9
failings of disciples 70–1
female discipleship 72–5
divorce 20
Dominicans 141
Donum Vitae (The Gift of Life) 24

early Christians/Church 69, 70, 71, 80, 120–1
Elizabeth, mother of John the Baptist 40
embryo selection 25
equality of sexes 11
ethical issues/principles 14
    forgiveness of sins 108–9
    IVF 24–5
    oppressed people 52–3
    ordination in Catholic Church 82–3
    shrines and relics in worship 138–9
Eucharist 125, 133
Eucharist Prayer 135
evangelical counsels 79
evil, forgiveness of 109

faithful women 32, 36–9, 42–3
feast days 134, 135, 138
fertility problems 24
foetus, rights of 17
forgiveness 98, 108–9, 112
Fra Angelico 35
France, Marian devotion 143
freedom 13, 14
furniture recycling 155

Gabriel, archangel 134, 135
Gaudium et Spes (Joy and Hope) 19
Genesis, Book of 8, 10–11, 34
Giusto de' Menabuoi 123, 140
God
    creation 8, 12
    existence of 26
    forgiveness of sin 108
    grace of 102
    gratitude for 38–9, 41
    judgement 52–3
    justice 41
    love 12

praise for 38–9, 40, 41
Temple of 106, 107
worship of 107
grace 102
gratitude 38–9, 41
guardian angels 134, 135
guide to using this book 6–7

Hannah 36–9
He Qi 85
heaven 132
Hebrews, letter to the 99
hell 132
Herod's Temple 96–7
High Priest 97, 98, 106, 128
holiness 12, 103, 123, 126–7
Holocaust 112
Holy Communion 81, 105, 125
Holy of Holies 95, 97, 98, 101
Holy Orders 80–1, 82
Holy Spirit 105, 121
hospice movement 28–9
how to use this book 6–7
human person 14
    respect for 150, 151, 152–3
    value of 8, 12
human rights 152, 153
humble 36, 37, 39, 41

icons 142–3
imago Dei 8, 10, 12–13, 26–7
Immaculate Conception 45, 46–7
in vitro fertilisation (IVF) 24–5
inalienable dignity 18
incarnate 46, 137
intercession 50, 51, 131, 133
intercultural dialogue 148
International Young Catholic Students (IYCS) 87
interreligious dialogue 148–9
Isaac 43
Israel 43
IVF (in vitro fertilisation) 24–5

Jacob 43
Jeremiah 16
Jerusalem 95
Jesuit Refugee Service UK (JRS UK) 153
Jesus Calls His Disciples (He Qi) 85

Jesus Christ
   and Adam 34–5
   anointing at Bethany 73
   brothers and sisters of 48
   crucifixion, women present at 74
   depictions of 103, 104, 140, 141
   disciples of 62, 64–71, 84–5
   forgiveness 108, 109
   as head of Church 128–9
   heavenly sanctuary in 99
   as High Priest 106, 128
   incarnation 46
   as Lamb of God 104–5
   Last Supper 104
   and marginalised people 39, 52
   marriage, teachings on 20
   and Mary 35, 45, 51
   as Messiah 104, 105
   miracles 70
   New Covenant 99, 104, 107
   Peter's denial of 71
   relics of 138, 139
   Resurrection 75, 101, 104
   and the Rich Young Man 66–7
   Sacred Heart 103
   sacrifice of 92, 100–1, 102, 106, 107
   salvation in 37
   as Temple of God 106, 107
   and women 72–5
Jewish people 94–9, 112
John's Gospel
   Jesus as Temple of God 106
   worship of God 107
Joseph (son of Jacob and Rachel) 43
JRS UK *see* Jesuit Refugee Service UK
Judaism 94, 98, 99
judgement 52–3
justice 41, 112, 113

laity 124
Lamb of God 104–5
Last Supper 104
lay people 86–7
Lectionary 5
Levi, the tax collector 64
life
   beginning at conception 16–17

   dialogue of 149
   sanctity of 8, 16–17
Litany of the Saints 81, 136–7
literal sense 66
liturgical worship, saints and angels in 135
liturgical year 135
Lourdes, Our Lady of 143
love 12
Luke's Gospel
   Annunciation 44
   Magnificat 40
Lumen Gentium (Light of the Nations) 128

Magnificat 40–1, 50, 52–3, 56–7
marginalised/oppressed people 39, 52–3
Mark's Gospel
   audience for 62, 64
   crucifixion 74
   discipleship 62, 64–71, 74–5
   marriage 20
   Resurrection 75
   Rich Young Man, story of 66–7
   Syrophoenician Woman's Faith, story of 72–3
marriage 8, 18, 19, 20–3, 76
martyrs 68, 69
Mary, mother of Jesus 32, 44–55
   Annunciation 35, 40, 44
   Assumption 47
   Bernadette's visions of 143
   as Bride of Christ 49
   depiction of 140, 142
   devotion to 54–5, 142–3
   and Eve 34–5
   as Ever Virgin 48–9
   Immaculate Conception 45, 46–7
   intercession 51
   Magnificat 40–1, 50, 52–3, 56–7
   Marian dogmas 46–9
   Mother of the Church 51
   as Mother of God 40, 46
   as New Eve 35
   Our Lady 50
   prophecies 50–1
   relationship with Jesus 45
   and salvation 42

   shrines dedicated to 54–5
   'singular dignity' of 45
   virginity of 35, 48–9
Mass 105, 135
matriarchs 42
Matrimony, Sacrament of 8, 20–3
Meeting God in Friend and Stranger 146, 148–9
'Mercy Seat' 97
Messiah 104, 105
Mexico City 54
Michael, archangel 134, 135
Middle East, CAFOD's work in 157
miracles 70, 139
mission 77
monks 78
moral choices 13, 14–15
Moses 94, 97, 99, 104
Mother of the Church 51
Mother of God 40, 46
mystery of redemption 100–1

Nash, Molly and Adam 25
Nazi regime 53
Nebuchadnezzar, King 95
New Covenant 99, 104, 107
New Eve 35
New Testament 39, 54, 55, 99, 105, 120, 121, 123, 127
   see also John's Gospel; Luke's Gospel; Mark's Gospel
Nicene Creed 126
Noah's Ark 34
nuns 78
Nuptial Mass 22–3

obedience, vow of 79
Old Covenant 99, 104, 107
Old Testament
   covenants 99, 104, 107
   faithful women 32, 36–9, 42–3
   salvation theme 42
   stories of 8
   typology 34
oppressed/marginalised people 39, 52–3
orders (religious communities) 78
Ordinatio Sacerdotalis (Priestly Ordination) 82
ordination 80, 81, 82–3

Original Sin 47, 49, 103
Our Lady 50
Our Lady of Częstochowa 142
Our Lady of Guadalupe 54
Our Lady of Lourdes 143
Our Lady of Walsingham 55

Pacem in Terris (Peace on Earth) 113
palliative care 28
patron saints 57, 131, 136
Pax Christi 112–13
peace and security 112, 113, 150, 151, 156–7
penitents 133
person
   respect for 150, 151, 152–3
   value of 8, 12
Pilgrim Church 124
pilgrims 124, 143
Poland, Marian devotion 142–3
Pope 129
poverty, vow of 79
praise 38–9, 40, 41
prayers
   Angelus 137
   for the deceased 133
   Eucharist Prayer 135
   Hannah's prayer 38, 41
   intercessory prayers 50, 51, 131, 133
   litanies 136–7
   Magnificat 40–1, 50, 52–3, 56–7
   St John Henry Newman's prayer 76–7
pregnancy 17, 24, 43
prehistoric art 26–7
priests 80, 81, 82–3, 129
Prodigal Son, story of 111
prophecies
   of Jesus 35
   of Mary 35, 50–1
prophets 32, 42
Protestant Church, objections to shrines and relics 138–9
Protoevangelium 35
purgatory 122, 132, 133
purification 122, 126, 127, 132
purity 49

Rachel 42–3

Raphael, archangel 134, 135
rational 12, 13
Rebecca 42–3
reconciliation 108, 110–11, 112
Reconciliation (de Vasconcellos) 110
Reconciliation, Sacrament of 108
recycling initiatives 155
redemption 34, 35, 99, 100–1, 102–3
refugees 153
relational 12
relics 138, 139
religious experience, dialogue of 149
religious life 76, 78–9
religious orders 78
reparation 103
repentance 108
respect for the person 150, 151, 152–3
Resurrection 75, 101, 104
Revelation, Book of 54, 55, 105
Rich Young Man, story of 66–7
rings, giving of 23
Romans 64, 65
the Rosary 50

Sacrament of Baptism 77
Sacrament of Holy Orders 80–1, 82
Sacrament of Matrimony 8, 20–3
Sacrament of Reconciliation 108
Sacrament of Salvation 125
sacraments 21, 22
Sacred Heart 103
sacredness 13
sacrifice 92, 100–1, 102, 106, 107
St Andrew 131
St Bernadette Soubirous 143
St John XXIII, Pope 113
St John Henry Newman 76–7
St Josephine Bakhita 56–7
St Juan Diego 54
St Paul 101, 118
   Corinthians, first letter to 121, 123, 127
   dignity of human body 18–19
   and early Church 120, 121
   feast day 135
St Paul VI, Pope 126, 130

St Peter 68, 71, 102, 135
St Teresa of Calcutta 131
St Vincent de Paul Society (SVP) 146, 154–5
saints 55, 103, 122, 123, 124
   in art 140–1
   Church in heaven 130–1
   Litany of the Saints 81, 136–7
   patron saints 57, 131, 136
   personal devotion to 138
   veneration of 54, 118, 136–9, 142
   within liturgy 135
   see also communion of saints
salvation 32, 36, 37, 41, 42–3, 45, 99
   and Mary's virginity 49
   redemption as 102–3
   Sacrament of 125
Samuel 36, 37
sanctification 102, 103
sanctity of life 8, 16–17
sanctoral cycle 135
sanctuaries 94, 99
Sarah (wife of Abraham) 42–3
Saunders, Dame Cecily 28
'saviour siblings' 25
sculptures 110
Second Vatican Council 113, 146
security and peace 112, 113, 150, 151, 156–7
selfishness 67
sexual relationships 18–19
   see also celibacy; chastity, vow of
shrines 54–5, 138, 142
sin 14, 35, 99, 101
   of Adam and Eve 100
   forgiveness of 98, 108–9, 112
   see also Original Sin
Sinai covenant 94
slavery 56
social development 150, 151, 154–5
social justice 153
Social Teaching 150
social wellbeing 150, 151, 154–5
solidarity 156
Solomon, King 95
statues 138, 139
stewardship 13, 16
suffering 28, 56, 101
Sulawesi cave painting 26

SVP *see* St Vincent de Paul Society
synagogues 94
synoptic Gospels 66, 67
Syrophoenician Woman's Faith,
    story of 72–3

Tabernacle 94, 95
tax collectors 64
Temple 92, 94–7, 98, 99
   history of 94–5
   second Temple 94, 96–7
Temple of God 106, 107
Tennant, F.R. 26
Théas, Bishop Pierre Marie 112
theological exchange 149
Torah 94
tradition 82, 83, 128
typology 34

venerated 44, 45, 136–9, 142
virginity, Mary's 35, 48–9
vocation 62, 76–7, 80, 84
volitional 12, 13
volunteers, social wellbeing
    projects 154–5
vow of chastity 79

vow of obedience 79
vow of poverty 79
vows 21, 36, 76

Walsingham, Our Lady of 55
warfare 112, 113, 156, 157
wealth, attachment to 67
wedding ceremony 22–3
women
   discipleship 72–5
   equality with men 11
   faithful women 32, 36–9, 42–3
   ordination of 82, 83
   and Resurrection 75
   role in Jesus' ministry 72–3
worldview (religious or non-
    religious) 148
worship
   saints and angels in 135
   shrines and relics in 138–9

Youth Catechism (YC) 5, 122, 126

ACKNOWLEDGEMENTS

The publisher and authors would like to thank the following for permission to use photographs and other copyright material:

Photos: p11, 111: Jean and Alexander Heard Libraries / Vanderbilt University; **p13:** FatCamera / E+ / Getty Images; **p14:** Mike_shots / Shutterstock; **p17:** Henrik5000 / E+ / Getty Images; **p18:** Tim Robberts / DigitalVision / Getty Images; **p20:** wideonet / Shutterstock; **p21:** Jodie Nash / Alamy Stock Photo; **p22:** Bogdan Sonjachnyj / Shutterstock; **p25:** Sipa US / Alamy Stock Photo; **p26:** MAXIME AUBERT / PA WIRE; **p27:** R.M. Nunes / Shutterstock; **p28:** ADRIAN DENNIS / AFP / Getty Images; **p29:** Jiri Hubatka / Alamy Stock Photo; **p35, 47:** Photo Josse / Bridgeman Images; **p37, 121:** Zvonimir Atletic / Shutterstock; **p39, 123, 140, 141:** Historic Images / Alamy Stock Photo; **p41:** Frank Wesley / Vanderbilt Divinity Library; **p42, 126, 139:** Godong / Alamy Stock Photo; **p44:** Librairie de l'Emmanuel / Vanderbilt Divinity Library; **p48:** Anne Landell / Diocèse de Martinique; **p50:** Masterpics / Alamy Stock Photo; **p53:** Ukrainian Marian Collection / University of Dayton; **p54:** SandroSalomon / Shutterstock; **p55:** Diocese of Westminster; **p56:** INTERFOTO / Alamy Stock Photo; **p57:** Independent Photo Agency Srl / Alamy Stock Photo; **p64:** Duccio di Buoninsegna / Samuel H. Kress Collection / National Gallery of Art; **p66:** Carlo Bollo / Alamy Stock Photo; **p68:** Freedom Studio / Shutterstock; **p71:** Michael O'Brien; **p72:** Michael Cook; **p74:** Heritage Image Partnership Ltd / Alamy Stock Photo; **p76(l):** The Photolibrary Wales / Alamy Stock Photo; **p76(r):** redsnapper / Alamy Stock Photo; **p78(t):** Joerg Boethling / Alamy Stock Photo; **p78(b):** BSIP SA / Alamy Stock Photo; **p80:** Pontino / Alamy Stock Photo; **p83(t):** Maria Grazia Picciarella / Alamy Stock Photo; **p83(b):** PA Images / Alamy Stock Photo; **p84:** incamerastock / Alamy Stock Photo; **p85:** He Qi © 2013 All Rights Reserved; **p87:** International Young Catholic Students / Jeunesse Etudiante Catholique Internationale; **p95:** Dima Moroz / Shutterstock; **p98:** ArtMari / Shutterstock; **p100:** Dinodia Photos / Alamy Stock Photo; **p103:** Godong / Universal Images Group Editorial / Getty Images; **p104:** CURAphotography / Shutterstock; **p107:** Eraza Collection / Alamy Stock Photo; **p108:** Roman Zaiets / Shutterstock; **p110:** Andrew Michael / Alamy Stock Photo; **p112:** Yad Vashem / The World Holocaust Remembrance Center; **p113:** Pax Christi; **p125:** Hariyanto teng / Shutterstock; **p129:** dpa picture alliance / Alamy Stock Photo; **p131, 134:** Holmes Garden Photos / Alamy Stock Photo; **p133:** Radiant Light / Bridgeman Images; **p136:** Alex Ramsay / Alamy Stock Photo; **p138:** Papal Artifacts; **p142:** Dipper Historic / Alamy Stock Photo; **p143:** Delpixel / Shutterstock; **p148:** ALESSANDRA TARANTINO / AFP / Getty Images; **p151(t):** 1000 Words / Shutterstock; **p151(m):** k_samurkas / Shutterstock; **p151(b):** Phanphen Kaewwannarat / Shutterstock; **p153:** Caritas Social Action Network; **p154:** Amy Fitzgerald / Youth St Vincent de Paul team; **p156:** Catholic Agency for Overseas Development's partner; **Throughout:** andromina / Shutterstock.

Artwork by Eleanor Grosch, Peter Bull and Kamae Design.

Every effort has been made to contact copyright holders of material reproduced in this book. Any omissions will be rectified in subsequent printings if notice is given to the publisher.

We are grateful to the authors and publishers for use of extracts from their titles and in particular the following:

Scripture quotations are from the **ESV® Catholic Edition with Deuterocanonical Books (ESV-CE)** copyright © 2017 by Crossway, a publishing ministry of Good News Publishers. Used by permission. All rights reserved. The ESV-CE text may not be quoted in any publication made available to the public by a Creative Commons license. The ESV-CE may not be translated in whole or in part into any other language. Users may not copy or download more than 500 verses of the ESV-CE Bible or more than one-half of any book of the ESV-CE Bible.

Extracts from **Catechism of the Catholic Church**, published by Vatican Publishing House. © Dicastero per la Comunicazione – Libreria Editrice Vaticana. Reproduced with permission by the Publisher.

Extracts from **Credo of the People of God 15, 29**, published by Vatican Publishing House. © Dicastero per la Comunicazione – Libreria Editrice Vaticana. Reproduced with permission by the Publisher.

Extracts from **Pastoral Constitution on the Church in the Modern World,** *Gaudium Et Spes*, promulgated by His Holiness, Pope Paul VI on December 7, 1965. © Dicastero per la Comunicazione – Libreria Editrice Vaticana. Reproduced with permission by the Publisher.

Extracts from prayer composed by Saint Josephine Bakhita on the occasion of her consecration to God with the Final Religious Profession, December 8th, 1896; Prepared by Pontifical University Urbaniana, with the collaboration of the Missionary Institutes. © Dicastero per la Comunicazione – Libreria Editrice Vaticana. Reproduced with permission by the Publisher.

Extracts from *Pacem in Terris*, **Encyclical of Pope John XXIII, On Establishing Universal Peace In Truth, Justice, Charity, And Liberty**, April 11 1963. © Dicastero per la Comunicazione – Libreria Editrice Vaticana. Reproduced with permission by the Publisher.

Extracts from **Dogmatic Constitution on The Church,** *Lumen Gentium*, solemnly promulgated by His Holiness, Pope Paul VI, on November 21, 1964. © Dicastero per la Comunicazione – Libreria Editrice Vaticana. Reproduced with permission by the Publisher.

Extracts from **Apostolic Constitution of Pope Paul VI,** *Indulgentiarum Doctrina*. © Dicastero per la Comunicazione – Libreria Editrice Vaticana. Reproduced with permission by the Publisher.

Extracts from *Dialogue and Proclamation*, **Reflection and Orientations on Interreligious Dialogue and the Proclamation of the Gospel of Jesus Christ (1)**, Pontifical Council for Interreligious Dialogue, May 1991. © Dicastero per la Comunicazione – Libreria Editrice Vaticana. Reproduced with permission by the Publisher.

Extracts from **Educating to Intercultural Dialogue in Catholic Schools, Living in Harmony for a Civilization of Love**, Congregation for Catholic Education, 2013. © Dicastero per la Comunicazione – Libreria Editrice Vaticana. Reproduced with permission by the Publisher.

Extracts from Instruction **'Relics in the Church: Authenticity and Preservation'**, 2017. © Dicastero per la Comunicazione – Libreria Editrice Vaticana. Reproduced with permission by the Publisher.

Extracts from **'Reflections and Orientations on Dialogue and Mission 3'** © Dicastero per la Comunicazione – Libreria Editrice Vaticana. Reproduced with permission by the Publisher.

Extracts from **'Pax Christi – our vision'** © Pax Christi UK – Christian Peace Education Centre. Reproduced with permission of Pax Christi.

Extract from a joint statement from Sarah Teather, Director of JRS UK, and Raymond Friel, Chief Executive of CSAN. Reproduced with permission of Jesuit Refugee Service UK.

Extract form **'The SVP and Synodality, a Beneficiary'** St Vincent de Paul Society. Reproduced with permission of Dr Greg Ryan.

Extracts from **'Meeting God in Friend and Stranger' 21, 9, 110–114**, published by Catholic Bishops' Conference of England and Wales International Affairs Department. © Catholic Bishops' Conference of England and Wales. Reproduced with permission by the Publisher.

Extracts from **Youth Catechism of the Catholic Church**, Ignatius Press, San Francisco. © 2011 Ignatius Press. Reproduced with permission by the Publisher.

Extracts from **'CAFOD's work in the Middle East'** © The Catholic Agency for Overseas Development (CAFOD). Reproduced with permission by the Publisher.

Although we have made every effort to trace and contact all copyright holders before publication this has not been possible in all cases. If notified, the publisher will rectify any errors or omissions at the earliest opportunity.

Links to third party websites are provided by Oxford in good faith and for information only. Oxford disclaims any responsibility for the materials contained in any third party website referenced in this work.

Thank you

This series is dedicated to Professor Anthony Towey – a friend to all in RE. Your spirit, inspiration and legacy lives on in these books.

Andy Lewis: Thank you, as always, to my amazing family – Emily, Tommy and Joseph. I am incredibly grateful to everyone who helped transform this dream of resourcing the new RED into a reality. It's been an incredible journey with everyone at OUP, but especially Minh Ha who has worked on this from the beginning. A personal thanks to all the authors who have put everything into this series – you are amazing. Thanks also to all our reviewers, we couldn't do it without you. Finally, thanks to every person who had faith in the project and used the resources in their classrooms, with their students.

Rebecca Jinks: Thank you to my husband, Sean, and my sons Isaac and Hugh who have been endlessly encouraging and supportive of me, particularly in the writing of this book. To them and my wider family, my colleagues at work and the team at OUP, thank you for having faith in me.

Laura Skinner-Howe: As ever thank you to my husband and family for their constant support and encouragement. A huge thank you to all the team at OUP, your support and guidance whilst writing this book has been invaluable.

Ann-Marie Bridle: As we draw closer to the completion of this substantial project, I hope we have contributed to enriching the lives of many young people. I thank my family, particularly Kevin, Liam and Lizzy and my parents, for enabling me to be part of this important work. And I thank the team at OUP who have remained so kind, professional and supportive throughout.

Mateusz Boniecki: The list of people to whom I am grateful for support and encouragement grows with each year: first and foremost, thank you to my wonderful wife Olimpia, for her unshakable faith in me; to my son Octavian who is and always will be a primary source of motivation in all that I do; to my parents and rest of my family, for smalls acts of practical support that allowed me to focus on work. To my God-mother, Ewa, who early in my life planted literary seeds. To my friends and colleagues – especially Daniella and Suzan – who revealed to me the true meaning of faith in daily life.

The publisher would like to thank the following people for their invaluable contribution to the development of this book: Philip Robinson, Dr Maureen Glackin, Jacob Phillips, Julia Naughton, Harriet Power, Julie Haigh, Robert Bowie, Jess Bailey and Susan Kambalu (CAFOD), Raymond Friel (CSAN), Pax Christi England and Wales, St Vincent de Paul Society, International Young Catholic Students, Rabbi Benjy Rickman, Revd Mark Griffiths, Fr Martin Hardy and Smrithi Devaiah. The publisher would also like to thank James Helling for compiling the index for this book.